ALSO BY TOM FITTON

The Corruption Chronicles
Clean House

A REPUBLIC UNDER ASSAULT

THE LEFT'S ONGOING
ATTACK ON AMERICAN FREEDOM

TOM FITTON

THRESHOLD EDITIONS

NEW YORK   LONDON   TORONTO   SYDNEY   NEW DELHI

Threshold Editions
An Imprint of Simon & Schuster, Inc.
1230 Avenue of the Americas
New York, NY 10020

First Threshold Editions hardcover edition October 2020

THRESHOLD EDITIONS and colophon are trademarks of Simon & Schuster, Inc.

For information about special discounts for bulk purchases, please contact Simon & Schuster Special Sales at 1-866-506-1949 or business@simonandschuster.com.

The Simon & Schuster Speakers Bureau can bring authors to your live event. For more information, or to book an event, contact the Simon & Schuster Speakers Bureau at 1-866-248-3049 or visit our website at www.simonspeakers.com.

Interior design by Davina Mock-Maniscalco

Manufactured in the United States of America

10 9 8 7 6 5 4 3

Library of Congress Cataloging-in-Publication Data

Names: Fitton, Thomas, author.
Title: A republic under assault : the left's ongoing attack on American freedom / Tom Fitton.
Description: First Threshold Editions hardcover edition. | New York : Threshold Editions, 2020. | Includes bibliographical references. |
Summary: "In this explosive new book, *New York Times* bestselling author and president of Judicial Watch Tom Fitton explains how the Radical Left and the Deep State are trying to destroy the Trump presidency"—Provided by publisher.
Identifiers: LCCN 2020033164 (print) | LCCN 2020033165 (ebook) | ISBN 9781982163655 (hardcover) | ISBN 9781982163662 (trade paperback) | ISBN 9781982163679 (ebook)
Subjects: LCSH: United States—Politics and government—2017– | Right and left (Political science)—United States. | Political culture—United States. | Trump, Donald, 1946–
Classification: LCC E912 .F494 2020 (print) | LCC E912 (ebook) | DDC 306.20973—dc23
LC record available at https://lccn.loc.gov/2020033164
LC ebook record available at https://lccn.loc.gov/2020033165

ISBN 978-1-9821-6365-5
ISBN 978-1-9821-6367-9 (ebook)

CONTENTS

INTRODUCTION
Never Let a Crisis Go to Waste   1

SECTION ONE
Our Republic Under Assault . . . from the Deep State   23

SECTION TWO
Our Republic Under Assault . . . from the Impeachment-Coup
    Attack on President Trump   127

SECTION THREE
Our Republic (Still) Under Assault . . . from Hillary Clinton   151

SECTION FOUR
Our Republic Under Assault . . . at the Ballot Box   233

SECTION FIVE
Our Republic Under Assault . . . at Our Border   273

SECTION SIX
How to Protect and Save Our Republic   293

ACKNOWLEDGMENTS   301
APPENDICES   303
NOTES   309

A REPUBLIC UNDER ASSAULT

Never Let a Crisis Go to Waste

As this book goes to print, our nation's cities are being burned by radical, violent leftists seeking to overthrow our republic. This follows unprecedented restrictions on our constitutional freedoms, our ability to work and other God-given rights by mostly left-wing governors and local officials under the guise of controlling the coronavirus. Many leftist governors and mayors were quick to suspend constitutional rights and destroy businesses of the law-abiding but slow to protect citizens from rioters.

In one way or another, for good, and sometimes unfortunately, for bad, a crisis always reveals who we are as individuals and as a people. Always.

During the late winter and spring of 2020, the multiple individual, governmental, health-care, and private sector responses to the Wuhan

COVID-19 crisis serve as a timely case study—one that should and will be examined in great detail over the course of the coming months and years.

A crisis, of course, should and does bring out the very best in a majority of us. We have seen that time and again in the past, and time and again at the height of the Wuhan COVID-19 pandemic. Neighbors helping neighbors; major-league sports teams and professionals paying laid-off employees or providing other financial support; a grocery store chain donating at least 6 million meals to those hit hardest by the crisis; grocery store employees going way above and beyond the call of duty to stock shelves, ring up our orders, and keep their stores open; America's truck drivers working endless hours and driving past the point of exhaustion to fill those stores and pharmacies with the supplies and medications our nation so desperately needed; and most important of all, our doctors, nurses, and their support staff who heroically manned the front lines of that pandemic to help and save as many infected as humanly possible.

Unfortunately, a crisis can also quickly or instantly reveal some troubling proclivities of those hoping to use it as a means to an end. Even, quite alarmingly and tragically, the Wuhan COVID-19 crisis.

There are a number of ways our republic can be—and is—under assault. One of the most unsettling, and truly vile, would be to attempt to weaken its freedoms, its laws, its borders, and the accountability of its government by exploiting a global pandemic for partisan or personal gain.

And yet, as we now know, there was a great deal of evidence that points exactly to that tactic. It was as if some politicians and activists were using the confusion, the trillions of dollars, and tragedy surrounding the Wuhan COVID-19 crisis to achieve political objectives, such as imposing long-sought changes to election integrity measures—

such as ending voter ID, while pushing massive vote-by-mail schemes and ballot harvesting. Judicial Watch called for a rollback of the calling to "Liberate America" from the draconian dictates of the "cure."

This pandemic "cure" was destroying millions of American jobs, the very economy of our nation, and our freedoms in the process.

There is no doubt that the Wuhan COVID-19 virus was quite serious and especially dangerous to the elderly and other susceptible populations.

The doubts and the questions surfaced over, first, how best to treat the virus without destroying our nation and the economic, mental, and physical well-being of tens of millions of Americans in the process. And second was the real concern regarding the World Health Organization's (WHO) seemingly corrupt relationship with the People's Republic of China and its leadership, and how that corrupt relationship might negatively impact the American people. For instance, based on rather obvious China lies, the WHO minimized the threat of coronavirus by suggesting the risk of human-to-human transmissibility was low. President Trump was so livid about WHO's coddling of China that he withdrew the United States from the international organization.

Be it in our nation, or around the world, too many on the left and their allies in the mainstream media had no intention of letting the paralyzing fear and uncertainty over the Wuhan COVID-19 pandemic go to waste.

It was the intention of the Left to exploit the crisis from day one.

As reported in March 2020 during a conference call held between House Democrats, House Majority Whip James Clyburn—third in line among House Democratic leadership and a strong ally of Speaker Nancy Pelosi—spelled out their selfish, biased, and truly anti-American strategy with one sentence.

Said Clyburn: "This is a tremendous opportunity to restructure things to fit our vision."

Clearly meaning to use the panic and fear over the virus as a means to advance their leftist policy agenda.

President Barack Obama's former chief of staff Rahm Emanuel—who, after leaving the White House, went on to become mayor of Chicago—must have been quite proud of Clyburn. For it was Emanuel who, as White House chief of staff, infamously said: "You never want a serious crisis to go to waste. And what I mean by that is an opportunity to do things that you think you could not do before."

That you "could not do before." A better and more accurate translation of that being what you were not *allowed* to do before.

Such as using the pandemic crisis as an excuse to strip the American people of their Second Amendment rights. This was a tactic multiple liberals and their handmaidens in the media immediately tried as they loudly advocated for the outright ban on the sale of guns and ammunition during the early days of the pandemic. They did so because they noticed the immediate uptick in gun and ammunition sales—an uptick caused by Americans nervous about the draconian measures being hinted at or outright advocated by many on the left.

Or when—as mentioned in *Issues & Insights*—a number of liberal politicians and operatives—the Los Angeles City Council, made up of 14 Democrats and 1 independent, for example—made it clear they should have been given the power to *completely* take over private businesses under the guise of "Saving the people."

Operatives from the Far Left seeking to take complete control of a business built from the ground up from the blood, sweat, and tears of hardworking, law-abiding American citizens is a scheme we have seem time and again. This is the tactic of totalitarian or dictatorial regimes.

Another tactic is rigging or stealing elections. When better to try than in the confusion of a national and international crisis?

As was noted in numerous news accounts, precisely because of the Wuhan COVID-19 pandemic, many leftists instantly pushed a vote-by-mail "free for all" scheme that would give fraudsters a much easier chance to rig or steal the 2020 elections—and elections in the future. Naturally, with no voter ID needed or wanted.

As Judicial Watch has long pointed out, voter fraud is a key *civil rights* issue. This issue demands increased attention and, more important, action. Much of that action being to not only stop fraudulent vote-by-mail efforts, but also to oppose any cleanup of the existing voter rolls, which are littered with quite possibly millions of suspect names. *Millions.*

Calling back to Rahm Emanuel's point, they sought to use the pandemic as an opportunity to aggressively push "what they could not do before." Again, what would *never* be allowed under "normal" circumstances.

As liberal politicians worked as one to exploit the crisis for their own partisan agenda at the direct expense of the welfare of the American people, the liberal mainstream media continually sought to silence the voice of President Donald J. Trump during the crisis by not only smearing him every chance they got, but by ignoring and not broadcasting his then live updates to the nation regarding the Wuhan COVID-19 pandemic.

While suppressing Trump, too many in the media were happy to defend the People's Republic of China.

Shills for the communist leadership of the nation that, unintentionally or not, unleashed the virus upon the world.

Shills who, while still making millions of dollars, were also involved in a truly heinous cover-up.

For instance, the *Washington Post* has a long and ongoing business relationship with *China Watch*, which is a branch of *China Daily*, a newspaper and media outlet directly controlled by the Chinese Communist Party and the Chinese military.

For over thirty years, both the *Washington Post* and the *New York Times* have featured advertorial inserts from *China Watch* at a reported price of over $100,000 per page. The basic math on that spells out millions of dollars of Chinese government money going into the corporate bank accounts of the *Washington Post* and the *New York Times.*

It is little wonder then that during the weeks and months before the Wuhan COVID-19 was proven dangerous and highly contagious, the *Washington Post,* the *New York Times,* and a number of other media outlets benefiting financially from business relationships with and in the People's Republic of China continually raised doubts about how serious the pandemic truly was while simultaneously smearing anyone—most especially President Trump—who dared to suggest that not only did COVID-19 *originate* in China, but that the Chinese government was actively trying to cover up that fact.

Over the coming months and years, good and decent people in and outside of various governments and organizations will try to ascertain approximately how many lives could have been saved had the world caught the Chinese Communist Party earlier in its vicious lies and deceptions regarding the Wuhan COVID-19.

Lies and deceptions aided and abetted by certain U.S. media outlets.

While we will long examine and debate which was the correct strategy to follow to save our nation and the world in a time of highly flawed pandemic computer models, there is no debating the initial motivations of much of the mainstream media in creating panic and hysteria over the Wuhan COVID-19 pandemic.

Knowing that, it is critically important to examine and contrast the conduct of that *same* media—and even certain infectious disease experts who advised President Trump—with the coverage and advice surrounding the swine flu pandemic that hit our nation and the world in 2009 and 2010.

While most of the media and a few of those "experts" would prefer that we forget, when that swine flu pandemic finally ran its course in 2010, it infected 1.5 billion people on earth and killed upward of 700,000.

Here in the United States, the swine flu pandemic infected 61 million Americans, hospitalized over 300,000, and killed upward of 18,000. Many of them were children and young people.

And yet, in the media of that time, there was no hysteria. They created no panic. They did not weaponize it. All the opposite, in fact. They played it down.

Be it CNN, the *New York Times,* the *Washington Post,* or the major television networks, all either completely ignored the swine flu pandemic at first, or pushed it deep within their papers, relegated it to a sidebar story on their sites, or a minute or two on the nightly news.

Not by coincidence, as the swine flu pandemic and its real threat to the safety and lives of American citizens was swept under the rug by the media, the nation remained "totally open for business."

No lockdowns. No "social distancing." Were the medical experts wrong not to do so then? Did they overreact in the late winter and spring of 2020?

Also, and as we know, there were no threats of a massive fine, or arrest, or prison time for violating the edicts of those in power.

To further understand and explain some of that conduct of the time, let's cast our minds back to 2009 and 2010 and try to remember who the president of the United States was at the time.

Oh, right: it was Barack Obama.

Next, it becomes mandatory to examine the actual mainstream media coverage of President Obama as it pertained to the "Crisis" that was . . . barely covered.

What a difference ten years, another pandemic, and a different president make. One who is totally despised by most of the mainstream media, Hollywood, and academia.

More than anything else, certain behavior within the media, academia, and now even medicine and science is driven by an unhinged and incurable hatred of President Trump, a condition some have named Trump Derangement Syndrome.

To underscore that, we need only go back to the last two major pandemics before the swine flu of 2009–10. Those would be the Asian flu of 1957 and the Hong Kong flu of 1968–69.

The Asian flu hit during the last administration of President Dwight D. Eisenhower. By the standards we use today, it was an incredibly dangerous pandemic, one that, by the time it ran its course, had infected tens of millions of Americans, hospitalized hundreds of thousands, and killed approximately 116,000 Americans out of a then population of about 175 million.

And yet, no lockdowns, no social distancing, no destruction of the American economy.

In 1968, during the last year of the administration of President Lyndon Johnson, came the Hong Kong flu pandemic. Again, by today's Covid-19 standards, truly quite dangerous. A virus that in many ways was a mirror image to COVID-19 in that it was highly infectious and could be primarily lethal to those over sixty-five years of age with preexisting conditions. By the time that pandemic ran its course in 1969, it had infected tens of millions of Americans, hospitalized hundreds of thousands, and killed approximately 100,000 out of a population of about 200 million. Worldwide, it killed upward of 4 million people.

But again, the media that existed during the last year of President Johnson's term and the first year of President Richard Nixon's term remained calm and induced no panic whatsoever into the population.

Consequently, once again, no lockdowns, no social distancing, no destruction of the American economy or way of life.

Knowing that historical context, it then becomes fair to ask two questions. The first: Did some on the left in the media, academia, medicine, and science react differently because Trump was president? And second, because of that bias, were they holding President Trump to a much different and much higher standard than say, Presidents Obama, Nixon, and Eisenhower?

Or did they simply—and tragically—paint our entire nation into a corner with their panic and draconian measures and then were too cowardly to admit to their mistakes and refuse to choose the actual best course of action to fight the Wuhan COVID-19 pandemic?

While the answers to those questions seem clear to most of us, many on the left—because of hate and ideology—still choose blanket denials as the way to go.

What can't be denied by anyone who was paying attention in the late winter and spring of 2020 is that the emergence of the Wuhan COVID-19 pandemic led to the deliberate and dangerous abuse of that crisis by some of the usual suspects, which led to the emergence of a new tyranny at the state and local level.

It is instructive that left politico-media concerns about the "spread" and being on lockdown "together" went out the window as soon as radical leftists needed to riot, burn, and loot after the death in police custody of George Floyd on May 25, 2020, in Minneapolis, Minnesota.

So how did this new tyranny emerge?

Certain—and instant—responses to the Wuhan COVID-19 by some of our "leaders" gave us all a crystal-clear look at that truly disturbing process.

Close on the heels and soon coupled with the deliberately fear-induced media panic came the "End of the World" COVID-19 computer model projections. Projections that exponentially accelerated the panic and lockdowns.

A number of those projected and highly flawed computer models emanating from either far-left universities and university professors, or from far-left organizations that stood to benefit from the billions of dollars of stimulus money forked over involuntarily by U.S. taxpayers as well as other hardworking taxpayers around the world.

The most notable and infamous of these "End of the World" computer models was produced by a professor by the name of Neil Ferguson and his team from Imperial College in London. As an aside, in May 2020 Ferguson had to resign his position after it was alleged that he violated his own "safe distance" and "lockdown" orders to spend the night with the wife of another man.

With regard to the lack of accuracy or even danger associated with computer models, back in the glory days of NASA during the 1960s, when the United States was racing the then Soviet Union to the Moon, our truly courageous astronauts offered up an incredibly accurate description of such models, a description that has most certainly stood the test of time.

Observed those astronauts who were risking their very lives on the whims of calculations and predictions: "Garbage in, Garbage out."

With that truism in mind, in March 2020 as the Wuhan COVID-19 began to spread, the team at Imperial College fed "garbage assumptions" based upon what little real on-the-ground evidence they had at the time into their computer and came out with a computer model stating that approximately 500,000 would die from the virus in the United Kingdom and approximately 2,200,000 in the United States.

These numbers, uncritically pushed by media, panicked political leaders.

Never mind that the general rule with computer models such as that—or those predicting landfall for a hurricane in Florida or say, Hillary Clinton crushing Donald Trump in the 2016 presidential election—is that they are almost *always* wrong for the simple reason that either their sample size is way too small, or they were fed incorrect or biased information from the start.

Specifically with regard to the Imperial College computer model, *National Review* correctly stated: "Models like this will always turn out to be wrong in some way or other because they rely on very strong assumptions about aspects of the disease we haven't thoroughly studied yet. If nothing else, the original Imperial model will be obsolete soon."

With that fact in mind, no one should have been surprised when the Imperial College computer model was made obsolete by Imperial College itself just days after making that "End of the World" prediction. After getting a bit more real-time accurate statistics, the projected death rate for the United Kingdom went from 500,000 to just under 20,000.

It should be noted that in a normal year with absolutely no pandemic the United Kingdom loses approximately 18,000 people to the common flu.

Again, the Wuhan COVID-19 pandemic was quite serious and did merit the strongest response possible from all of us. But . . . a reasoned response.

Sadly, reason was left behind by many.

As we saw and experienced, the doom-and-gloom computer model projections are what set off not only that initial mindless panic, but greed and . . . the first hints of totalitarianism.

Not letting this good crisis go to waste, a number of governors and mayors in our country soon realized that thanks *entirely* to the growing panic and draconian lockdowns spawned from especially the error-filled computer model projection, they could suddenly exercise close to complete dictatorial powers within their respective states, cities, and towns and issue edicts that greatly curtailed or outright forbade the God-given rights and freedoms of their citizens. One couldn't go to church, earn a living, run a business, protest, travel. Our most basic freedoms and liberties were restricted on a scale never seen before in American history.

All, of course, under the guise of protecting us.

Shockingly, in the United States of America, citizens could be fined or even imprisoned if found violating one of these arbitrary, indiscriminate, and indefinite edicts that shut businesses, required social distancing, and, now, mandated wearing a mask.

Fined or imprisoned.

And indeed, a number of Americans were arrested or taken into custody protesting the lockdowns.

We are not talking about North Korea, the People's Republic of China, or Iran, but right here in the United States of America.

In many cases when countries, regions, or even states and cities lose their freedoms, it is not because the tyrant or dictator of the time forcibly took it from them. More often than not, it is because the people in those countries, regions, states, or cities slowly but surely began to surrender those freedoms in return for promised protection against the terrifying external threat of the moment. In this particular case, that terrifying—dialed up to truly mind-numbing—external threat is the Wuhan COVID-19 pandemic.

Within just *two weeks* after the pandemic computer-model projections, American citizens within the *United States of America* were told by state and local officials that they could be arrested and possibly imprisoned if they violated the hastily put together edicts instantly put in place "for their protection."

With our "leaders," "experts," and politicians having absolutely no clue as to whether their draconian actions would in fact work—or what the final societal, financial, mental health, or criminal costs to the nation would be—we were all collectively—and indeed *forcibly*—plunged into that unknown together.

The American people were literally given no say in their own fate or that of their families.

And, as we all fell toward that unknown, a select number from the left leapt at the chance to strengthen and expand that emerging tyranny, greatly expanding the alleged authority of government to run and restrict our day-to-day activities.

The radioactive dust and damage from this crisis is going to take months and even years to settle. As that process and evidence of mismanagement and especially deliberate wrongdoing unfolds, the millions of Americans and *voters* who lost their jobs, and life savings, and watched in desperation as their families suffered beyond comprehension must never lose sight of the life-altering lessons brought about by the virus . . . or . . . those who sought to exploit it.

One of the most telling takeaways was that many who instantly and even coldly advocated for a complete "lockdown" of our nation and the instant elimination of the jobs of tens of millions of hardworking Americans had nothing to lose themselves.

Nothing.

If they were federal, state, or local politicians, they had guaranteed salaries, health care, and more often than not a lifelong pension awaiting them.

If they were academics, they had tenured and protected jobs, paid health care, and pensions awaiting them.

If they were senior federal employees, they had their guaranteed jobs and health care.

And if they were many of the liberal media talking heads pushing for the complete "lockdown" of our nation, they had their often seven-figure plus salaries and full bank accounts to bring them comfort as millions of their fellow citizens suffered the severe consequences of those lockdowns.

As we close out this section, it is also critically important to remember that those who had no hesitation about using the world's pandemic crisis to further their political agendas are the same individuals, organizations, and entities who are part of the Deep State, seeking to eradicate our borders, steal our elections, and transform the United States of America into something truly unrecognizable and frightening.

THE PROMISE JUDICIAL WATCH REPRESENTS

"Enlighten the people generally, and tyranny and oppression of body and mind will vanish like evil spirits at the dawn of day."
—THOMAS JEFFERSON, APRIL 24, 1816

There—encapsulated within the wise and increasingly relevant words articulated by the third president of the United States; the principal author of our Declaration of Independence; and a driving force behind our Constitution more than two hundred years ago—is revealed the overriding mission of Judicial Watch. We always stand at the ready to enlighten the American people so their precious freedoms and rights cannot be taken from them by those using oppression for an orchestrated tyrannical outcome.

But . . . as we focus on Jefferson's quote about "Enlightening the People," the question of our time is: Whom do we trust with such a critically important responsibility? The media? Our media of *today*?

One can only wonder what arguably our nation's most powerful advocate of liberty would think of the United States and the world of today. Because, as we continue to witness, in a number of freedom-depriving ways, some things have changed dramatically for the worse since Jefferson walked the earth.

For instance . . . that very media.

Knowing that to be a fact, let's examine his often quoted and high-lighted remarks regarding the need for newspapers and their power to *truthfully inform* the American people.

In a letter written in 1787 from Paris to Edward Carrington—whom Jefferson had sent as a delegate to the Continental Congress—he spoke to the importance of a free press to keep government in check. The then minister to France said in part:

> The people are the only censors of their governors; and even their errors will tend to keep these to the true principles of their institution. To punish these errors too severely would be to suppress the only safeguard of the public liberty. The way to prevent these irregular interpositions of the people is to give them *full information of their affairs thro' the channel of the public papers* and to contrive that those papers should penetrate the whole mass of the people. *The basis of our government being the opinion of the people, the very first object should be to keep that right,* and were it left to me to

decide whether we should have a government without newspapers or newspapers without a government, I should not hesitate a moment to prefer the latter. . . .

In principle—and in 1787—Jefferson is and was correct.

But Jefferson's stated belief and desire that "were it left to me to decide whether we should have a government without newspapers or newspapers without a government, I should not hesitate a moment to prefer the latter . . ." is predicated *entirely* upon the hope and assumption that said "newspapers" were ethical, honest, and only had the best interests of the American people in mind.

Flash ahead over two hundred years to 2020 and we find that many of the mainstream "newspapers" of today are not ethical, honest, nor have the best interests of the American people in mind, but are joined in their malfeasance by other powerful institutions and professions.

It is quite possible that in 1787, the great mind of Thomas Jefferson simply could not imagine that "newspapers" or any organizations or professions that commanded tremendous sway over the lives of his fellow citizens of the time could become so corrupt that they would embrace and espouse the liberty-robbing beliefs he had spent a lifetime fighting.

But . . . unfortunately, we *don't* have to imagine and contemplate it because it is a part of our *everyday* lives. Not only are we living it, but watching as it seeks to erode the platform atop which sits the republic that Thomas Jefferson and our Founding Fathers sacrificed so much to create.

The catalyst for this destructive behavior is called "groupthink."

The Merriam-Webster dictionary defines "groupthink" as: "A pattern of thought characterized by self-deception, forced manufacture of consent, and conformity to group values and ethics."

Back in his day, Thomas Jefferson may have seen pockets of such "groupthink." Unfortunately, two-hundred-plus years later, we have "Liberal Groupthink" which has come to dominate not only the mainstream media, but academia, science, medicine, and entertainment. A domination enabled and spread primarily by blatant and illegal discrimination against conservative, libertarian, faith-based, pragmatic, and dissenting thought of any kind.

The fact that this liberal groupthink is so crushingly dominant shows itself in issues pertaining to the Wuhan COVID-19 pandemic, the rule of law, terrorism, border security, global warming, energy independence, health care, education, corrupt public employee unions, and the political leaders of our nation.

As Judicial Watch has uncovered and detailed repeatedly over the last number of years, the liberal groupthink coverage of President Bill Clinton, President Barack Obama, and former first lady, senator, and secretary of state Hillary Clinton has not only been fawning to the point of embarrassment, but repeatedly deceptive as it sought to shield the Clinton and Obama teams from negative coverage and, more important, needed serious criminal investigations.

The inverse of that of course is their rabidly negative and unethical coverage of former president Ronald Reagan, former president George H. W. Bush, former president George W. Bush, and most especially, current president Donald J. Trump.

Incredibly, but not the least bit shockingly to those who follow Judicial Watch, many liberal to far-left members of this groupthink coalition of the media, academia, science, medicine, and entertainment have openly and proudly proclaimed themselves to be part of the "Resistance" against President Trump.

Let that sink in for a minute.

Countless "professionals" from these highly influential professions and arenas have openly come out to reveal themselves as part of the "Revolution" to topple a president legally and constitutionally elected by the people of the United States of America.

Had these people existed in the time of Thomas Jefferson, he would not only have *never* put his faith in such truth and freedom-destroying groupthink, but indeed would have vocally and loudly called it out as an enemy of democracy, liberty, and the rule of law.

Unfortunately—but *always* purposefully—the information flowing today from these professions or groups on a regular basis is often biased, ill-informed, deliberately deceptive, and often insulting or threatening to the opinions, narratives, or even lives of the American citizens who dare to differ with their preapproved narratives and dogma.

A fact of our everyday lives that will *never* change unless *someone* stands up to hold them accountable.

_____

For those not quite familiar with the work of Judicial Watch, I am here to tell you that is what we do: hold government and other important institutions *accountable* to the rule of law

Since the very day we were established in 1994, we have been doing *precisely* that. Often, as a lone voice in the wilderness.

Our core mission remains to fight for transparency, honesty, accountability, and integrity in government, politics, and the law.

Judicial Watch was created as, and remains, a conservative, non-partisan educational foundation that seeks to promote the highest standards of ethics and morality in our nation's public life. While we do believe in limited government, individual liberty, the free market, and a strong national defense, our organization favors no party as it stands as one to ensure that our elected and judicial officials never abuse the powers we, as the American people, entrust to them.

Some—most especially the liberal mainstream media—like to claim, and inwardly wish, that our supporters are only "Republican." Far from it.

Because our mission is to fight for transparency, honesty, accountability, and integrity in government, politics, and the law for *all* Americans, that means Americans from every walk of life support us and our cause. Americans who are Democrats, independents, Republicans, or simply those who attach themselves to no labels but are sick and tired of the corruption stealing their nation from them and their children.

With that background and mission in mind, our motto remains:

"Because no one is above the law!"

How does Judicial Watch go about carrying out such a crucial mission? One day, but often, multiple cases at a time.

On a regular basis, we employ a multipronged strategy of litigation, investigation, and public outreach. As many on the wrong side of the law or adverse to the welfare of the American people have found out, we use the freedom-of-information laws as one of the most powerful tools in our arsenal of getting to the truth and uncovering wrongdoing. In fact, almost all of our investigations into wrongdoing begin with a freedom-of-information request.

The federal Freedom of Information Act allows most anyone to request documents from executive branch agencies about government activities. And if these agencies ignore or improperly withhold information, requestors can go to federal court! (States have similar freedom-of-information laws.)

While we don't sue at the "drop of a hat," we will sue when needed to gather information or inform and educate the American people about the operations of our government and those seeking to subvert those operations for their own means.

Not surprisingly, no one understands the power of our freedom-of-information laws to expose the corrupt or the guilty more than those who operate anonymously out of the deepest, darkest, and most cowardly shadows of the Deep State.

Ultimately, no matter if it is a famous or even *infamous* politician or branch or branches of our own government, Judicial Watch's work is designed to uphold the rule of law and drag government wrongdoing out into the light, where it can been seen for the danger it is by the American people.

Not only do we strive to continually protect the rights of the American people via our litigation and civil discovery process, but many times, as soon as those actions are made known to those we are investigating, the alleged corruption by those public officials or government agencies suddenly grinds to a halt. Imagine that.

In that sense, it can be most accurately stated that we are doing the work for the government that it often won't undertake itself for a number of not so convincing or sound reasons.

With regard to our investigations, we have often been kiddingly or even sarcastically asked if Judicial Watch also watches the judiciary. The answer to that question is a loud and underscored "Yes."

We would be remiss in our mission and our duties to the American people if we did not. Human nature is human nature, which means that no one from *any* walk of life is either infallible or is always resistant to temptation. That includes the official third branch of our federal government.

As judges *are* human, they can be biased, run into ethical issues, or occasionally be outright corrupt. As the judiciary does maintain a critical role in the running and the governance of our nation, it is imperative that we continually monitor it, and hold everyone in it who holds sway over our laws and lives accountable.

Precisely because Judicial Watch is at the forefront—and often initiating—these critically important investigations, more and more Americans reach out to us to learn not only about our activities, but most especially, the outlook and results of those activities and investigations. And, similarly, a judiciary that acts beyond its power and outside the Constitution is also an "ethics" issue. Judicial decision making that is nothing more than "legislating from the bench" is also a threat to the rule of law.

To respond to the public's increasing requests for information, we expanded our educational outreach. We do so via direct television and radio outreach, as well as regular speeches, op-eds, and public service announcements.

As those who do follow and support Judicial Watch know, all of that information, background, and daily updates are housed and ready to be viewed 24/7 on our website, www.JudicialWatch.org.

It is there because it *has* to be there. We want and *need* it to be there.

The general public and honest and ethical media must know that our research, our lawsuits, our open-records searches and documents, and, most especially, our findings and evidence are accessible to them around the clock.

Full transparency is *everything*.

Darkness of the sort we investigate can *only* be defeated by that constant light of truth. The brighter and more penetrating, the better.

As we have learned over the years and now, decades, that darkness always has two constant allies. Those being secrecy and corruption. Both of them not only help to spread the darkness, but deepen its stain into the very fabric of our republic.

Judicial Watch believes it is our moral obligation and duty to cleanse that fabric, brighten and restore it to its original and intended red, white, and blue hues, and ultimately protect it.

As we approach the 2020 election and beyond, you can be assured that Judicial Watch will remain ever vigilant in our defense of the Constitution and the rule of law. And you will see we are relentless:

✦ in our pursuit of the full truth surrounding the Obama-Clinton CIA/DOJ/FBI/DNC Obamagate/Spygate ring that abused President Trump;

✦ in ensuring accountability for the coup cabal that pursued (and is pursuing) abusive impeachment;

✦ in revealing the truth about Hillary Clinton's illegal email activities;

✦ in ensuring election integrity; and

✦ in protecting our border security and enforcing our immigration laws.

These matters can seem overwhelming, and, indeed, together they form one of the gravest crises our nation has ever faced.

OUR REPUBLIC UNDER ASSAULT . . . FROM THE DEEP STATE

George Orwell described the "memory hole" in his dystopian critique of the totalitarian Left, *Nineteen Eighty-Four*:

> When one knew that any document was due for destruction, or even when one saw a scrap of waste paper lying about, it was an automatic action to lift the flap of the nearest memory hole and drop it in, whereupon it would be whirled away on a current of warm air to the enormous furnaces which were hidden somewhere in the recesses of the building.

Many would like nothing more than to use a memory hole to disappear the misdeeds of the Clintons, the Obamas, and their legion of cronies. Judicial Watch seeks to preserve history and ensure accountability by saving the evidence of these misdeeds from being lost to a Deep State memory hole.

For instance, by getting Obama administration documents about the 2010–13 IRS targeting of the Tea Party and conservative opponents of Barack Obama, we showed, as detailed in our book *Clean House*, how the Obama Gang and its multiple allies within and outside our very own government used the IRS, the FBI, and the DOJ to undermine, overwhelm, and ultimately destroy Tea Party conservative groups they perceived to be a threat. This abuse helped suppress the most significant political movement in a generation and helped ensure the 2012 reelection of Barack Obama.

Following this pattern of election year "cheating," we now have Obamagate. We fight inch by inch for documents that show the unholy alliance of the Obama Gang and Clinton machine to use the Deep State CIA, FBI, NSA, Defense, and State Departments to attempt at first to stop the candidacy of Donald J. Trump. And when they failed miserably at that, they engaged in a perpetual coup to remove him from power.

Orwell's warning about totalitarianism was on my mind in February 2020 when I stepped to the podium to address the Conservative Political Action Conference (CPAC).

I have had the great privilege of representing Judicial Watch—and all who support us—at CPAC for a number of years. But this time felt more imperative. Things were much more uncertain. More perilous.

If anyone would understand that, it would be the attendees of CPAC. Including, in 2020, President Donald J. Trump. For it was he, more than anyone else, who represented the constant and *ultimate* target of the Deep State and its allies.

As CPAC does bring together thousands of conservative leaders and organizations, I did want to remind them that thanks to the steadfast and growing support of all who believe in us and our mission, we are more active and vigilant than ever.

But more than even that, I *needed* to remind them why we *have* to be so vigilant. I wanted to wave a bright red flag warning that the heinous agents and operatives from the Left were now more brazen and dangerous than ever as they worked in concert to shade or hide that past, so they could condemn us to repeat it all over again.

But this time, so they could finally grab—and *never relinquish*—absolute power across the board of our republic. And with that power grab, extinguish our rights and freedoms forever.

With that in mind, the title of my presentation to CPAC was turned into the title of this very book:

Our Republic Is Under Assault

My excerpted speech follows:

The republic is under assault.

You can see this through the continuing lawless attacks on President Trump.

For almost four years now we have been busy uncovering the truth about the widest—and most destructive corruption in American history, the Deep State coup against President Donald Trump.

The coup began as an attempt by high-ranking members of the Obama administration to rig the 2016 presidential election in favor of Hillary Clinton. Failing that, it developed into a full-blown effort to overthrow a legitimately elected president of the United States. Comey effectively spied on Trump with Obama's implicit approval. And, the Deep State coup plotters in the DOJ and FBI talked of wearing wires in the Oval Office and invoking the 25th Amendment.

Then, after Robert Mueller's special counsel partisans failed to deliver the goods, the coup cabal led by Adam Schiff, abused whistleblower laws in one of the gravest abuses of Congress ever. President Trump was "impeached forever" as Nancy Pelosi so childishly put it. But he was also acquitted forever in the Senate.

The Mainstream Media won't use the word "coup" to describe

these continuing plots against the president, but that is what it is. And I'm using the present tense because, despite a few setbacks, the coup continues to this day.

The biggest enemy of the coup plotters, and the thing they have fought most vigorously against, is one thing—the truth. And despite their best efforts at covering up what they have done, the truth is coming out.

In a sane world the whole Obama/Clinton/Deep State gang would be worried about prosecution and accountability. I mean Obama, Clinton, Brennan, Clapper, both the Bidens, Rice, Comey, McCabe, Kerry, Bruce Ohr (and Nellie), the Fusion GPS crowd, and, of course, Strzok and Page—the two figures whose texts exposed the true motive behind the attacks on Trump. BTW, you heard me right—I said Obama. Obama knew. Frankly, if we are going to be impeaching presidents then we should impeach Obama. It isn't too late.

And, of course, there is the heavy lifting by Judicial Watch to expose the abuse of the president. Who needs an IG when you have Judicial Watch? We exposed that the FBI, in a joint operation with the Clinton campaign, paid the foreign spy Steele for dirt on Trump. That's right—your tax dollars helped pay for Hillary Clinton's foreign spy to target President Trump. We also exposed that the FISA warrant fraud and the fact the FISA court held not one darn hearing on spy warrants targeting candidate Trump and then President Trump. And we exposed how Bruce and Nellie Ohr funneled what they should have known was misinformation into the DOJ and FBI, used to try to implicate Trump. We uncovered that Bruce Ohr got a $28,000 bonus in the middle of the Russiagate spying on Trump—and then got a raise *after* he was caught for improperly colluding with Clinton spy Christopher Steele. Why is Ohr still at DOJ!

I tell you what—the best FISA reform would be to prosecute those who illegally spied on President Trump (and Lord knows who else)—to prosecute the Spygate ring and put them in jail.

Unfortunately, the Justice Department has been frozen when it comes to prosecuting the *real* bad guys. Comey got a pass. McCabe got a pass. And there's no evidence of major prosecutions against any other significant players. Worse yet, the Justice Department is *still* protecting Hillary Clinton as Judicial Watch forces out more emails and more evidence of criminal conduct. The statute of limitations has not run on Hillary Clinton, by the way!

And, in the meantime, the president ought to start pardoning Flynn, Stone, Manafort, and the other Americans caught up the abusive Mueller machine.

The craven Left is not just attacking our republic through its assault on President Trump.

Our republic is also facing the continuing challenge of border security.

Borders are critical to our country. They protect us and keep us safe. They define us as a nation. And, as you can see with the coronavirus, secure borders also protect the public health.

But open borders activists encouraged, aided, and funded mass caravans that further stressed our southern border. President Trump has taken strong action to control the assault on our sovereignty, but he's faced dishonest opposition from anti-Trump activist judges and sanctuary politicians who placed politics over the public safety.

[And] we have sanctuary cities and states where police and other officials are told not to cooperate with federal law enforcement trying to enforce the law. These sanctuary policies are illegal and dangerous. Judicial Watch is suing to stop them in California, particularly in San Francisco.

So we have tens of millions of legal and illegal aliens present in the United States and we're expected to believe none of them vote?

Also of grave concern are the attacks on clean elections that highlight how our republic is also under threat at the ballot box. Judicial Watch has a massive project to force states and counties across the nation to clean up their voter rolls. The Justice Department should be doing this, but it is largely AWOL, so we have to—because dirty election rolls can mean dirty elections.

We just found (in 2019) that there are least 2.5 million extra names on the voting rolls. Believe it or not, this is good news. Because our prior analysis found 3.5 million extra names on the rolls. So our pressure and lawsuits are working. In Los Angeles County, our federal lawsuit resulted in a settlement agreement requiring the county to remove as many as 1.6 million "inactive" voters over the next few years!

And, let me ask you this. Why would the Left so reflexively oppose clean election rolls, voter ID, and citizenship verifications for voting, and promote dangerous practices like ballot harvesting? I think it is because they want to be able to steal elections when necessary.

The Soros-funded Left has hundreds of groups attacking clean elections and voter ID (and now even the Electoral College)! And on the other side is Judicial Watch and one or two other groups. As I say, we are happy to do the heavy lifting but we all have to realize all our debates about taxes and abortion and health care don't mean a lick if the Left can steal our elections to maintain and expand power.

Never before in our nation's history have we seen such a sustained attack on our republican form of government.

And remember, the assault on our borders continues. Rising leftists openly call for open borders and seek to erase the distinction between citizens and noncitizens. I tell you what, if you erase our borders, you erase our country.

And now voter fraud is the civil rights issue of our time. Who stands for the civil rights of voters who votes are stolen? The Left would pretend voter fraud is no big deal. How many fraudulent votes are too many? In this era of close elections, even one is too many.

In too many ways, our republic is tottering. They tried to overturn our elections and they are trying to erase our borders.

What do we do? Judicial Watch has shown the way—enforce the law, put the coup cabal in jail, and dry up the swamp by bringing the sunlight of transparency!

And my simple advice for President Trump: Pardons, Prosecutions, and Transparency.

In the body of those remarks I gave before the CPAC conference were the most chilling words any American who believes in the rule of law could possibly hear:

"A Deep State coup attempt against a president of the United States of America." In this particular case, Donald J. Trump.

A coup attempt—initially—begun by high-ranking members of the Obama administration to rig the 2016 presidential election in favor of Hillary Clinton. Once that effort failed and Trump was elected in November 2016, it instantly evolved into a full-blown effort to overthrow a legitimately elected president of the United States.

Please think about that for a moment. Operatives from the Deep State whose only duty and obligation is to protect the security of our nation and all in it conspired as one to overthrow a constitutionally, legally, and legitimately elected president of the United States.

As a tagline from the old horror movie *Black Christmas* once stated: "If that doesn't make your skin crawl, it's on too tight."

But, the truth is, this real-life plot against President Trump by the

Left would have been deemed utterly ridiculous by Hollywood producers if it had been written as a screenplay.

"There's no way," one of these liberal Hollywood producers would have proclaimed, "that moviegoers are going to remotely believe that an FBI director would spy on the opposition party's candidate with the former president's complete approval. No way. And then on top of that, this idiot screenwriter is including Deep State operatives from the FBI and the DOJ joining in on this political hit job as they talk about wearing wires into the Oval Office to entrap the now opposition party's president and they would talk about invoking the Twenty-Fifth Amendment to get rid of him. Come on! Do you think that our moviegoers are that stupid?"

And yet, as we know, every bit of it is true; every bit happened.

All of this betrayal followed by Robert Mueller's failed, special counsel partisan circus, which was then followed by Adam Schiff's pathetic impeachment-coup-cabal show, which openly abused the whistleblower laws so Schiff and Nancy Pelosi could say President Donald J. Trump was "impeached forever" in the House of Representatives.

In a number of real ways, this plot began on June 16, 2015. That was the day when then private citizen and businessman Donald J. Trump rode down that escalator at Trump Tower in New York City with his wife, Melania Trump, to announce his candidacy for president of the United States.

The wheels of unethical and clearly criminal intent began to turn that very day in the minds of those who were determined to retain the status quo of the Obama-Clinton years at all costs.

A QUICK REFRESHER COURSE

For those who may have forgotten all of the sordid details of the birth of that—still ongoing—coup attempt, what follows is a bit of a refresher course.

Let's name the course: **The Deep-State Betrayal 101.**

Let us cast our minds back to April 2016. It was then that a firm by the name of Fusion GPS, headed up by former journalists turned political hatchet men Glenn R. Simpson and Peter Fritsch, was hired by the Democratic National Committee and Hillary Clinton's presidential campaign to dig up dirt on then candidate Donald J. Trump.

Please focus on one of the most pertinent facts in this case. The firm *was hired by the Democratic National Committee and Hillary Clinton's presidential campaign.*

Hired solely to dig up dirt on Donald J. Trump.

While most in the liberal mainstream media and all in the Democrat Party tried to at first deny this, or at best, sweep it under the rug, even the liberal *Washington Post* finally had to report on the connected dots of the case.

Said the *Washington Post* in part: "Marc E. Elias, a lawyer representing the Clinton campaign and the DNC, retained Fusion GPS, a Washington firm, to conduct research . . . in April of 2016 on behalf of the Clinton campaign and the DNC."

Fusion in turn hired one of Britain's former top spies on Russia. An ethically challenged operative by the name of Christopher Steele. Remember him?

Steele, as it turned out—and it is completely no surprise considering the people involved in this truly amateur plot—did indeed have very murky connections to assorted bad characters in Russia as well as our very own FBI and other three-letter U.S. agencies. Imagine that.

Steele, then seemingly anxious to cobble together something for the very large amount of money Fusion GPS was paying him, produced a thirty-five-page report filled with ludicrous, salacious, and completely unfounded allegations against Donald J. Trump.

As we now know, all were totally discredited, leaving some to wonder if some or all of the charges simply flowed from Steele's fertile and biased imagination.

Leaving aside the outright salacious, one of the more ridiculous allegations in the dossier was that Trump was offered bribes of more than one billion U.S. dollars by the Russian state-controlled oil monopoly Rosneft to end U.S. trade sanctions on Russia if he won the election in November 2016.

The other highly absurd, provably false allegation against Trump in the Steele dossier—and the one that became the fuel for the unhinged minds of the Democrats and liberal mainstream media—was that Trump officials secretly met with Russian officials to collude on "hacking" the Democrats during the 2016 election.

Again, all of this was a political hit job and fairy tale orchestrated by those on the left determined to ensure Hillary Clinton's victory in November 2016.

The hardworking people of the United States ultimately paid tens of millions of their tax dollars to have the eighteen-month long, highly biased, highly tainted, highly incompetent, and highly disgraced Comey-Mueller-FBI investigations forced to finally admit what every honest American already knew—that there was absolutely no collusion between Trump and Russia. None. Snake eyes.

And yet, look at the great and lasting damage that piece of fictional trash has done to our nation.

A majority of that damage coming from the fact that the disgraceful, disgusting, and discredited "Steele Dossier" was used as a pretense by some Deep State operatives in the FBI to convince a FISA court to let the FBI spy on the Trump campaign and some of its officials.

See how that works? Bad actors within our very own FBI use false information from a fictional report to give themselves permission to spy on innocent fellow Americans.

The Federal Bureau of Investigation—sworn to protect the United States of America and her citizens—used a completely fake dossier paid for by the Democratic National Committee and the Hillary Clinton presidential campaign to spy on Donald Trump.

Nauseating, dangerous, and treasonous are but the first three words that come to mind to describe such un-American conduct.

But wait. Naturally, it gets worse and much sleazier.

Inventing the fictional and discredited report was just the beginning of the mission to smear Trump and steal an election.

Next, came the main course. The "Steele Dossier" had to be leaked to the media. And it was.

Not only was it liberally and promiscuously shared with numerous reporters and democratic operatives, but with those in the U.S. intelligence community as well. Long before the American public learned of this corrupt and immoral dossier, it had become an open secret within official Washington.

This open secret landed loudly and squarely on the desk of pro–Hillary Clinton, anti–Donald Trump FBI director James Comey.

But wait, again . . . just like when ordering a "As seen on TV" product . . . there is still much, much more.

While the Democrats, the liberal mainstream media, and the founders of Fusion GPS bent over backward to keep it from the American people, it should be screamed from the mountaintops that Glenn Simpson and Peter Fritsch also had a secret, high-level meeting with . . . drumroll please . . . senior Department of Justice official

Bruce Ohr during the campaign. But wait, it gets even more comically disgraceful. As it turns out, Fusion GPS also hired Bruce Ohr's CIA-connected wife, Nellie, to do some "investigative" work for them. Next, how about Justice Department official Bruce Ohr also meeting with the Russia-connected, former British spy Christopher Steele.

Talk about unethical and potentially criminal conflicts, the tangled webs of deception and outright lies that gave birth to that wasteful Robert Mueller investigation.

Oh, and it should also be noted and seared into our memories that the DNC continued to pay Fusion GPS for its "research" right up until the end of October 2016—in other words, just days before the presidential election.

Ironically—at least for those of us who do believe in the rule of law and the republic it protects—some very dark clouds do indeed have a silver lining. Even a dark cloud created to pour acid rain down upon the Trump presidential campaign and our very Constitution.

That ironic silver lining appeared because of the release of the fraudulent FISA application to "investigate" the alleged—and now know to be fictional—"collusion" between the Trump presidential campaign and Russia.

Because of its release, we were able to learn of the deeply troubling background that seemed to trace the very beginnings of this conspiracy against Trump and his presidential campaign all the way back to the Oval Office of . . . President Barack Obama.

Not only does it appear that President Obama *knew* about this scheme, but he may have pushed and directed at least parts of it.

Luckily, we don't have to imagine that may have happened. James

Clapper, Obama's then director of national intelligence, was more than happy to spell it out for Anderson Cooper on CNN.

Said Clapper in part in July 2018:

"If it weren't for President Obama, we might not have done the intelligence community assessment that we did that set up a whole sequence of events which are still unfolding today. Including Special Counsel Robert Mueller's investigation. President Obama is responsible for that. It was he who tasked us to do that intelligence community assessment in the first place."

What? President Obama may have known much more about this plot to take down a political opponent than he let on? Say it ain't so.

But, as we have all learned by now, it wasn't just President Obama, but his highly compromised CIA director John Brennan as well.

Not surprisingly, while the mainstream media refused to make anything out of Clapper's jaw-dropping bit of information, we can still surmise ourselves that President Obama and John Brennan knew the allegations against Trump were false, but pushed them anyway.

Over the course of the last few years, former CIA director John Brennan has proven himself to be unhinged when it comes to President Trump. His animus against the president is not only deep felt, but disturbing.

For instance, after President Trump held a mini-summit with Russian leader Vladimir Putin in July 2018, Brennan bizarrely tweeted out that Trump's remarks, stating that he hoped to strengthen relations with Russia and that he had more trust in some of what Putin was saying compared to some in the U.S. Deep State, were "nothing short of treasonous," and "the threshold of high crimes and misdemeanors."

That someone with such demented thinking became the director of the CIA under the leadership of President Barack Obama speaks volumes about the ethics, values, and judgment of both men.

But, while we know *now* that Brennan suffers from an incurable case of Trump Derangement Syndrome, we did not know that in the summer of 2016 when he was actually in charge of the Central Intelligence Agency.

It was then that he felt certain that his beloved candidate Hillary Clinton was almost a shoo-in to become the next president of the United States. And if so, she could keep him on as director of the CIA.

With that devotion and his ambition stated, it's easy to see why he would want to *make certain* Hillary Clinton was elected in November 2016.

But, while Brennan's mind was deeply clouded by partisan hatred, it was still clear enough to remember that it was against the law for the CIA to engage in domestic spying operations.

No problem. Let's connect a few more dots.

Remember, the vile and discredited "Steele Dossier" had already been widely leaked and was an open secret within the media and Democratic power centers of Washington, DC.

Obviously—because of his job title and his loyalty to Hillary Clinton—one of the first people who would have gotten a hold of that document would have been CIA director John Brennan.

But, because Brennan knew he had a very serious legal constraint in the fact that the CIA could not *operate domestically*, he had to figure out a clandestine way for him to continue spreading the dossier within the most powerful circles to smear and take down Trump without being discovered.

What better way than to have a secret meeting with then Senate Minority Leader Harry Reid in August 2016, tell him about the "shocking" contents of the dossier, and let nature take its course.

It worked.

Reid—then one of the most powerful people in Congress—fired

off a letter to FBI director James Comey citing the "evidence" that he came across showing a "direct connection" between the Trump campaign and Russia.

The fix was now in across the liberal media, throughout the Democrat Party hierarchy, and at the highest levels of our intelligence agencies.

Don't take our word for it. John Brennan himself was anxious to brag about it and cover himself in "glory" with the Far Left out to take down a legally and legitimately elected president of the United States.

Brennan appeared on MSNBC with Rachel Maddow in August 2018 to crow about the collusion of intelligence agencies marshalled together to smear President Donald J. Trump.

Admitted Brennan in part: "We put together a Fusion-Center at the CIA that brought NSA and FBI officers together with CIA to make sure those proverbial dots would be connected."

Wow. Simply wow.

This plot was hatched under the Obama FBI designation "Crossfire Hurricane." This is the code name the FBI gave to its *own* bogus counterintelligence operation, which it launched under false pretenses against the Trump campaign and numerous innocent individuals.

A "Hurricane" indeed. A storm of epic governmental corruption that left a wake of personal destruction in its path.

The FBI investigation; the Mueller investigation; the fraudulent FISA applications and searches; the tens of millions of taxpayer dollars wasted. Lives and reputations destroyed, all because of a phony and discredited dossier created by former British spy Christopher Steele on behalf of Fusion GPS. A dossier that was bought and paid for by the Democratic National Committee and the Hillary Clinton presidential campaign with the sole mission of smearing and taking down candidate and then President Donald J. Trump.

The dossier was used by the Obama administration (and the Mueller operation) even as the leadership of the Obama administration and top Deep State leadership at FBI, CIA, and NSC knew or should have known that it was false and politically motivated.

But then, that was the whole point.

The "Steele Dossier" was meant to be weaponized from day one as the instrument to take down a political opponent whom President Obama and his Deep State hacks at the FBI, the CIA, and the NSC despised and saw to be a threat to their own personal and partisan ambitions.

The more we learn of this plot to take down a political opponent and subvert our Constitution, and the rules of law, the more questions we have.

For instance: Was *then* President Barack Obama a ringleader of this failed coup attempt or was he merely a tool to be used by Comey, Brennan, Clapper, and other Deep State operatives to achieve their objectives?

If Obama *was* a willing and eager ringleader—as documents and testimony seem to suggest—then why?

Did he want to facilitate a Hillary Clinton victory to protect his legacy while ensuring that his secrets and multiple failings remained buried under the layers of Obama and then Hillary Clinton political appointees who had burrowed extensively into every federal agency?

As these and many other questions continue to be asked—and get answered—what remains crystal clear to the American people who believe in our republic and the rule of law is that the Obama, Clinton, and Deep State machines colluded as one to improperly interfere in the election of an American president.

An un-American collusion at the highest levels of our political, governmental, and intelligence apparatus that knowingly used false and tainted information as the basis to activate numerous federal assets to scam the FISA court and in order to smear and even jail numerous innocent Americans.

Such a collusion is often called something else: a crime.

More than that, those activities would be—and are—felonies punishable by years or decades in prison.

As this investigation continues to play out, we are faced with one overriding question: Is our own Justice Department—filled with former Obama and Clinton political appointees and loyalists, along with an assortment of "Never-Trump" Republican appointees—much too deeply compromised to bring those who committed these multiple crimes against our nation and the integrity of its electoral process to justice?

We ask that tough question precisely because of inconsistencies, obstruction, and falsehoods coming out of the FBI and the Justice Department.

Current FBI director Christopher Wray seems to have caught the disease of the "cover-up."

Wray and his top operatives clearly now know that the FBI's fake, counterintelligence "Crossfire Hurricane" operation against the Trump campaign and a number of innocent individuals was based on a completely discredited dossier. Because of that, it seems logical to assume that some FBI agents and some Justice Department officials involved in that operation and inwardly harboring ill-will toward then candidate and now President Trump might try all in their power to cover their tracks and obstruct a fair and honest investigation of their activities.

Does current FBI director Wray share that same assumption and deep concern? Does he know how truly tainted, shameful, and dangerous this internal rogue operation run from within his own organization was to the stability of our very republic?

We say that, because with each passing day, it becomes more and more clear that the FBI's "Crossfire Hurricane" operation was deeply infected by . . . wait for it . . . *Russian* disinformation.

Russian disinformation.

This is a fact that many in the mainstream media and the Democrat Party knew and tried to obscure at all costs.

With regard to the bogus "Crossfire Hurricane" being infected by Russian disinformation, Senate homeland security chairman Ron Johnson and Senate finance chairman Chuck Grassley called out the current director of the FBI. Stressed Johnson and Grassley in part:

> We are deeply troubled by the Crossfire Hurricane team's awareness of and apparent indifference to Russian disinformation, as well as by the grossly inaccurate statements by the FBI official in charge of the investigation and its supervisory intelligence analyst . . . what other parts of the FBI's investigation were infected by Russian disinformation?

As well they—and all of us—should be.

Especially in light of the fact that declassified intelligence footnotes showed that U.S. intelligence agencies determined that Russian Intelligence Services (RIS) were well aware of Christopher Steele's fraudulent investigation into then candidate Donald Trump during the summer of 2016 and that a number of Steele's sources supported Hillary Clinton.

On that point, Senators Johnson and Grassley dropped the hammer on the current director of the FBI. They said in part:

> The FBI knew that Russian intelligence was targeting Christopher Steele's company, that Steele relied on sources affiliated with Russian intelligence, and at least two of Steele's reports were described as the product of a Russian disinformation campaign. Because these facts show the intention, means, and ability to plant Russian disinforma-

tion in Steele's reporting, they suggest that the prevalence of such disinformation in the FBI's Crossfire Hurricane investigation may have been widespread.

Not only was the "Steele Dossier" that launched the FBI's "Crossfire Hurricane" investigation a political hit job from the start, but it was riddled with purposeful *Russian* disinformation as well.

Again, any wonder that some in the FBI and the Department of Justice may be doing all in their power to cover up this monumental screwup. I also suspect that even the Russian disinfo may have been Western intel smears made to look "Russian" as evidence suggests some of the sources may have had as many links to Western intelligence agencies as to the Russians.

In December 2019, Department of Justice inspector general Michael Horowitz blistered the Justice Department and the FBI for at least seventeen "significant errors and omissions" related to the bogus FISA warrants against Trump campaign associate Carter Page and for the FBI's reliance on the "Steele Dossier" created for the opposition research firm Fusion GPS and funded by the Democratic National Committee and Hillary Clinton's presidential campaign.

The Department of Justice and the FBI getting publicly spanked by their own inspector general is one thing. Getting outed as complicit is deeply troubling.

And outed they were.

Footnotes from Inspector General Horowitz's FISA investigation report revealed some significant bombshells. These bombshells are blowing up in the faces of those who hid them.

For instance, the inspector general revealed that the FBI's Crossfire Hurricane team was briefed on a document detailing that an individual dubbed "Person 1" and described as a "Key Steele sub-source" had been someone with "historical contact with persons and entities suspected of being linked to *Russian Intelligence Services.*" The document further revealed that "Person 1 was . . . a former *KGB/SVR* officer."

It gets much more troubling.

The footnotes from the inspector general also revealed that senior Department of Justice official Bruce Ohr told a senior FBI agent that he had met with Fusion GPS founder Glenn Simpson, who said that "Person 1" was a "Russian Intelligence Services Officer" central to connecting Trump to Russia.

As these despicable secrets—and potentially serious crimes—continue to leak and pour out, stonewalling by loyalists to Obama and Hillary Clinton within the FBI and the Department of Justice is to be expected.

Taking that as a given, we can assure you that Judicial Watch is doing everything in its power to expose the guilty and call attention to their intertwined illicit and illegal activities.

The reason we can say that with such confidence is that the absolute fact is that Judicial Watch has done more investigation of the Obama administration's and Deep State schemes to overthrow candidate and then President Donald J. Trump than any federal agency, media outlet, or Congress.

Period.

JAMES COMEY-DEEP STATE PERSONIFIED

One name, more than any other, has come to personify the despicable, and criminal conduct of the various Deep State operatives that worked overtime to overthrow the elected president of the United States of America.

That face belongs to disgraced former FBI director James Comey.

It truly boggles the mind to even state this, but as someone who had been director of the FBI, Comey was *leaking President Trump's FBI files/documents* to the liberals as part of a vendetta over Trump's well-considered firing of him.

He leaked as an act of pure revenge against a president—with the express and admitted purpose of spurring the appointment of a "special counsel."

In the act of leaking to harm President Trump, Comey also deliberately smeared the good name of a true American hero, that of retired lieutenant general Michael Flynn, a highly decorated U.S. Army commander who led forces into combat in both Iraq and Afghanistan.

More than smeared, we now know Comey purposely planned to set a trap for and frame this innocent man. He set out to frame an American hero who put his life on the line countless times to protect us all.

Don't just take my word for it. James Comey himself bragged about it.

In 2018, during an interview with liberal "Never Trumper" NBC talking head Nicolle Wallace at a 92nd Street Y conference, Wallace asked Comey about this very subject:

"You look at this White House now and it's hard to imagine two FBI agents ending up in the Sit [Situation] room, how did that happen?" Wallace asked.

"I sent them," Comey brazenly admitted with a slight smile.

He personally sent the two FBI agents into the White House, who, records strongly suggest, entrapped the then national security adviser to the president of the United States.

Comey next admitted it was "[s]omething I probably wouldn't have done or even gotten away with in a more organized investigation, a more organized administration."

Something he wouldn't have "done or even gotten away with" before. Why? Because it was unethical, and likely unlawful.

Comey then went on about how he willfully took advantage of some of the confusion during the Trump transition—coupled with the goodwill of his target—to go after General Flynn. Later, we learned that General Flynn's son was targeted as well.

The disgraced former FBI director further admitted he never would have gotten away with this unethical behavior in the White Houses of Barack Obama and George W. Bush, where they had the normal protocols already established. Because of those past protocols, the FBI would have had to go through a series of steps *before* interviewing or interrogating a White House official.

But not during the first few days of the Trump White House.

"In both of those administrations there was process, so if the FBI wanted to send agents into the White House itself to interview a senior official, you would work through the White House counsel, and there would be discussions and approvals of who would be there and I thought it's early enough, let's just send a couple guys over," gloated Comey.

Meaning, let's take advantage of the fact that the Trump White House didn't have the normal protocols in place yet so let's sneak over and ambush General Flynn.

Which is exactly what Comey did through his invading FBI agents.

"And so," Comey continued. "We placed a call to Flynn and said 'Hey, we're sending a couple guys over, hope you'll talk to them.' He said 'sure.' Nobody else was there, they interviewed him in a conference room at the White House situation room."

Wallace then inadvertently asked a critically important question of Comey: What did Comey think General Flynn thought the interview was going to be about?

"I don't think he knew," Comey said. "We didn't tell him."

We didn't tell him.

On this very subject and from a book by one of Comey's *own assistants* within the FBI, Comey is further quoted as to why he would support this abuse of power.

Said Comey: "We just decided, you know, screw it."

Screw it.

No. It's not that simple. Comey can't let himself off the hook so easily.

He screwed over an innocent man. He screwed over the rule of law. And most important, he screwed over the United States of America.

Finally, and thankfully for General Michael Flynn, calmer and honest heads in the Department of Justice came to that exact same conclusion when in May 2020 they not only dropped the false and deliberately malicious case against Flynn but went out of their way to criticize those who set him up, saying in part it was "conducted without any legitimate investigative basis" and "untethered to, and unjustified by, the FBI's counterintelligence investigation into Mr. Flynn."

Translation: Some in the FBI were caught trying to frame an innocent man; those of us with integrity at the Department of Justice just uncovered that truth; we dropped all the charges against General Flynn; and, we're sorry.

For years, true American hero General Michael Flynn and his family paid a terrible price for an operation that came right out of the playbook from the former East German secret police. Michael Flynn incurred millions in legal bills, was forced to sell his home to try and pay those bills, and saw his sterling reputation for a lifetime of service to his nation destroyed by the actions of the truly corrupt.

James Comey was behind all of this, and there is absolutely no doubt that he will go down as the most corrupt director of the FBI in the history of our republic. He is truly beneath contempt.

So, the real questions still being: *Who* was controlling Comey and *why* set up Flynn?

The first question is the easiest to answer: Barack Obama.

Next. Why set up the general for a fall? The short answer is Comey, President Obama, and those illicitly serving them knew that Flynn—as the former director of the Defense Intelligence Agency—was *much* too experienced and *much* too street-smart not to spot their planned coup attempt against President Trump. For that reason, they had to get rid of him as fast as humanly possible.

With that mission in mind, one can only wonder what, on January 5, 2017, President Barack Obama, Vice President Joe Biden, James Comey, acting attorney general Sally Yates, National Security adviser Susan Rice, CIA director John Brennan, Office of the National Intelligence director James Clapper, and National Security Agency head Michael Rogers were all *really* discussing.

The official reason as stated by Obama and the others is that they were going over the report: "Assessing Russian Activities and Intentions in the Recent U.S. Elections." Not by coincidence, a report asked for and created for: *Barack Obama.*

See how this really works.

Let's keep in mind, that by January 5, 2017, now president-elect Trump had already named General Michael Flynn as his designated national security adviser.

That is important to know for the simple fact that *Barack Obama* truly despised Michel Flynn. He reportedly warned President Trump personally against hiring him. Flynn had a reputation for calling out the intelligence establishment and its radical politicization under the Obama-Clinton regime.

Knowing that, curious minds would then wander back to that

meeting *still* President Obama was holding with his with national security team on January 5, 2017.

We now know that Obama knew that Flynn was an innocent man. This has been further confirmed by documents finally released or declassified the Justice Department (at the insistence of General Flynn's heroic lawyer, Sidney Powell) and by Richard Grenell, who just recently served for three months as acting director of the Office of Director of National Intelligence.

The FBI had concluded that there was "no viable" case against Flynn the day before the meeting on January 4, 2017, but the "7th Floor" intervened and kept the case open. And, of course, they all had the transcripts of Flynn's calls with Russian ambassador Sergey Kislyak, which show no misconduct by General Flynn. In fact, they show Flynn deserves another medal for persuading the Russians *not* to escalate the tense situation with the United States in response to Obama sanctions that were more about embarrassing President-elect Trump than punishing Russia for immaterial interference in our elections.

What is even more intriguing about all of this subterfuge in the last days of the Obama White House is that as the meeting on January 5 was breaking up, Obama asked Comey and Sally Yates—two of the most compromised officials in his administration—to remain in place for a more *private* conversation with Obama himself, Joe Biden, and Susan Rice.

If anyone doesn't believe those five individuals engaged in a conversation about how to bring down the Trump presidency, how to get Flynn, their collective abuse of the FISA court, and gleeful gossip about the discredited and invented "Steele Dossier," then as the saying goes: Have I got a bridge to sell you.

In fact, Sally Yates admitted to the Mueller operation that she was surprised that Obama brought up the Flynn-Kislyak calls. And then the infamous Susan Rice CYA "by the book" memo written weeks later and minutes before President Trump was inaugurated confirms that Obama and Comey knew Flynn was an innocent man: "Director Comey affirmed that he is proceeding 'by the book' as it relates to law enforcement. From a national security perspective, Comey said he does have some concerns that incoming NSA Flynn is speaking frequently with Russian Ambassador Kislyak. Comey said that could be an issue as it relates to sharing sensitive information. President Obama asked if Comey was saying that the NSC should not pass sensitive information related to Russia to Flynn. Comey replied 'potentially.' He added that he has no indication thus far that Flynn has passed classified information to Kislyak, but he noted that 'the level of communication is unusual.'"

So Comey and Obama discuss that Flynn did nothing wrong but then talk about "potentially" and seditiously withholding classified information about one of the most important nations on earth from the incoming president of the United States! And yet this same gang at the Obama holdover-run FBI then tried to entrap Flynn in the Trump White House!

In fact, handwritten notes by the notorious Peter Strzok appear to document that Comey told Obama and others in the Oval Office (including Biden) in early January 2017 that Flynn's calls with the Russian ambassador appeared "legit." In May 2020, President Donald J. Trump addressed these subjects himself. First, with regard to the charges against General Flynn being dropped, the president said in part: "He was an innocent man. He is a great gentleman. He was targeted by the Obama administration and he was *targeted in order to try and take down a president.*"

Jaw-dropping does not begin to adequately describe what

Donald J. Trump—as the *sitting* president of the United States of America—understandably charged regarding the motivations of the previous administration.

Please tell me again the definition of a coup.

With regard to that coup attempt against him, President Trump continued:

> What they've done is a disgrace and I hope a big price is going to be paid. A big price should be paid. There has never been anything like this in the history of our country. What they did, what the Obama administration did, is unprecedented. It's never happened.

We at Judicial Watch have been stressing this from the very beginning. This coup attempt against Trump was like nothing else in the history of our country.

As we close out 2020 it is clear now that "a big price" will be paid by some of those plotting this sedition.

Now, back to the Obama lackey James Comey.

To focus once again on him, let's move up just a month later, when Trump is now president.

Other than as an act of illicit revenge, there is another major reason many believe Comey leaked the memo to the *New York Times* that he said he had "memorialized" on February 14, 2017, after a private conversation in the Oval Office between himself and President Trump regarding Lieutenant General Michael Flynn.

But first, with regard to that "memorializing" business, *come on.*

Who is he trying to kid?

Or, for that matter, former Obama National Security adviser Susan Rice, who hours after she was *out of her job* on January 21,

2017, magically "memorialized" that secret meeting held on January 5 with President Obama, Comey, and the rest of the Obama National *In*-Security team.

She did so for one reason and one reason only: to basically back-date the "conversation" to give them all cover should their corrupt dealings eventually blow up in their faces. Indeed, as this book goes to press, it has been reported that Rice wrote the "by the book" CYA memo at the direction of Obama White House lawyers!

Similarly, as discussed below, Comey then "memorialized" his *private* conversation with President Trump to paper the record. No other witnesses. Just Comey and President Trump.

Gee, wouldn't we all like to be able to do that after private conversations with someone we don't like or are unhappy with and then leak our "memorialized" one-sided version to a major news organization with the express purpose of making us look like the good guy and the person we disagreed with look like the bad or even . . . guilty . . . guy?

Now, back to that *other major reason* Comey not only leaked the conversation but then turned on President Trump so publicly. And it's a really important one that does not get nearly the attention it deserves.

That reason being *guilt*.

A number of people within the conservative community have long believed Comey has always been center-left to outright liberal, including *during* his time as the director of the FBI. Does anyone seriously believe Barack Obama would nominate a FBI director diametrically opposed to his policies?

As such, they also believed that during the 2016 presidential election, he not so secretly wanted Hillary Clinton to win.

But . . . there was a major roadblock to Hillary Clinton's path back to the White House. That being the fact that in July 2015, the FBI itself was forced (after enormous pressure . . . most of it from

Judicial Watch) to open a criminal investigation into Hillary Clinton's use of a private computer and email server while she was secretary of state. You know, the one that used to contain those 33,000 deleted emails.

Whoops.

Then former president Bill Clinton tried to ride to the rescue of his wife by secretly meeting with then Obama attorney general Loretta Lynch onboard her Department of Justice aircraft sitting on the tarmac at the airport in Phoenix.

Talk about both inappropriate and completely stupid.

As soon as the news of that *secret* meeting leaked, there were immediate calls for Lynch to be fired, or at the very least, to recuse herself from the Hillary Clinton email server investigation.

Like that was really going to happen.

Days after the tarmac meeting, on July 2, 2016, FBI agents completed their investigation with an interview of Hillary Clinton at FBI headquarters in Washington, DC, where she professed her total innocence.

Hey, that was *more* than good enough for FBI director James Comey and his gang of compromised associates. So good, in fact, that on July 5, 2016—just *three* days later—Comey held a nationally televised press conference to announce there was no basis for criminal indictments in the case.

Talk about a "Get Out of Jail Free" card.

Not only did all the air go out of the Trump campaign with that unprecedented public acquittal, but it made Hillary Clinton all but a shoo-in to be elected the next president of the United States in four short months.

But . . . then a funny thing happened on the way to the coronation of Queen Hillary. Comey seemed to get cold feet over the clearly unprofessional and biased way he and the FBI had *prematurely* cleared Hillary Clinton of the email scandal. Especially in light of the damning new evidence that was still pouring in to FBI headquarters.

Evidence that was *impossible to ignore,* as much as they wanted to try.

Damning evidence such as FBI agents investigating the *seemingly* totally unrelated case involving former congressman Anthony Weiner and his habit of sending pornographic photos of himself . . . potentially to underage minors. In the course of looking through that cesspool of a laptop computer, the agents discovered emails between Weiner's wife— senior Hillary Clinton aide Huma Abedin—and Hillary Clinton herself. Emails from the Clinton server were on the Weiner laptop!

Whoops, again. No way the FBI could bury *that* revelation.

So, on October 28, 2016, less than two weeks before the presidential election, Comey figuratively crawled out of his rat hole once again to send a sheepish letter to members of Congress alerting them to the fact that the FBI had stumbled upon the huge cache of emails between Abedin and Hillary Clinton and therefore, the investigation regarding the former secretary of state and her email server was being *reopened.*

Talk about an "October Surprise."

Just like that, all the air flew out of the Clinton campaign balloon *back* into the Trump campaign balloon.

As soon as it did, Hillary Clinton and her supporters went berserk and directed their instant, unhinged rage at FBI director James Comey.

So the question then becomes, if Comey was in reality more liberal than not, and was no fan, like many "Establishment Republicans," of Donald Trump, *why* would he reopen the investigation of Hillary Clinton less than two weeks before the election?

Three potentially very solid reasons:

First, because the new evidence was in fact so damning that he felt he had no choice and was worried about his own reputation and *legal exposure* should he not.

Next, because deep inside, he knew the dog-and-pony show he had put on in July 2016 to seemingly exonerate Hillary Clinton had crossed several professional and ethical lines and history would eventually record that fact and paint him as the stooge many knew him to be.

The last possible reason being that James Comey is a complete and utter weasel only interested in himself at the expense of anyone and anything—including the welfare of his own country.

As such, a part of him wanted to cover his bets *just in case* Trump somehow won. The last thing Comey needed was a newly elected President Trump coming after him for improper and possibly criminal behavior.

But then, of course, Trump did win.

Against all odds, against every poll, and against the entrenched elites in the Democrat Party, the media, academia, entertainment, and even the "Never Trumpers" within the Republican Party, Trump pulled off the impossible and made history in the process.

As a real-world businessman outsider with absolutely no political experience and virtually no campaign team, Donald J. Trump got himself elected president of the United States of America.

And because Comey did reopen the investigation of Hillary Clinton, he certainly did play a role in the historic outcome.

"What have I done?" he must have asked himself time and time again as Trump organized his transition team and prepared to take the oath of office as the next president.

Trump the next president . . . instead of Hillary Clinton.

Oh, the very horror of it all for Comey. He clearly had to be despondent.

We now know Comey had decided to let Clinton off the hook *long before* the FBI had completed its investigation of her. Long before. The FBI was forced to release a memo written by Comey on May 2, 2016, more than two months *before* his press conference to the nation and world to exonerate Hillary Clinton.

The FBI further revealed that in the *initial* draft of that May 2 exoneration letter, Comey stated that Clinton had committed "gross negligence" in handling classified information on her server.

Yikes. "Gross negligence" is wording from federal law that details a crime.

But, it seems one of Comey's fellow Trump-hating underlings caught that major mistake, which would have spelled doom for Hillary Clinton, and changed that charge to "extreme carelessness" instead.

Gee, whoever could have made that change to Comey's draft in the hope of saving Hillary Clinton? Why, it turns out it was none other than disgraced former FBI agent Peter Strzok.

As in the same Peter Strzok who was fired by the FBI for conduct (documented in countless text messages) seen as strongly anti-Trump and favoring . . . *Hillary Clinton.*

But, to the everlasting shame of the FBI and the DOJ, Strzok was not fired before he could inflict more damage upon the nation by joining Robert Mueller's witch-hunt probe against President Trump.

So, back to the heartsick James Comey.

Not only did liberal analysts on CNN and MSNBC say Comey was at least partially responsible for Hillary Clinton's embarrassing defeat, but Clinton herself would later claim the same thing.

In an interview after the loss with far-left CNN talking head Christiane Amanpour, Clinton said in part: "I was on the way to winning until a combination of Jim Comey's letter on October 28th and Russian WikiLeaks raised doubts in the minds of people who were inclined to vote for me and got scared off."

"Scared off" is the way Hillary Clinton would put it. Others would say voters were "reminded" of her shady lack of respect for the rule of law.

In January 2017, the inspector general for the Department of Justice launched a formal investigation into whether the FBI engaged in "improper considerations" regarding the investigation of Hillary Clinton.

In June 2018, Inspector General Michael Horowitz issued a report highly critical of former FBI director James Comey. Among other things, he found that Comey's handling of the Hillary Clinton email probe was "insubordinate." Horowitz further admonished that Comey made "a serious error in judgement," "usurped the authority of the Attorney General," "chose to deviate" from established procedures, and engaged "[i]n his own subjective, ad hoc decision making" by publicly announcing on July 5, 2016, that he wouldn't recommend any charges in the Hillary Clinton email investigation.

President Donald J. Trump himself may have summed it up best when he said: "Perhaps never in the history of our Country has someone been more thoroughly disgraced and excoriated than James Comey in the just released Inspector General's Report. He should be ashamed of himself!"

Leaving that humiliating public spanking of Comey aside, the Department of Justice also revealed that some of Comey's other leaked memos contained *classified information*.

This guy should not have been allowed to be the director of a Boy Scout troop, let alone an organization tasked with the protection of our nation and those who reside within her still sovereign borders.

Sadly, Comey *was* director of the FBI. And he did do significant harm to our republic. For it was from that lofty perch—and after being pushed from it—that he chose to engage in an open vendetta against President Donald J. Trump.

As to why, it was because men and women—like James Comey—took an oath to protect our nation. But instead, for partisan and personal reasons, they chose to try to destroy it from within instead.

Don't just take my word for it. We have the proof from FBI records. In fact, Judicial Watch just received the "Holy Grail" of Obamagate—the FBI "electronic communication" opening the spy operation against President Trump known as "Crossfire Hurricane"!

In fact, it was on May 20, 2020, that we finally uncovered one of the most important documents we have ever unearthed in the history of Judicial Watch.

The document is proof that Crossfire Hurricane was a scam, based on absurd gossip and innuendo. The document Judicial Watch obtained is Exhibit A to Obamagate—the worst corruption scandal in American history.

The document in question—which we obtained through a Freedom of Information Act lawsuit—is the previously classified, and deeply disturbing July 31, 2016, FBI "Electronic Communication" that was the scam excuse for launching the fraudulent counterintelligence investigation of the Trump campaign.

Thanks to our investigative work and lawsuit, Kevin Brock—among many others—was able to view the document for the very first time and then comment. Who is Kevin Brock? Only the former assistant director of intelligence for the FBI. Additionally, Brock not only served as an FBI special agent for twenty-four years, but was principal deputy director of the National Counterterrorism Center.

Upon viewing the FBI Electronic Communication created under

false pretenses at the organization where he served protecting our nation for over two decades, Brock said—among other things—in a piece for *The Hill* newspaper:

> What this FBI document clearly establishes is that Crossfire Hurricane was an illicit, made-up investigation lacking a shred of justifying predication, sprung from the mind of someone who despised Donald Trump, and then blessed by inexperienced leadership at the highest levels who harbored their own now well-established biases.[1]

And just which mind that "despised Donald Trump" did the document spring from? In this case, the document sprang from the mind of Peter Strzok, one of the two FBI "Lovers" who were out to get Donald Trump. Much more on both of them later in the book.

We should note that Judicial Watch had previously received a production of 144 pages of emails between Strzok and former FBI attorney Lisa Page in which this very electronic communication was discussed.

As Kevin Brock further stated, this FBI electronic communication was used as the pretext to try to stop the Trump campaign and then, when that failed, used to try to topple a legally and constitutionally elected president: "*Essentially . . . a document created by Peter Strzok, approved by Peter Strzok, and sent from Peter Strzok to Peter Strzok.*"

Beyond Strzok, we have—as Brock labeled them—the "inexperienced leadership at the highest levels who harbored their own now well-established biases" and "blessed" the document.

And just who are the names of the FBI leadership who "harbored" those biases against Trump and presumably in favor of Hillary Clinton? Well, the former assistant director of intelligence for the FBI goes a long way toward solving that mystery as well.

Explained Brock:

Names on an FBI document are always listed in cascading fashion, with the most senior at the top and on down to the least senior. On this EC, Strzok is listed last, so the redacted names should be more senior to him. Those names could well include then–FBI Director James Comey, then–Deputy Director Andrew McCabe and then–Counterintelligence Assistant Director Bill Priestap.

Taking a direct shot at Comey, Brock said:

To paraphrase a fired FBI director: "No reasonable FBI counterintelligence squad supervisor in the field would have approved and opened that Strzok EC. They know the rules too well."

Which again, is entirely the point. Those at the FBI intent on bringing down Trump at any cost could not care less about the rules. Brock closes out his column by stressing:

The rule of law, upon which the FBI rests its very purpose and being, was callously discarded by weak leaders who sought higher loyalty to their personal agendas, egos, biases and politics. Accountability is demanded by the American people. Let's pray we see some.

While we at Judicial Watch strongly believe in the power of prayer, we also believe that the Lord helps those who help themselves. That's why we filed the Freedom of Information Act lawsuit now creating the accountability that Brock rightfully stated is "demanded by the American people."

———

What follows is the text of the FBI "electronic communication" obtained by Judicial Watch through our Freedom of Information Act lawsuit.

Keep in mind as you read what the former assistant director of intelligence for the FBI said of the document: "To the trained eye, however, it is a train wreck."

FEDERAL BUREAU OF INVESTIGATION

Electronic Communication

Title: Crossfire Hurricane Date: 07/31/2016

Cc: [Redacted]

Strzok Peter P II

From: COUNTERINTELLIGENCE

[Redacted]

Contact: Strzok Peter P II, [Redacted]

Approved by: Strzok Peter P II

Drafted by: Strzok Peter P II

Case ID #: [Redacted]

CROSSFIRE HURRICANE;

FOREIGN AGENTS REGISTRATION ACT –

RUSSIA;

SENSITIVE INVESTIGATIVE MATTER

DOCUMENT RESTRICTED TO CASE PARTICIPANTS

This document contains information that is restricted to case participants

Synopsis: (S/ / CC/NF) Opens and assigns investigation

Reason 1.4 (b)

Derived from: FBI

NSISC-20090615

Declassify On: 20411231

[Redacted]

(S/NF) An investigation is being opened based on information received by Legat [Redacted] on 07/29/2016. The text of that email follows:

SECRET/ORCON/NOFORN
[Redacted]

Title: (S/ / CC/NF) CROSSFIRE HURRICANE
Re: [Redacted] 07/31/2016

BEGIN EMAIL

(U/ /FOUO) Legat [Redacted] information from [Redacted] Deputy Chief of Mission

Synopsis:
(U/ /FOUO) Legat [Redacted] received information from the [Redacted] Deputy Chief of Mission related to the hacking of the Democratic National Committee's website/server.

Details:
(S/ /REL TO USA[Redacted] On Wednesday, July 27, 2016, Legal Attaché (Legat) [Redacted] was summoned to the Office of the Deputy Chief of Mission (DCM) for the [Redacted] who will be leaving [Redacted] post Saturday July 30, 2016 and set to soon thereafter retire from government service, advised [Redacted] was called by [Redacted] about an urgent matter requiring an in person meeting with the U.S. Ambassador. [Note: [Redacted]. The [Redacted] was scheduled to be away from post until mid-August, therefore [Redacted] attended the meeting.

(S/ [Redacted]) [Redacted] advised that [Redacted] government had been seeking prominent members of the Donald Trump campaign in which to engage to prepare for potential post-election relations should Trump be elected U.S. President. One of the people identified was George Papadopolous [sic] (although public media sources provide a spelling of Papadopoulos), who was believed to be one of Donald Trump's foreign policy advisers. Mr. Papdopoulos [sic] was located in [Redacted] so the [Redacted] met with him on several occasions, with [Redacted] attending at least one of the meetings.

(S/ [Redacted]) [Redacted] recalled [Redacted] of the meetings between Mr. Papdopolous [sic] and [Redacted] concerning statements Mr. Papadopolous [sic] made about suggestions from the Russians that they (the Russians) could assist the Trump campaign with the anonymous release of information during the campaign that would be damaging to Hillary Clinton. [Redacted] provided a copy of the reporting that was provided to [Redacted] from [Redacted] to Legal [Redacted]. The text is exactly as follows:

(Begin Text)

(S/ [Redacted]) 5. Mr. Papadopolous [sic] [Redacted] also suggested the Trump team had received some kind of suggestion from Russia that it could assist this process with the anonymous release of information during the campaign that would be damaging to Mrs. Clinton (and President Obama). It was unclear whether he or the Russians were referring to material acquired publicly or through other means. It was also

unclear how Mr. Trump's team reacted to the offer. We note
the Trump team's reaction could, in the end, have little bearing
of what Russia decides to do, with or without Mr. Trump's
cooperation.

(End Text)

(s/ [Redacted]

[Redacted]

(s/ [Redacted] Legat requests that further action on
this information should consider the sensitivity that this
information was provided through informal diplomatic
channels from [Redacted] to the U.S. Embassy's DCM. It was
clear from the conversation Legal [Redacted] had with DCM
that [Redacted] knew follow-up by the U.S. government would
be necessary, but extraordinary efforts should be made to
protect the source of this information until such a time that a
request from our organization can be made to [Redacted] to
obtain this information through formal channels.

[[END EMAIL]]

(S/ / CC/NF) Based on the information provided by Legat
[Redacted] this investigation is being opened to determine
whether individual(s) associated with the Trump campaign are
witting of and/or coordinating activities with the Government
of Russia.

In March 2018, based upon the information contained in the DOJ
communication and other information, the Intelligence Committee
produced a 150-page report, the summary of which states: "We have

found no evidence of collusion, coordination, or conspiracy between the Trump campaign and the Russians."

In an interview after reviewing the electronic communication, U.S. representative Devin Nunes, ranking member of the House Permanent Select Committee on Intelligence, said, "We now know there was no official intelligence used to start this investigation."

No wonder the DOJ and FBI strongly and continuously resisted the public release of this infamous electronic communication that did disregard the rule of law and "opened" Crossfire Hurricane. Strzok sat down and literally wrote himself a memo full of vague innuendo, and then approved his own memo—and thereby launched an unprecedented spy operation on a presidential candidate. As intelligence expert Kevin Brock noted:

> On that basis alone, the document is an absurdity, violative of all FBI protocols and, therefore, invalid on its face. An agent cannot approve his or her own case; that would make a mockery of the oversight designed to protect Americans. Yet, for this document, Peter Strzok was pitcher, catcher, batter and umpire.

Unfortunately for the FBI and the coup cabal, Judicial Watch refused to take no for an answer and now the American people have more of the truth and the Justice Department has less cover to avoid holding Strzok and others accountable for this abuse of power to target Trump and mess with our elections.

Knowing what we know now, and as each day, week, and month does bring out more evidence regarding this coup attempt, it becomes clearer and clearer that then–president Barack Obama was behind much of it.

The emerging picture of the infamous Obama Oval Office meeting of January 5, 2017, accelerated Comey's Javert-like targeting of General Flynn and President Trump.

Hopefully one day, when we can once again rely on honest, fair, and unbiased historians, those scholars will conclusively agree that the one president who should have been impeached by the House of Representatives and convicted by the Senate was Barack Obama.

The "Chicago Way" disgraced the White House and shook the pillars of liberty, the repercussions of which we are still feeling and suffering from to this very day.

What follows is a deep dive into Judicial Watch's incomparable investigation and litigation into the Obamagate Deep State coup.

ALL HANDS ON DECK—DEEP STATE AGENCIES TARGET TRUMP

One of the underreported aspects of the seditious assault on the Trump presidency is how much of it was organized and originated out of the Kerry State Department. Multiple versions of the dossier were laundered out of the agency, and Obama officials worked desperately to undermine President Trump with the Russia smear up until the moment he was inaugurated.

The Justice Department, Congress, and the leftist media had little interest or ability in uncovering this scandal, so it was left to Judicial Watch to do all the heavy lifting. We did have some help though, as, together with the Daily Caller News Foundation, we released eighty-four pages of documents revealing that the Obama State Department was central to advancing the Russian collusion hoax narrative prior to the 2016 presidential election. Included in the documents is "a September 2016 email exchange between then–Assistant Secretary of State Victoria Nuland and Special Coordinator for Libya Jonathan Winer, a close associate of dossier author Christopher Steele, discussing a 'face-to-face' meeting on a 'Russian matter.'"[2]

According to an op-ed Winer authored in the *Washington Post* in 2018, Winer acknowledged he was part of the effort to push the infamous dossier. He wrote that, also in September 2016, "Steele and I met in Washington and discussed the information now known as the 'dossier.' . . . I prepared a two-page summary and shared it with Nuland, who indicated that, like me, she felt that the secretary of state needed to be made aware of this material."

The documents also show that State Department officials continued to use unsecure BlackBerry devices for the transmission of classified material more than a year after Hillary Clinton's use of an unsecure, nongovernment email system was revealed.

In June 2019, the *Daily Caller* also reported that Jonathan Winer "facilitated meetings between Christopher Steele and private consulting firms," and "had contact with Glenn Simpson, the founder of Fusion GPS, the opposition research firm that hired Steele on behalf of the Clinton campaign and DNC."

These documents show that Fusion GPS and Clinton spy Christopher Steele had a close relationship with the Obama State Department. The State Department under John Kerry turns out to be a key center of the Spygate conspiracy against President Trump.

Winer's involvement in advancing the Russia collusion hoax also includes disseminating information that would end up in the dossier to the State Department and with the media prior to the election.

Winer has said that during a meeting in summer 2016, Steele

provided him with information that would end up in the dossier. Winer wrote a two-page summary of the information and shared it with others at State. Here you can see how State Department resources were used to help write a version of the dossier!

Winer also helped with news stories about Steele's findings. He served as a background source for reporters Michael Isikoff and David Corn, who were the only two journalists to write stories about Steele's claims prior to the election. Isikoff published a story for Yahoo! on September 23, 2016, that laid out Steele's allegations about Carter Page.

Corn published a story on October 31, 2016, that quoted Steele anonymously claiming that the Russian government has compromised Trump.

Both reporters used Winer to vouch for Steele's credibility. Other emails obtained through the Judicial Watch lawsuit showed that Glenn Simpson reached out to Winer days before Isikoff published his story on September 23, 2016.

Winer "is also linked to a second dossier on Trump, this one authored by Cody Shearer, a controversial political operative who is closely allied to the Clintons." Winer reportedly obtained the "Shearer dossier" from longtime Clinton associate Sidney Blumenthal and then gave it to Steele, who provided it to the FBI.

"It's amazing how hard our government tries to keep the truth from the American people," noted Neil Patel, the president of the Daily Caller News Foundation. "Thankfully, with Judicial Watch filing a lawsuit on our behalf, we have been able to uncover phony dossier author Christopher Steele's previously hidden contacts with the Obama State Department."

THE STATE DEPARTMENT WORKS
OVERTIME TO UNDERMINE TRUMP

The "Obama-Kerry-Clinton" State Department was a multiheaded monster that quickly became a nest of desperate anti-Trump activity.

I remain astonished by the ninety pages of heavily redacted U.S. Department of State documents we uncovered detailing Obama State Department officials' efforts to disseminate classified information to multiple U.S. senators immediately prior to President Donald Trump's inauguration.[3]

The information, which included raw intelligence, purported to show "malign" Russian interference in the 2016 presidential election. Among the senators receiving the classified documents were Senator Mark Warner (D-VA), Senator Ben Cardin (D-MD), and then anti-Trump Republican senator Robert Corker from Tennessee.

We obtained the documents through our June 2018 Freedom of Information Act lawsuit filed against the State Department after it failed to respond to a February 2018 request seeking records of the Obama State Department's last-minute efforts to share classified information about Russia election interference issues with Democratic senator Ben Cardin (*Judicial Watch v. U.S. Department of State* [No. 1:18-cv-01381]).

A January 13, 2017, email from Hera Abbasi, a former congressional adviser in the State Department's Bureau of Legislative Affairs, suggests that the intelligence community was providing "raw intel" to Senator Warner. Such an exchange almost certainly would have been coordinated by the Office of the Director of National Intelligence (ODNI): "Yes, that is correct. Warner/raw intel stuff is going thru IC channels." (Abbasi previously worked in Speaker Nancy Pelosi's office and was a 2017 Next Generation National Security Fellow at the liberal

Center for a New American Security. Abbasi donated $725 to the Clinton campaign and Act Blue during the 2016 election cycle.)

The documents show that early in the process of gathering and clearing classified information—beginning a day after Senator Warner formally asked Secretary of State John Kerry for "intelligence products" and "raw intelligence" on Russian involvement in the 2016 election—Assistant Secretary of State Julia Frifield brings Senior Advisor and Investigations Counsel Zachary Schram into the loop in a January 5, 2017, email chain, in which she says Schram would help "figure out the best way to get these to the Hill." Frifield was an Obama appointee who previously served as Maryland Democratic senator Barbara Mikulski's chief of staff. (Frifield contributed $2,700 to the 2016 Clinton campaign.)

On January 11, 2017, former State Department senior congressional advisor Kathrine Harris sends an email to Abbasi; Naz Durakoglu, who was a senior advisor to the assistant secretary for European and Eurasian affairs; Kathleen Kavalec; and others that seems to confirm they were breaking the rules to get Trump: "If we are not going through our standard CDP [Collection Due Process] process, others in H need to weigh in on how to move these to the Hill."

In emails written on January 10 and 11, 2017, from Abbasi to Durakoglu and Kavalec, Abassi expresses the need to get the documents cleared "as soon as possible (ASAP)."

On January 17, 2017, three days before Trump's inauguration, Kavalec emails Abbasi, Durakoglu, and others emphasizing, again, that getting the documents to Cardin and Warner is a priority and urges the process to be sped up:

> Agree this is a priority . . . and I don't see why lengthy reviews are
> required. I would suggest we send up the things that can go immedi-

ately, and if there is any concern about specific internal documents, those be adjudicated separately and sent up as a follow-on.

In a January 18, 2017, email from Naz Durakoglu to Elizabeth Lawrence, Abbasi, former Foreign Service officer Kerem Bilge, and others regarding the processing of the request, Durakoglu writes, "there is a time sensitivity to these docs."

Shedding additional light on possible irregularities in the release process, a January 17, 2017, email reveals that ODNI, then led by James Clapper, was involved in clearing cables for release to the Hill. State Department official Cody Walsh emails Schram and Lauren Gills that the ODNI is "fine" with the State Department "sharing . . . cables with the Hill."

On January 13, 2017, at 10:27 a.m., Durakoglu emails more than a dozen State Department employees, invoking the name of then assistant secretary of state Victoria Nuland to reiterate the need to accelerate the process of getting materials prepared to go to the Hill: "Hi All. This is a priority for our Assistant Secretary . . . Is there anything we can do to better facilitate the process?"

Two minutes later, Durakoglu emails Kerem Bilge and two others: "Where are we on clearances? Do I need to ask Toria to raise with Julia? The clock is ticking." Durakoglu, at the time, was a senior advisor to Nuland. Durakoglu currently works for the Atlantic Council. She contributed $1,600 to the Clinton campaign in 2016.

The concluding, unredacted section of an otherwise heavily redacted email sent on Friday, January 13, 2017, by Kerem Bilge to numerous State employees indicates the intense time pressure under which State officials were operating to beat the Inauguration Day deadline:

**** Please clear the action memo by noon TUESDAY [Jan. 17].
****** Please clear on the actual package of documents, if
you have not done so already, by noon TUESDAY** [Jan. 17].
[Emphasis in original]

I want to get the whole package into the EUR front office today.
This means we can get it out of EUR and to M [Undersecretary
for Management] on Wednesday [Jan. 18], then H can courier it
to the Hill on Thursday [Jan 19].

In a January 18, 2017, email, as time was running out, Elizabeth
Lawrence described getting the package of cables to Cardin and Warner as "urgent": "This is an urgent package from EUR that they're trying to get to the Hill ASAP. Please review so we can get it up to M."
(Lawrence is a career foreign service officer, now the Consul in New
Delhi, and was previously a Foreign Policy Advisor to Illinois Democratic senator Dick Durbin. A DC-based State Department employee,
her name is on record as having donated a cumulative total of $1,000
to the Clinton campaign in 2016.)

The final batch of cables was stored in Kavalec's safe.

President Trump was inaugurated less than twenty-four hours later.

These documents show how the Obama State Department, staffed
by Clinton donors, improperly, and perhaps illegally, rushed classified
information to their anti-Trump allies in the U.S. Senate. The Obama
State Department was central to the conspiracy to smear President
Trump with Russiagate lies and innuendo. The Justice Department
must expand any Spygate criminal investigation to include this agency.

We also uncovered other documents showing classified information
was researched and disseminated to multiple U.S. senators by the
Obama administration immediately prior to President Donald Trump's
inauguration. The documents reveal that among those receiving the

classified documents were Senator Mark Warner (D-VA), Senator Ben Cardin (D-MD), and Senator Robert Corker (R-TN). A January 19, 2017, email from Durakoglu sums it up: "We made the deadline! Thank you everyone for what was truly a Department-wide effort!"

Made the deadline? If the dissemination of this material was appropriate, why would Inauguration Day be a "deadline"? It is only a deadline, it seems, because shoveling classified information out the door to political allies on the Hill was an essential part of a get-Trump effort. We also previously released an email exchange between then assistant secretary of state Victoria Nuland and Special Coordinator for Libya Jonathan Winer, a close associate of dossier author Christopher Steele, discussing a "face-to-face" meeting on a "Russian matter."

In May 2019, we uncovered documents showing a conversation between Kavalec and former associate deputy attorney general Bruce Ohr, discussing the targeting of Donald Trump with Steele dossier material.

In June, we made public documents revealing that State Department "Special Coordinator for Libya" Jonathan Winer played a key role in facilitating Steele's access to other top government officials and prominent international business executives.

We also uncovered documents showing Nuland and Winer coordinating with then House minority whip Steny Hoyer's (D-MD) national security advisor, Daniel Silverberg, to work on Russia dossier materials provided by Steele.

Are you beginning to see the pattern here? That pattern being: "Smear Trump at any price."

Once again, what happens to a free society and nation when those tasked with protecting it turn against their duties and oaths for their own partisan and personal means?

By "smearing Trump" and attempting to take him down, many in our powerful and secretive spy agencies made a mockery of their oaths while unleashing themselves against the rule of law. And once they did, the Justice Department and the FBI made it purposefully difficult for us and even Congress to get to the bottom of it.

Too bad for them. Judicial Watch is *always* eager to get to the bottom of it.

CHRISTOPHER STEELE JUMPS INTO BED WITH TOP OBAMA STATE DEPARTMENT OFFICIALS

Of course, to have as massive a conspiracy as we are describing above, you need conspirators and co-conspirators.

Christopher Steele was one of the first to step forward. In fact, he oozed into the State Department much earlier than suspected. But it was no surprise to us, as we were onto him from practically the very start.

As mentioned earlier, Judicial Watch and the Daily Caller News Foundation released 146 pages of State Department documents revealing that former British spy and dossier author Christopher Steele had an extensive and close working relationship dating back to May 2014 with high-ranking Obama State Department officials.[4]

The documents obtained by Judicial Watch in a Freedom of Information Act lawsuit show that, from May 2014 to November 2015, Steele filed dozens of reports with his close associate at State, Special Coordinator for Libya Jonathan Winer, who would then pass them to Assistant Secretary of State Victoria Nuland. The reports focused mainly on the Russia-Ukraine crisis and U.S. sanctions on Russia.

The documents show that Steele's work was also distributed to State Department Coordinator for Sanctions Policy Daniel Fried and

Principal Deputy Assistant Secretary Paul Jones, whose focus in the Bureau of European and Eurasian Affairs was on Russia and Ukraine policy.

By way of example, an early Steele report was passed by Winer to Nuland on May 19, 2014. It discusses Russia-Ukraine policy. Winer writes: "Toria, another piece that is not in my lane but which I wished to pass on to you. My friend Chris Steele (Orbis Intelligence, former MI-6 Russia expert), provided me the enclosed memo yesterday, describing a recent conversation (redacted) on Russian Ukraine policy. As I was provided it from a person in private sector, I am treating it as low side."

In a November 20, 2014, email exchange, Winer offers to introduce Principal Deputy Assistant Secretary of State Paul Jones to Steele while Steele was to be in town, and he provides Jones and Nuland with three Steele reports, discussing: "Ukraine looking towards [redacted]"; "Ukraine economy shrinking due to loss of East [redacted]"; and "President Putin's current priorities [redacted]." Winer writes to Jones: "Paul, if you are still free, does 3 pm work to meet with Chris Steele? I would pick him up downstairs, get him to your office, and sit in. Will be sending you another Orbis report regardless in a few minutes, it just arrived but I haven't had chance to open it and manicure it yet."

These new documents show that Clinton spy Christopher Steele had an outsized influence, to put it mildly, at the Obama State Department that proved useful when the Clinton campaign needed help smearing Trump in 2016 and beyond. Steele, you can see, was not just a tool of the Clinton campaign, but was an operative of the Kerry State Department. The documents show Steele shared nearly three dozen reports with Obama-run Foggy Bottom—*before* Russiagate. He may as well as have had a desk at the Obama State Department.

In May 2019, a related Judicial Watch lawsuit produced information from the DOJ showing a conversation between former deputy assistant secretary of state for the Bureau of European and Eurasian Affairs Kathleen Kavalec and Bruce Ohr, discussing the targeting of Donald Trump with Steele dossier material. In discussing a meeting with the potential source for a *Mother Jones* article accusing the Trump campaign of taking money from a Russian-American oil magnate, as well as Steele's connection to that source, Kavalec emails Ohr citing the accusatory *Mother Jones* article. Ohr says, "I really hope we can get something going here." You can see that Ohr had it in for Trump.

In March 2019, Judicial Watch uncovered emails from Bruce Ohr showing that he remained in regular contact with former British spy and Fusion GPS contractor Steele after Steele was terminated by the FBI in November 2016 for revealing to the media his position as an FBI confidential informant. The records show that Ohr served as a go-between for Steele by passing along information to "his colleagues" on matters relating to Steele's activities. Ohr also set up meetings with Steele, regularly talked to him on the telephone, and provided him assistance in dealing with situations Steele was confronting with the media.

RUSSIANS? WHO WAS *REALLY* DEALING WITH THEM?

As we have been outlining, Steele, Ohr, and a number of others were either in direct contact with Russian assets, or were being used by those Russian intelligence operatives.

We uncovered blockbuster State Department documents revealing that on December 23, 2016, twenty-eight days before the inauguration of President Donald Trump, State Department special coordinator for Libya Jonathan Winer had a ten-minute phone call with Alexey Vladimirovich Skosyrev, the "political chief" at the Russian embassy in Washington, D.C.[5]

Following Winer's December 23 call with Russian political operative "Skosyrev," State Department official Anne Sackville-West provides a "read-out" of the call to department colleagues in which she updates the "S-Lavrov points" (Russian foreign minister Sergey Lavrov). The body of the readout is entirely redacted as classified for reasons of national security or foreign policy. Despite the classification, Eric Green, then director of the Office of Russian Affairs in the Eurasian Bureau of the State Department, forwarded the exchange via his unsecure BlackBerry to Deputy Assistant Secretary of State for the Bureau of European and Eurasian Affairs Kathleen Kavalec, to Obama assistant secretary of state for European and Eurasian affairs Ambassador Victoria Nuland, and to Principal Deputy Assistant Secretary John Heffern. Kavalec then responds, saying "Jonathan called me after first trying to get through to Toria and John. He relayed this readout, noting that Skosyrev emphasized that [redacted]."It is shameful that the Deep State Department, as President Trump has called it, is covering up the details of this Russia collusion by the Obama administration. But we can see how the Kerry State Department and Jonathan Winer worked hand in glove with the Clinton Fusion GPS spy Christopher Steele. It is suspicious, to say the least, that Winer was in contact with a senior Russian government official as the Kerry State Department was simultaneously pushing the Russia smear against then president-elect Trump.

Judicial Watch also uncovered State Department documents showing that Winer played a key role in facilitating Steele's access to other top government officials, prominent international business executives. Winer was even approached by a movie producer about making a movie about the Russiagate targeting of President Trump. In September 2019, Judicial Watch released State Department documents revealing that former British spy and dossier author Christopher Steele had an extensive and close working relationship dating back to May 2014 with Winer and Nuland.

STATE DEPARTMENT OFFICIAL IMITATES HILLARY TO USE PERSONAL EMAIL IN SECRET AND CORRUPT WAYS

Those out to get Trump were seemingly disseminating false or invented information after he announced his candidacy; during his campaign; hours before he took office; hours after he took office; and ever since.

As you are learning, no matter when or where we looked, we continued to find evidence of Department of Justice, FBI, State Department, and other Deep State activists acting as one to get out that fake information with the express goal of bringing down candidate and then President Trump.

As we all know, much of this is either learned behavior, or being done to impress someone important and to curry favor with them.

One such person all of these conspirators and coconspirator continually wanted to impress or emulate was: Hillary Clinton.

And to be sure, Hillary Clinton loves to be a role model . . . for those she can use. Most especially it seems, when she is schooling others on the art of deception.

We surmise this because people in Obama's State Department

other than Hillary Clinton were oblivious, to put it charitably, to the fact that using personal email for government business is a security risk and can also thwart federal record-keeping laws.

We uncovered the use of personal email by a State Department official involved with the notorious British spy Steele.

In our lawsuit filed together with the Daily Caller News Foundation we uncovered eleven pages of State Department documents revealing a discussion about the use of private email to transmit potentially sensitive information from Steele.[6]

We obtained the documents in a Freedom of Information Act (FOIA) lawsuit filed on April 25, 2018, on behalf the Daily Caller News Foundation against the State Department after it failed to respond to three separate FOIA requests (*Judicial Watch v. U.S. Department of State* (No. 1:18-cv- 00968)).

Here's the story.

On December 8, 2014, Principal Deputy Assistant Secretary for European Affairs Paul Jones suggests to Special Coordinator for Libya Jonathan Winer that he "flip" reports from Steele's firm, Orbis Business Intelligence, to a more secure email system, "given our ongoing concerns about security of opennet . . ."

Jones added, "We just want to be sure we don't inadvertently undermine a very good source of info or worse." Winer responds, "Flipping to the high side will result in delays whenever the reporting takes place and I am out of the office, which includes weekends plus when I am overseas. . . . " Then assistant secretary of state Victoria Nuland replies, "Let's do high side."

Winer replies that he would "have [his assistant] Nina Miller send them to you on my behalf high side. . . . I will send them to her from my non-State email account, not copying myself. She will then send them to us. You know who they are coming from, so even high side from here I will just refer to them as 'O Reports,' and strip out any other identifying information as to sourcing."

On February 9, 2016, a heavily redacted email exchange with the subject "Urgent—[redacted]" begins with an email from Justin Siberell, former principal deputy coordinator of the State Department's Counterterrorism Bureau, to multiple senior State Department officials including Winer. In this exchange, Siberell mentions that they are "meeting later today with OSD/SOLIC [redacted]." OSD/SOLIC is the office run by the Assistant Secretary of Defense for Special Operations/Low Intensity Conflict.

Siberell notes that the "DOD will work on press guidance and a strategic messaging plan that will be cleared with/through State," which implies that it is a matter of public relations concern.

Later in the redacted discussion, Winer changes the distribution list and writes, "For this group only—[redacted]." Secretary John Kerry's chief of staff Jonathan Finer responds, "As Jonathan predicted [redacted]."

One of the other recipients, Deputy Assistant Secretary for Europe John Heffern, then forwards the entire exchange to two colleagues, Deputy Assistant Secretary of State for Western Europe Conrad Tribble and then office director for Western European affairs, Robin Quinville, saying, "Do not circulate widely."

Tribble replies the next day asking Heffern and Quinville, "Anything further on this? No real action for EUR [State Department's Bureau of Europe and Eurasian Affairs] yet, but obviously of some concern."

No wonder Jonathan Winer, Steele's ally at the State Department, refused to talk to the DOJ inspector general who investigated the Russiagate/Obamagate affair. He seems to have circumvented the rules in pushing Steele's unreliable reports to his Obama State Department colleagues. Our lawsuits have documented that the Obama-Kerry State Department was a hotbed of anti-Trump activity. Attorney General

William Barr and U.S. Attorney John Durham would do well to focus like a laser on the State Department.

Again, the State Department was a center of the Obamagate storm: Steele had an extensive and close working relationship dating back to May 2014 with high-ranking Obama State Department officials including Winer and Nuland. And less than a month before the presidential inauguration Winer had a ten-minute phone call with Alexey Vladimirovich Skosyrev, the "political chief" at the Russian embassy in Washington, DC.

Another mail exchange between Nuland and Winer discussed a "face-to-face" meeting on a "Russian matter" in New York in September 2016.

Again, Winer was even approached by a movie producer about making a movie about the Russiagate targeting of President Trump.

No surprise to us that some in Hollywood are willing to team up with the Deep State to take down President Trump. And the State Department's role in the assault on President Trump wouldn't end with the Obama administration; it would continue with his holdovers during the Trump administration and culminate, as we'll see later, in the outrageous impeachment attack on the president.

BRUCE AND NELLIE OHR— THE "BONNIE AND CLYDE" OF THE ATTEMPT TO TAKE DOWN TRUMP

Bruce and Nellie Ohr were and *are* a very infamous and compromised couple—by anyone's standards. Bruce Ohr is a senior official in the Justice Department whose wife, Nellie, was hired by Fusion GPS to assist with its dossier work against then-candidate Trump. In an outrageous conflict of interest, Bruce Ohr worked closely with both Nellie Ohr and her fellow Clinton campaign spies at Fusion GPS, including Christopher Steele, to launder Russia smears against President Trump into the DOJ and FBI. He was subsequently "demoted" from his position as U.S. associate deputy attorney general in December 2017 after his conflicts of interest were "discovered."

For instance we found 330 (!) pages of Justice Department documents showing Bruce Ohr discussing information obtained through his wife, Nellie Ohr. This information contained anti-Trump dossier materials, including a spreadsheet that tries to link President Trump to dozens of Russians.[7]

Remember: Nellie Ohr *worked for Hillary Clinton* through Fusion GPS.

On December 5, 2016, Bruce Ohr emailed himself an Excel spreadsheet, seemingly from his wife, Nellie Ohr, titled "WhosWho19Sept2016." The spreadsheet purports to show relationship descriptions and "linkages" between Donald Trump, his family, and criminal figures, many of whom were Russians. This list of individuals allegedly "linked to Trump" include: a Russian involved in a "gangland killing"[8]; an Uzbek mafia don; a former KGB officer suspected in the murder of Paul Tatum; a Russian who reportedly "buys up banks and pumps them dry"; a Russian money launderer for Sergei Magnitsky; a Turk accused of shipping oil for ISIS; a couple who lent their name to the Trump Institute, promoting its "get-rich-quick schemes"; a man who poured him a drink; and others.

On December 5, 2016, Bruce Ohr emailed himself a document titled "Manafort Chronology," another Nellie Ohr–Fusion GPS document, which details Paul Manafort's travel and interactions with Russians and other officials.

FBI interview reports from December 5 and December 12, and

December 20, 2017, show that Bruce Ohr "voluntarily" gave these anti-Trump and Manafort materials, created for the Clinton campaign by Fusion GPS, to the FBI.

On January 25, 2017, Bruce Ohr's wife, Nellie Ohr, forwarded text messages to him that she'd sent to her "colleagues," where she refers to the Steele dossier as the "yellow rain dossier" and the "yellow showers dossier."

In the same set of forwarded texts, Nellie speculates that Department K of the Russian intelligence service FSB "would be a pretty good candidate for listening in on Hillary."

On February 14, 2017, Obama appointed and then deputy assistant secretary of state for the Bureau of European and Eurasian Affairs, Kathleen Kavalec, forwarded Ohr a *Huffington Post* article touting the Steele Dossier's claim that an alleged deal between Russian oil company Rosneft and Trump supporter Steve Schwarzman constituted a "high crime of treason worthy of impeachment." Ohr forwarded the article to the FBI's Washington field office the same day.

Remember, four months prior to this exchange, Kavalec had found Christopher Steele not credible because of factual inaccuracies that he had relayed to her in October 2016!

Nellie Ohr seems to have been a go-to source for Ohr's buddies at DOJ. Fusion GPS hit pay dirt by hiring her. On May 23, 2016, DOJ prosecutor Lisa Holtyn emails Bruce Ohr to see if he could connect her as well as prosecutors Joe Wheatley and Ivana Nizich with his wife, Nellie Ohr, as she could be a "great resource" for them. He replies, "I'm sure Nellie would be delighted to speak with them. I'm pretty sure there is no conflict of interest since they aren't paying her or anything like that." Congressman Mark Meadows suggested this email shows that Nellie Ohr "knowingly provided false testimony" to Congress that she had no role in DOJ investigations.

These documents show a crazed DOJ-FBI effort to use the Clinton spy ring at Fusion GPS, *namely Nellie Ohr,* to smear President Trump—even *before he was sworn in as president.* Clinton campaign operative Nellie Ohr may as well have had a desk at the Justice Department.

Here is some recent history on our discoveries about the Ohrs.

We received documents showing that Bruce Ohr in his January 2018 preparation to testify to the Senate and House intelligence committees wrote to a lawyer about "possible ethics concerns." Bruce Ohr forwarded the email to Nellie Ohr, who had been hired by Fusion GPS, the Hillary Clinton campaign–Democratic National Committee vendor who compiled the anti-Trump dossier.

We also uncovered key documents, discussed below, showing he remained in regular contact with former British spy and Fusion GPS contractor Christopher Steele after Steele was terminated by the FBI in November 2016 for revealing to the media his position as an FBI confidential informant.

As you can see, we're still uncovering the sordid details of this attempted coup d'état.

NELLIE OHR PUSHES ANTI-TRUMP DISINFORMATION

As discussed above, Bruce and Nellie Ohr trafficked in salacious gossip of the worst kind in their effort to topple a U.S. president.

How bad? *Really* bad.

As in *Russian* bad.

We have yet another batch of details in the form of seventy-two pages of DOJ documents containing Russia-related emails sent from

Nellie Ohr to DOJ official Lisa Holtyn (whom Bruce Ohr supervised!) at the time Nellie Ohr worked with anti-Trump dossier firm Fusion GPS.[9]

In an email to Holtyn dated November 22, 2016, revealing her anti-Trump sentiments, Nellie poses a question in the subject line: "Who stands behind the Russian 'friends of Trump,'" which she answers enthusiastically in the first line of the email: "Pornographer-turned-pro-Kremlin-media-impresario Konstantin Rykov!!!"

The documents show that Nellie Ohr was providing the Justice Department significant amounts of information on Russia via email from January 2016 to November 2016. She testified to Congress that she worked as a contractor for Fusion GPS in "October of 2015, give or take a couple weeks, and into the end of September 2016." Much of the material Ohr sent to the DOJ is untranslated Russia-language reports.

Once again, Fusion GPS is the firm paid by the Hillary Clinton campaign and the Democratic National Committee to create the anti-Trump dossier.

The documents show Nellie Ohr's providing Justice Department officials much the same kind of open-source research and investigative services she was paid to provide Fusion GPS.

Nellie Ohr told Congress that she worked at Fusion GPS on "a project looking into the relationship of Donald Trump with [Russian] organized crime," for which she would "write occasional reports based on the open source research that I described about Donald Trump's relationships with various people in Russia." She also testified she gathered information during the 2016 campaign about Paul Manafort, Michael Flynn, Carter Page, President Trump, his wife, Melania Trump, and his children for Fusion GPS.

Nellie Ohr funneled anti-Trump smears to her husband's underlings in the DOJ, who were running an illicit spy operation against President Trump.

Nellie Ohr is obviously a key figure in the Clinton–DNC–Fusion GPS spy ring. More than that, she may have also worked with her husband to delete critically important material

NELLIE OHR TAKES HINT FROM HILLARY TO: DELETE, DELETE, DELETE

When the wife of a top Justice Department official tells her husband that she's "deleting these emails now," it may well be innocent. But when *both of them* are up to their necks in plotting against a president of the United States, this potential destruction of evidence needs to be investigated.

In May 2019, we released records from the Justice Department that included an email exchange between Ohr; his top aide Lisa Holtyn; his wife, Nellie Ohr, who worked for Fusion GPS; and First Secretary at the German Embassy Stefan Bress. The email discusses a meeting with German analysts for an "analytical exchange" on topics including the "Impact of Russian influence operations in Europe ('PsyOps/InfoWar')."

According to the emails, Bress had initiated the offer of the meeting to which Holtyn responds, "I haven't had a chance to confer with Bruce yet, but would certainly love to meet with the 'A Team'!" Bruce Ohr says, "That time works for me as well." Bress then provides the personal details/passport numbers of the German analysts who will be meeting with Holtyn and Ohr. Holtyn tells Bress that the Ohrs would like to host the German delegation for dinner and notes that

Joe Wheatley and Ivana Nizich (a husband/wife team of DOJ Organized Crime prosecutors, and friends of the Ohrs) would join them as well.

Included in that email exchange were records revealing that Nellie Ohr informed her husband that she was deleting emails sent from his DOJ email account. Here's the smoking gun:

From: Nellie Ohr

Sent: Wednesday, April 20, 2016 12:49 PM

To: Ohr, Bruce (ODAG)

Subject: Re: Analyst Russian Organized Crime—April 2016

Thanks! I'm deleting these emails now

Here's the crucial question: *Was Bruce Ohr directing his wife, Nellie Ohr, who worked for the Clinton spy ring at Fusion GPS, to delete emails about Russia?*

We are on top of this scandal with several smoking gun disclosures.

In August 2019, we released FBI 302 interviews with Bruce Ohr showing the efforts of the FBI, DOJ, and State Department to find allegedly incriminating material about President Trump through communications with Fusion GPS and Clinton-funded dossier author Christopher Steele. Also released were documents containing Russia-related emails sent from Nellie Ohr to Holtyn during the time Nellie Ohr worked with Fusion GPS.

In June 2019 we uncovered documents showing the removal of Bruce Ohr from the position of associate attorney general in 2017; his transfer from the Organized Crime Drug Enforcement Task Force to International Affairs in 2018; and that Ohr received a total of $42,520 in performance bonuses during the Trump/Russia investigation. Ohr's bonus nearly doubled from $14,520 (received in November 2015) to *$28,000* in November 2016.

Apparently, there is good money to be made in selling out your president.

BRUCE OHR PLAYED
ANTI-TRUMP SPYMASTER

To get a full understanding of the scope of the desperate Obama administration plotting against Donald Trump, you first have to look at the corrupt relationship with Clinton-DNC spy Christopher Steele. Judicial Watch uncovered that Steele was not only a source for the Obama FBI but a paid source!

More than two years ago, our litigation and investigative team uncovered an extraordinary cache of documents that show that Steele was cut off as a "Confidential Human Source" (CHS) after he disclosed his relationship with the FBI to a third party. The documents show at least eleven FBI payments to Steele in 2016 and document that he was admonished for unknown reasons in February 2016.

The documents include a "source closing communication" that states that Steele (referred to below as "CHS") "is being closed" because:

> CHS confirmed to an outside third party that CHS has a confidential relationship with the FBI. CHS was used as a source for an online article. In the article, CHS revealed CHS' relationship with the FBI as well as information that CHS obtained and provided to FBI. On November 1, 2016, CHS confirmed all of this to the handling agent. At that time, handling agent advised CHS that the nature of the re-

lationship between the FBI and CHS would change completely and that it was unlikely that the FBI would continue a relationship with the CHS. Additionally, handling agent advised that CHS was not to operate to obtain any intelligence whatsoever on behalf of the FBI.

The documents also show that Steele was paid repeatedly by the FBI and was "admonished" for some unknown misconduct in February 2016. The documents include:

+ Fifteen (15) FD-1023, Source Reports.

+ Thirteen (13) FD-209a, Contact Reports.

+ Eleven (11) FD-794b, Payment Requests. (It appears Steele was paid money eleven of the thirteen times he met with the FBI and gave them information.)

+ An Electronic Communication (EC) documenting that on February 2, 2016, Steele was admonished in accordance with standard Justice Department guidelines and the FBI CHS Policy Manual.

These documents show the shady, cash-based relationship the Obama FBI had with Clinton operative Christopher Steele. The anti-Trump Russia "investigation" had Steele at its center and his misconduct was no impediment to using information from his Russia intelligence collaborators to spy on the Trump team. The corruption and abuse is astonishing.

But it gets worse.

The Steele Dossier garbage wasn't panning out and the Deep State FBI was desperate to try to reestablish a relationship with Steele in order to continue to get more shady information on the incoming president. And they found a willing—and compromised—go-between in

Ohr. Our friends at the *Washington Examiner* analyzed our material in a story titled "FBI used Steele dossier in FISAs despite knowing about flaws and bias."

> Following a November 2016 meeting with Ohr, the interviewing FBI agents wrote that Ohr told them Steele "was desperate that Donald Trump not get elected and was passionate about him not being the U.S. President." Ohr said he believed Steele "wanted to blunt or foil the Kremlin's plans." Steele's explicit motivations were also not made clear to the FISA court.
>
> Ohr told agents in November 2016 he "never believed" Steele was "making up information or shading it" and that he believed Steele was just passing along what his sources in Russia were telling him, but added "that doesn't make that story true." And Ohr raised the specter of possible Russian disinformation, noting "there are always Russian conspiracy theories that come from the Kremlin" and providing a redacted example.[10]

By January 2017, some FBI agents trying to verify the dossier's allegations had reportedly concluded some of the dossier's contents may *have been based upon rumors and hearsay passed from source to source and originated as Russian disinformation.* Former CIA Moscow station chief Daniel Hoffman told the *Washington Examiner* the dossier likely contained "FSB disinformation."

Agents said in a series of notes from December 2016 that Ohr told them Simpson from Fusion GPS "directed" Steele to speak to press "as that was what Simpson was paying [Steele] to do." Michael Isikoff, the chief investigative correspondent for Yahoo News whose September 2016 news article based on the dossier was used to bolster the FISA applications, later said the media should have shown more skepticism over Steele's dossier, which he described as "third-hand stuff." Steele also passed along information to numerous other media outlets.

Agents also noted in December 2016 that Ohr told them his wife, Nellie, was hired by Simpson to work for Fusion GPS during the presidential election, and Ohr provided the FBI with all the work his wife conducted for Simpson.

Agents further wrote in February 2017 that Ohr reminded them that Deputy Assistant Secretary of State Kathleen Kavalec spoke with Steele several times prior to the presidential election. Steele met Kavalec ten days before the first FISA application was submitted, and he admitted to her that he was encouraged by his client to get his research out before the 2016 election.

The notes were just the beginning. Judicial Watch then forced out the release of about a dozen FBI 302 reports that provided more evidence that the Steele operation was a hit job and the FBI knew all about it.

Again, Bruce Ohr *was removed from his post of associate deputy attorney general on December 6, 2017, after it was uncovered that he was working with his wife and Christopher Steele on the Trump dossier.*

Ohr was corruptly used by the FBI as a conduit to Clinton spy Christopher Steele and the Clinton-DNC spy ring at Fusion GPS, and we now have thirty-four pages of "302" report material from the FBI interviews of Ohr—documents that Congress has been seeking but have been unable to get for over a year. (FBI agents use a Form 302 to summarize interviews and record notes taken during an interview.) Here is what we found:

On November 22, 2016, Bruce Ohr said that "reporting on Trump's ties to Russia were going to the Clinton Campaign, Jon Winer at the U.S. State Department and the FBI."

In late September 2016, Ohr describes Christopher Steele as "desperate that Donald Trump not get elected and was passionate about him not being the U.S. President."

"Ohr knew that [Fusion GPS's] Glen[n] Simpson and others were talking to Victoria Nuland at the U.S. State Department."

Glenn Simpson directed a person whose name is redacted to speak to the press. It appears as if the press that person went to was the far-left-leaning *Mother Jones*.

On December 5, 2016, Ohr promised to "voluntarily" give his wife Nellie Ohr's Fusion GPS research to the FBI. He also provided the FBI with a report on Paul Manafort titled "Manafort Chronology."

On December 12, 2016, Simpson gave Ohr a thumb drive with Fusion GPS research on it. Ohr claims to not know what is on that drive. During the meeting Simpson, based evidently on a meeting with Glenn Simpson, identified Michael Cohen, President Trump's former personal lawyer, as having "many Russian clients." Simpson also told Ohr that Cohen "may have" attended a meeting in Prague.

Ohr describes Simpson directing someone to talk to the *Mother Jones* reporter as "Simpson's Hail Mary attempt."

On December 20, 2016, Ohr provided the FBI with his wife's Fusion GPS research, "which contained the totality" of her work, "but the Fusion GPS header was stripped."

On January 23, 2017, Ohr tells the FBI that Steele told him that Steele "spoke with a staff member of Senator John McCain's office sometime prior to October 2016."

The FBI interviews show that Ohr texted and talked to Christopher Steele using the WhatsApp application.

On February 2, 2017, the FBI tells Ohr to see if Steele would be "comfortable getting the name of an FBI agent" as a contact. Ohr tells the agents that State Department official Kathleen Kavalec spoke with "Steele several times prior to the U.S. Presidential election and believed Steele's reporting to have [been] generated mainly from [REDACTED]."

On February 14, 2017, Ohr tells the FBI that Steele communicated with him via FaceTime that Steele was "beginning to worry about his business." Steele discussed brokering new business with the FBI and told Ohr, "You may see me re-emerge in a couple of weeks."

On May 3, 2017, Steele called Ohr to tell him that he "had been worried about Director Comey's upcoming testimony to Congress, especially his response to questions that would be raised by [Senator] Grassley." Although what he was specifically worried about is redacted, Steele was "happy with Director Comey's response."

Steele also stated that he was limited in "his ability to testify before Congress" because of disclosure laws in the United Kingdom being more narrow than the United States.

On May 12, 2017, Steele called Ohr to discuss a letter the Senate Intelligence Committee sent him. According to Ohr, "The letter requested answers to the following questions":

Had Steele provided information to the U.S. government?

What was the scope of Steele's investigation?

Did Steele have any additional information to provide?

In May 2017, Ohr was asked by the FBI to ask "Steele if he would be willing to have a conversation with FBI agents in the UK." Steele responded that he would, but he would need to check with a redacted name.

These new Bruce Ohr FBI 302s show an unprecedented and irregular effort by the FBI, DOJ, and State Department to dig up dirt on President Trump using the conflicted Bruce Ohr, his wife, and the

Clinton/DNC spies at Fusion GPS. The FISA courts weren't informed of this corrupted process when they were asked to approve and reapprove extraordinary spy warrants targeting President Trump.

One would think that a senior DOJ official such as Ohr would think that something was off after his third, let alone twelfth, interview with the FBI about his spy game communications with Steele *and* Ohr's wife. In what universe is this appropriate! To this day, Ohr remains employed by the DOJ. Which is outrageous enough on its own, but as Judicial Watch found, in addition to the bonuses we uncovered, got a pay increase after his misconduct was exposed!

Bruce Ohr was removed because of his tainted conflict of interest role as a conduit for Fusion GPS material. The documents show that Ohr was removed from his position as associate deputy attorney general on December 6, 2017. On January 7, 2018, Ohr was reassigned from his position of director of the Organized Crime Drug Enforcement Task Force (OCDETF) and shifted to Counselor for International Affairs in the Department of Justice Criminal Division. Ohr received a $2,600 pay increase.

Unusual bonuses and a raise after misconduct is exposed—this is how the Deep State "punishes" its operatives.

IF YOU FLIP OVER ENOUGH ROCKS, YOU FIND MUELLER'S PUPPET MASTER

Part of uncovering that truth means we have to flip over a bunch of rocks. And what lives and thrives under those large, slime-covered flat rocks? Creepy and even venomous things, as it turns out.

One in particular.

As Daniel John Sobieski at *American Thinker* pointed out:

Robert Mueller—the former director of the FBI under George W. Bush and whom Rod Rosenstein appointed special counsel for the Department of Justice investigating Trump—was revealed to be an empty suit during his feeble performance before the House Judiciary and Intelligence Committees [. . .], unable to answer questions on a report that it became painfully clear he could not defend because he did not write it. The true author is likely longtime associate Andrew Weissmann, often called Mueller's "pit bull," who perhaps should also have the title of Mueller's "Rasputin."[11]

Sobieski also highlighted Congressman Louis Gohmert (R-TX) regarding Weissmann's immense power:

"It's also clear . . . that Weissmann was the driving force behind all this."[12]

To the congressman's point, Weissmann's record speaks to his ruthlessness in pursuing a target, doing such things as withholding exculpatory evidence. As noted at USAPoliticsToday.org:

The top attorney in Robert Mueller's Special Counsel's office was re-ported to the Department of Justice's Inspector General by a lawyer representing whistleblowers for alleged "corrupt legal practices" more than a year before the 2016 presidential election and a decade before to the Senate.[13]

Weissmann, among his other jobs, was lead prosecutor in the trial of former Trump campaign manager Paul Manafort. Weissmann was the point man in the predawn raids on Manafort's home and offices, which involved more armed force than we employed at Benghazi, and was condemned by a judge for withholding exculpatory evidence in a criminal case. As the Daily Caller News Foundation reported:[14]

Weissmann has a reputation for pushing the boundaries on prosecutions. *The New York Times* called him a "pit bull" who used "scorched-earth tactics" against opponents.

In the 1990s, Chief Judge Charles P. Sifton reprimanded Weissmann as "reprehensible" during a trial regarding the Colombo crime family for withholding evidence.

"The judge described then (Assistant U.S. Attorney) Weissmann's conduct as the 'myopic withholding of information' and 'reprehensible and subject, perhaps, to appropriate disciplinary measures,'" according to a February 2018 article by investigative reporter Sara Carter.

As our friends at *American Thinker* further noted when referring to our investigations:[15]

Mueller's professed lack of knowledge regarding Fusion GPS is inexplicable since . . . as former deputy assistant attorney general Bruce Ohr's closed-door testimony before Congress shows, Weissmann had full knowledge of the fake nature of the Steele dossier that was a major predicate of the Russian witch-hunt that became the Mueller probe.

Bruce Ohr was the number four official at the Justice Department as U.S. Deputy Associate Attorney General and the highest ranking non-appointee in the building with an office a *couple of doors down from* Deputy AG Rod Rosenstein. Ohr continually kept Weissmann "*in the loop*" about the fake dossier and its journeys through the deep state swamp, along with a myriad of other co-conspirators in a web of conspiracy and deceit so vast that Watergate trivia question Carl Bernstein may be right in a way he did not intend when he suggested this whole matter might be bigger than Watergate. It seems only the DOJ janitor was not involved.

Weissmann had to know the dossier was fake and that its use in obtaining FISA warrants to conduct surveillance on Team Trump and provide a predicate for the Mueller witch hunt was a fraud committed upon the FISA court. If he knew, Robert Mueller should have known.

Weissmann is a partisan hack and Mueller thug who sent an email to Acting Attorney General Sally Yates, one of those who signed the fraudulent FISA applications, congratulating her for refusing to defend in court President Trump's travel ban.

It is shocking that a senior member of special counsel Robert Mueller's investigative team, set up to reassure Americans that justice will be impartially pursued, said he was in "awe" of former acting attorney general Sally Yates the day she was fired for refusing to defend President Trump's controversial travel ban.

"I am so proud and in awe," Weissmann wrote, according to emails obtained by Judicial Watch through a Freedom of Information Act request. "Thank you so much."

He also attended Hillary Clinton's 2016 *almost-victory* party, probably shedding a tear over her loss and fueling his desire to overturn Trump's surprising victory.

Andrew Weissmann is a virulent Trump-hater who, the record shows, had no interest in going after Fusion GPS and the real collusion between Team Hillary, the DNC, Christopher Steele, and the Russians.

Sadly for our nation, people like Andrew Weissmann—and countless like him—littered the Department of Justice while working on several missions simultaneously.

The first mission was to *always* cover up for any Obama-Clinton mistakes or crimes. Next, to do all in their power to stop candidate Trump. And then, when they failed at that, orchestrate an illicit and un-American soft coup against then President Trump. And finally, use every resource at their disposal to cover up that high crime.

Knowing all that, it is little wonder why the FBI could never seem to see or expose the coup attempt hiding in plain sight before their very eyes.

This truly is the biggest corruption scandal in American history.

SEVEN DAYS IN MAY—THE COUP ACCELERATES AGAINST PRESIDENT TRUMP

There's a leftist fantasy book and movie from the sixties, *Seven Days in May,* in which far-right military leaders unsuccessfully plot to overthrow a liberal president in a coup. In reality, it turned out to be the anti-conservative Left who plotted a coup. And, ironically, it happened over a seven- to ten-day period in May 2017, after President Trump fired corrupt FBI director James Comey on May 9.

Comey's firing unhinged Deputy Director McCabe (who became acting FBI director for a time) and Deputy Attorney General Rosenstein. Rosenstein was "acting" attorney general for the purposes of all things Russia because of Attorney General Jeff Sessions's precipitous and unneeded "recusal" decision.

Leaky DOJ officials soon disclosed that three issues popped up immediately—all elements of the coup attack against President Trump:

Rosenstein and McCabe discussed invoking the Twenty-Fifth Amendment to remove President Trump. (The Twenty-Fifth Amendment is designed for the transfer of power if a president is incapacitated, not as a punishment for exercising his power as president to fire a FBI director!)

Rosenstein discussed wearing a wire while in the Oval Office with President Trump to somehow entrap him.

Rosenstein appointed anti-Trump former FBI director Robert Mueller as a roving special counsel to investigate the nonsense theory of Russia collusion.

The Mueller appointment and its woeful abuses and aftermath are in the books, but Rosenstein, most recently earlier this year, in Senate testimony has downplayed or denied the other coup discussion topics.

But Judicial Watch uncovered documentary evidence of these seditious discussions.[16]

The records show that, following a September 21, 2018, report on Rosenstein suggesting he would wear a wire to secretly record Trump and his discussions on using the Twenty-Fifth Amendment, Rosenstein sought to ensure the media would have "difficulty" finding anyone in the DOJ to comment and a concerted effort within the DOJ to frame the reporting as "inaccurate" and "factually incorrect."

The records show DOJ officials had also discussed characterizing Rosenstein's reported offer of wearing a wire to record Trump as merely "sarcastic."

Additionally, the records show that DOJ public affairs officer Sarah Isgur Flores, after conferring with other top DOJ officials and Rosenstein's office about her email exchange with *New York Times* reporter Adam Goldman, waited twelve hours to forward the email exchange to DOJ chief of staff Matthew Whitaker. Former White House chief of staff John Kelly had referred to Whitaker as the president's "eyes and ears" in the DOJ.

We obtained the records through a Freedom of Information Act lawsuit filed after the Justice Department failed to respond to three separate FOIA requests dated September 21, 2018 (*Judicial Watch v. U.S. Department of Justice* (No. 1:19-cv-00388)). The lawsuit seeks all written and audiovisual records of any FBI/DOJ discussions regarding the Twenty-Fifth Amendment and plans to secretly record President Trump in the Oval Office.

The records we obtained include a September 21, 2018, email from Assistant U.S. Attorney (DOJ/NSD) Harvey Eisenberg to Rosenstein informing the deputy attorney general that *Washington Post* reporter Ellen Nakashima had called inquiring about a *New York Times* report on the Twenty-Fifth Amendment/wire discussion, Rosenstein responds: "Thanks! Hopefully we are being successful, and the reporters are having difficulty finding anybody to comment about things. [Remainder of email redacted.]" Apparently in response to the redacted portion of Rosenstein's reply, Eisenberg responds, "I'm aware. Besides letting you know, [redacted]. My best to you and the family." Rosenstein replies, "I don't mean about me. [Redacted.]"

The emails also detail the DOJ's response to the initial story as it was being prepared by the *New York Times*. On September 20, 2018, the *Times'* Goldman emailed DOJ's Flores that he and fellow reporter Mike Schmidt were working on a story and wanted a DOJ response to certain questions, including that at a May 16, 2017, meeting of senior federal law enforcement officials, Rosenstein offered to wear a "wire" to record his conversations with Trump. "He also said McCabe could wear a wire."

In a second request for comment, Goldman alleges that in a separate conversation between Rosenstein and McCabe, they discussed using the Twenty-Fifth Amendment "to remove President Trump" and "Rosenstein said that he may be able to get (then–Attorney General Jeff) Sessions and Kelly to go along with the plan."

In a third request for comment, Goldman said he'd learned that

Rosenstein in a May 12, 2017, conversation at the DOJ Command Center "appeared 'upset' and 'emotional' over the Comey firing."

In a fourth request for comment, Goldman said that in a May 14, 2017, conversation with McCabe, "Rosenstein asked McCabe to reach out to Comey to seek advice about appointing a special counsel. McCabe believed that was a bad idea."

In a fifth and final request for which he sought DOJ comment, Goldman wrote, "Rosenstein considered appointing (former Deputy Attorney General) Jim Cole as the special counsel."

On September 20, 2018, Flores forwarded the Goldman email to "Annie" and "Bill"—apparently White House deputy counsel Annie Donaldson and White House communications director Bill Shine— telling Donaldson, "Boss calling Don re the below—if you think appropriate, share with Don [presumably referring to White House Counsel Don McGahn]." She tells Shine, "We've sent a response from the DAG that's below and had someone in the room dispute the 'wire' part noting the dag was being sarcastic." She then includes the DAG response, which reads, "The New York Times's story is inaccurate and factually incorrect. I will not further comment on a story based on anonymous sources who are obviously biased against the Department and are advancing their own personal agenda. But let me be clear about this: based on my personal dealings with the President, there is no basis to invoke the 25th Amendment."

Shine thanks Flores and asks her to "share with Elliott ASAP." Flores responds that if Shine is directing her to share with Elliott, "I don't think I know who that is referring to." Flores sent that response at 10:09 p.m. on September 20, but Flores waited until 10:00 a.m. the next day to forward the entire exchange to DOJ chief of staff Whitaker, saying: "Should have sent this to you last night."

A mostly redacted email exchange on the evening of September

20, 2018, shows the efforts of officials in the Public Affairs and DAG's office to produce a response to the impending news article. DOJ official Bradley Weinsheimer forwarded to Flores the "DAG response" to the allegations in the article, saying "DAG has cleared this, which is what we just discussed." He then provides the official DAG response about the allegations over Rosenstein wanting to invoke the Twenty-Fifth Amendment against Trump as being "inaccurate and factually incorrect." Deputy attorney general's office official Ed O'Callaghan responds, "Think good." The rest of his response is redacted under (b)(5)—deliberative process.

In the final draft of the official DAG response approved by O'Callaghan, the statement is changed from "Based on my dealings with the President, there is no basis to invoke the 25th Amendment" to "Based on my personal dealings with the President, there is no basis to invoke the 25th Amendment."

What a difference one word makes! By adding the word "personal" to his careful statement, one can see how Rosenstein leaves open the possibility that others, rightly he believes, would want the president removed!

Nowhere do these documents, even the material directly from Rosenstein, suggest that the wire and coup discussions did not take place.

And then we found the extraordinary two-page memo, dated May 16, 2017, by McCabe detailing how Rosenstein proposed wearing a wire into the Oval Office "to collect additional evidence on the president's true intentions." McCabe writes that Rosenstein said he thought it was possible because "he was not searched when he entered the White House."

The Justice Department turned over the document thanks to a February 2019 FOIA lawsuit for documents about any FBI/DOJ discussions regarding the Twenty-Fifth Amendment and plans to secretly record President Trump in the Oval Office (*Judicial Watch v. U.S. Department of Justice* [No. 1:19-cv-00388]).[17]

The memo, which is redacted in key sections, purports to serve as a "contemporaneous recollection" of a meeting that day ("12:30 pm on 5/16/2017") in Rosenstein's office. The meeting included Rosenstein, Deputy Assistant Attorney General for Intelligence Tashina Gauhar, and Principal Associate Deputy Attorney General Jim Crowell in Rosenstein's Justice Department office. McCabe writes he began the meeting by telling Rosenstein that he "approved the opening of an investigation of President Donald Trump . . . to investigate allegations of possible collusion between the president and the Russian Government, possible obstruction of justice related to the firing of FBI Director James Comey, and possible conspiracy to obstruct justice." In justifying his investigation, McCabe refers to the memos Comey secretly wrote on meetings he had with President Trump and an NBC interview with Lester Holt. McCabe writes he "informed DAG [Rosenstein] that as a result of his role in the matter, I thought he would be a witness to the case." Rosenstein responded by recounting his discussion with President Trump, then attorney general Sessions, and then White House counsel Don McGahn about Comey's imminent firing and that President Trump wanted him to write a "memo explaining the reason" for Comey's firing. McCabe writes:

> As our conversation continued the DAG proposed that he could potentially wear a recording device into the Oval Office to collect additional evidence on the President's true intentions. He said he thought this might be possible because he was not searched when he entered the White House. I told him that I would discuss the opportunity with my investigative team and get back to him.
>
> We discussed the issue of appointing a Special Counsel to oversee

the FBI's Russia investigation. The DAG said he has two candidates ready, one of whom could start immediately.

Additionally, McCabe admits that Rosenstein told him that Mc-Cabe had a "credibility problem" because a Rosenstein staffer had provided him with photos of McCabe wearing his wife's campaign T-shirt, in contradiction to McCabe's "assurance" he had no role in her campaign. McCabe writes he told him the photos were not from campaign events and that he confirmed with "my ethics counsel at FBI" that wearing such a shirt did not "constitute proscribed political activity."

This incredible memo details the conflicted and conniving coup effort against President Trump. It is astonishing and shocking that McCabe thought he could have the FBI conduct a "counterintelligence" operation on the president and that Rosenstein thought it would be appropriate to wear a wire to secretly record President Trump in the Oval Office. That the DOJ and FBI sat on this smoking gun for a year shows the need for urgent housecleaning at those agencies.

The full text of the redacted McCabe memo is printed below:

Tuesday, May 16, 2017

At 12:30 pm on 05/16/2017, I met with Deputy Attorney General (DAG) Rod Rosenstein in his office at the Department of Justice. Also present were Tashina Gauhar and Jim Crowell. The following is a contemporaneous recollection of the main topics we discussed.

I began by telling him that today I approved the opening of an investigation of President Donald Trump. I explained that the purpose of the investigation was to investigate allegations of possible collusion between the president and the Russian Government, possible obstruction of justice related to the firing of FBI Director James Comey, and possible conspiracy to obstruct justice. The DAG questioned what I meant by collusion and I explained that I was referring to the investigation of any potential links between the Trump campaign and the Russian government. I explained that counterintelligence investigations of this sort were meant to uncover any existence of any threat to national security as well as whether or not criminal conduct had occurred. Regarding the obstruction issues, I made clear that our predication was based not only on the president's comments last week to reporter Lester Holt (that he connected the firing of the director to the FBI's Russia investigation), but also on the several concurring comments the president made to Director Comey over the last few months. These comments included the President's requests for assurances of loyalty, statements about the Russia investigation and the investigation of General Michael Flynn. I also informed the DAG that Director Comey preserved his recollection of these interactions in a series of contemporaneously drafted memos. Finally, I informed the DAG that as a result of his role in the matter, I thought he would be a witness in the case.

The DAG then related his experiences at the White House on Monday, 05/08/2017. He began by stating that he had the feeling that the decision to fire the Director had been made before he arrived. At the White House, he first met with White House Counsel Donald McGahn, who told him that the President had drafted a letter to Director Comey that McGahn did not want the President to send. Shortly thereafter they met with the President and Attorney General Jeff Sessions, and possibly others, in the Oval Office. President Trump told the DAG he had written a letter to Director Comey, asked the DAG if he had seen the letter, and instructed McGahn to provide the DAG with a copy. The DAG described the letter to me as being a long list, possibly several pages, of the President's complaints with Director Comey. Among those complaints was a discussion about the FBI's Russia investigation, as well as a paragraph about the FBI Deputy Director. The DAG indicated to me that he retained a copy of the President's letter. The DAG said he told the President [redacted]. The President then directed the DAG to write a memo explaining the reasoning for Director Comey's termination and that the DAG should include Russia. The DAG said to the President he did not think this was a good idea and that his memo did not need to include Russia. The President replied that he understood, but that he was asking the DAG to include Russia anyway. As our conversation continued the DAG proposed that he could potentially wear a recording device into the Oval Office to collect additional evidence on the President's true intentions. He said he thought this might be possible because he was not searched when he entered the White House. I told him that I would discuss the opportunity with my investigative team and get back to him.

We discussed the issue of appointing a Special Counsel to oversee the FBI's Russia investigation. The DAG said he has two candidates ready one of whom could start immediately. [Redacted] The DAG said that he left a copy of the delegation with Acting Assistant Attorney General for National Security Dana Boente to execute in the DAG's absence if the DAG were suddenly removed from his position. [Redacted] He anticipated that he may be terminated when he puts the Special Counsel in place, in light of the president's anger with AG Sessions when the AG recused himself from the Russia investigation. The DAG further stated that he was told that others heard the President tell the AG "you were supposed to protect me."

[Redacted]

The DAG related to me that on Sunday, 05/14/17, the AG asked him to participate in the interview of [redacted] for the position of FBI Director. [Redacted.]

The DAG told me that he informed the AG that I should remain in my role as Acting Director until the permanent Director was chosen. The DAG opined that my only "problem" was that some people believe that I was involved in my wife's 2015 campaign for State Senate in Virginia. The DAG said it was a "credibility problem" because after having told him during my May 13 interview that I played no role in her campaign and attended no campaign events, the DAG said a staffer had provided him with a photograph found on the internet of me and my wife wearing Dr. Jill McCabe campaign t-shirts. The DAG suggested that this photograph contradicted my statement that I had not campaigned for my wife. I pointed out to the DAG that the photograph he saw was taken not at a campaign event, but rather at [redacted.] I further informed the DAG that I confirmed with my ethics counsel at FBI that the Hatch Act does not prohibit wearing a campaign button or shirt away from the office, and that attending [redacted] wearing such a shirt does not constitute proscribed political activity.

Doesn't this memo read as if Rosenstein and McCabe were two animals in a box fighting it out?

McCabe isn't exactly the most trustworthy witness but this contemporaneous record persuasively confirms that there was a plot to get Trump. Ironically, as best we can tell, the part of the coup discussion from those "seven days in May" that was acted upon was the creation of the Mueller special counsel harassment operation against Trump.

A PENTAGON DEEP STATE OPERATIVE LEAKS TO THE *WASHINGTON POST*

As President Trump was rightfully slamming McCabe, the FBI "lovers," and others, there were still more out to get him.

Many more.

Which is *entirely* the point here.

The tentacles of this plot extended into every dark and deceitful corner of our government.

Knowing that to be the case, no one should be surprised that they reached the Pentagon.

On that very subject, we released 143 pages of new records from the U.S. Department of Defense, showing extensive communications between the Pentagon's director of the Office of Net Assessment James Baker and *Washington Post* reporter David Ignatius.[18]

Lawyers for Lieutenant General Michael Flynn alleged in a November 1, 2019, court filing that Baker "is believed to be the person who illegally leaked" to Ignatius the transcripts of Flynn's December 29, 2016, telephone calls with Russian ambassador Sergey Kislyak. The *Washington Post* published Ignatius's account of the calls on January 12, 2017, setting in motion a chain of events that led to Flynn's February 13, 2017, firing as national security advisor and subsequent prosecution for making false statements to the FBI about the calls. U.S. Attorney John Durham is reportedly investigating the leak of information targeting Flynn.

Citing "the government's bad faith, vindictiveness and breach of the plea agreement," in January 2020 Flynn's attorney, Sidney Powell, moved to withdraw Flynn's 2017 guilty plea during the Mueller investigation. Flynn claims he felt forced to plead guilty "when his son was threatened with prosecution and he exhausted his financial resources." Recently, prosecutors provided Flynn's defense team with documentation of this threat, according to additional papers Flynn's lawyers filed April 24, 2020, in support of the motion to withdraw.

Judicial Watch obtained the records in a November 2019 Freedom of Information Act lawsuit filed after the DOD failed to respond to a September 2019 request (*Judicial Watch v. Department of Defense* [No. 1:19-cv-03564]). Judicial Watch seeks:

All calendar entries of Director James Baker of the Office of Net Assessment.

All records of communications between ONA director James Baker and reporter David Ignatius.

The time frame for the requested records was May 2015 through September 25, 2019.

The records include an exchange on February 16, 2016, with the subject line "Ignatius," in which Baker tells Pentagon colleague Zachary Mears, then deputy chief of staff to Obama secretary of defense Ashton Carter, that he has "a long history with David" and talks with him regularly.

In an email exchange on October 1, 2018, in a discussion about artificial intelligence, Baker tells Ignatius: "David, please, as always, our discussions are completely off the record. If any of my observations strike you as worthy of mixing or folding into your own thinking, that is as usual fine." Ignatius replies, "Understood. Thanks for talking with me."

Ignatius and Baker's email exchanges per year are summarized below:

In 2015, Ignatius and Baker had a total of seven email conversations to set up meetings or calls, two simply to complement one another and one exchange where Ignatius invited Baker to speak at the Aspen Strategy Group conference.

In 2016, Ignatius and Baker had a total of ten email exchanges to set up meetings or calls and two to complement each other.

In 2017, Ignatius and Baker had a total of ten email exchanges to set up meetings, one exchange where Ignatius forwarded one of his articles, and one exchange where Ignatius asks Baker for his thoughts on the JCPOA (the Iran nuclear deal), because Baker wasn't available on the phone.

In 2018, Ignatius and Baker had a total of nine email exchanges to set up meetings, four where Ignatius forwarded articles and one where Ignatius asks Baker for tips on what to say at a quantum computing conference where he was speaking.

As I stated with the release of these critically important documents: "These records confirm that Mr. Baker was an anonymous source for Mr. Ignatius. Mr. Baker should be directly questioned about any and all leaks to his friend at the *Washington Post.*"

In a related case, in October 2018, Judicial Watch filed a FOIA lawsuit against the U.S. Department of Defense seeking information about the September 2016 contract between the DOD and Stefan Halper, the Cambridge University professor identified as a secret FBI informant used by the Obama administration to spy on Trump's presidential campaign. Halper also reportedly had high-level ties to both U.S. and British intelligence.

Government records show that the DOD's Office of Net Assessment (ONA) *paid Halper* a total of *$1,058,161* for four contracts that lasted from May 30, 2012, to March 29, 2018. More than $400,000 of the payments came between July 2016 and September 2017, after

Halper reportedly offered Trump campaign volunteer George Papado-poulos work in London to entice him into disclosing information about alleged collusion between the Russian government and the Trump campaign.

General Michael Flynn's attorney told the court that Baker was Halper's "handler" in the Office of Net Assessment in the Pentagon.

MUELLER'S SPECIAL COUNSEL— A DEEP STATE SPECIAL

We must keep this in mind at all times: if dirty and highly compro-mised operatives from the Deep State can band together to try to take down a legitimately and constitutionally elected president of the United States while also destroying the life and reputation of a man who was not only the head of the Defense Intelligence Agency, but a true and lasting American hero, then they can come after any of us, at any time.

The Mueller special counsel operation was built on corruption. I've already described how the special counsel operation flowed out of the coup discussions by senior anti-Trump leaders of the FBI and DOJ. But the corruption behind the appointment runs deeper than that. Mueller was appointed as a result of the illegal leak of the FBI files of President Trump by James Comey, the corrupt Obama holdover whom President Trump had rightly fired.

How do we know this? Because Comey confessed. First, Comey dishonestly created memos on his private conversations with Presi-dent Trump, including a February 14, 2017, conversation in which Trump asked him to drop the FBI's investigation of ousted national security advisor Lieutenant General Michael Flynn, allegedly saying,

"I hope you could see your way to letting Flynn go. He's a good guy. I hope you can let this go." Comey never considered this obstruction (and it wasn't, even if Trump did say it) but decided to try to use his memo of this conversation against Trump as part of a vendetta for being fired by him.

On May 12, 2017, a Judicial Watch lawsuit uncovered how FBI agents went to Comey's home to inventory and take possession of any FBI property Comey kept there. The agents inventoried and removed all government property from the home except the four "originals" of the memos, including the February 14 Flynn memo, that Comey kept in his personal safe. Comey failed to disclose to the agents that he retained the memos and later admitted that he never requested the FBI's permission to retain the memos.

A few days later after he misled the FBI, Comey took digital photos of the February 14 memo, texted the photos to his friend Daniel Richman, and directed Richman to disclose the contents of the memo, but not the memo itself, to *New York Times* reporter Michael Schmidt. Richman reportedly passed on the contents of the February 14 memo to Schmidt, by telephone, "very quickly" after receiving Comey's text.

Comey later admitted that he believed making the contents of the Flynn memo public would cause a special counsel to be appointed to investigate Trump. He confessed to this admission in an interview with investigators from the Justice Department's Office of Inspector General (OIG) and on other occasions. He told OIG that disclosing the memo would "change the game" and create "extraordinary pressure on the Department of Justice, which [Comey did] not trust, to appoint someone who the Country can trust." He also told OIG that he sent the Flynn memo to his buddy Richman because Comey "had a specific assignment for him" and wanted to "spur [the appointment of a special counsel] by putting this out." In the interview with IG, leaker Comey confirmed Richman as "acting at [his] direction to release something to the media."

On May 16, 2017, the *New York Times* published a report by Schmidt titled "Comey Memo Says Trump Asked Him to End Flynn Investigation," about the Flynn memo and its contents. The next day, May 17, 2017, Rosenstein, in his capacity as acting attorney general, had his excuse to appoint former FBI director Robert Mueller to serve as special counsel.

As far as Comey was concerned: mission accomplished. No matter that it involved leaks and lies in violation of law. The DOJ inspector general, by the way, referred Comey for possible prosecution but the Justice Department, under Attorney General William Barr, refused.

So the Mueller operation, corruptly formed from coup discussions and illegal leaks, went on to harass the president of the United States and victimize many others for nearly two years.

COUP—MUELLER PHASE

The appointment of Robert Mueller as special counsel was a key goal of the seditious coup cabal at the Justice Department and FBI. The agencies already had an active criminal and spy operation targeting President Trump, operations that began in 2016.

Using the illegal release of President Trump's FBI files as a corrupt pretext, Deputy Attorney General Rosenstein appointed Mueller in May 2017 under DOJ regulations created during the Clinton administration after the independent counsel law lapsed.

In theory, a special counsel subject to daily supervision by a

Senate-confirmed official might be kosher. But the Clinton-era special counsel regulations effectively prohibited the day-to-day supervision of any special counsel. In fact, the regulations suggest that Rosenstein or any other constitutionally accountable supervisor of Mueller could only countermand special counsel decisions after the fact, which gave the Mueller special counsel operation latitude and lack of accountability available to no other "career prosecutor" in the Justice Department. This resulted in an uncontrolled investigation by what effectively is a DOJ temporary employee into the official actions of the president of the United States. This was wildly unconstitutional.

The attorney general has no power to appoint "inferior officers," such as a special counsel, unless Congress authorizes such appointments. As acting attorney general because of then–attorney general Sessions's precipitous recusal, Rosenstein's authority to appoint a special counsel flowed from laws and appropriations passed by Congress. This arrangement is constitutionally untenable for a special counsel appointed to target the president.

This congressional special counsel scheme, as applied to Mueller's investigation of President Trump for his official acts, is unconstitutional because it disrupted the proper balance between the coordinate branches of the federal government. Mueller's investigation, made possible only by appointment authority vested by Congress in the attorney general and by expenditures of money specifically appropriated by Congress for the investigation, impaired (and arguably continues to impair) the president's exercise of his core constitutional duties, including the enforcement of federal law, the conduct of foreign affairs, and management of the executive branch.

So the Mueller special counsel was corruptly formed and unconstitutional. But it was also corruptly pursued, as President Trump repeatedly pointed out, by a group of "angry Democrats" who opposed him. A top deputy of the Mueller brigade is Andrew Weissmann, a "career" Justice Department prosecutor notorious for his aggressive approach to prosecutions.

In an October 2017 article describing Andrew Weissmann as Robert Mueller's "Pit Bull," the *New York Times* wrote, "He is a top lieutenant to Robert S. Mueller III on the special counsel investigation into Russian interference in the 2016 election and possible links to the Trump campaign. Significantly, Mr. Weissmann is an expert in converting defendants into collaborators—with either tactical brilliance or overzealousness, depending on one's perspective."[19] Weissmann, under Mueller, oversaw the predawn home raid of former Trump aide Paul Manafort in what one former federal prosecutor described as "textbook Weissmann terrorism."[20]

Weissmann should never have been near a special counsel operation that was put in place supposedly to increase confidence in the fair administration of justice. He is an anti-Trumper who had reportedly attended the Hillary Clinton election night party in New York.

And Weissmann seemed to bring his politics to the office. As mentioned above, Judicial Watch uncovered an illuminating email from Weissmann that exposed him as a cheerleader for Obama holdover Acting Attorney General Sally Yates's undermining of the rule of law and President Trump.[21]

Sally Yates was appointed by President Obama as U.S. attorney in northern Georgia and was later confirmed as deputy attorney general. In January 2017 she became acting attorney general for President Trump. Rather than serve as an honest caretaker for her president's incoming attorney general, on January 30 Yates unethically ordered the

Justice Department not to defend President Trump's January 27 executive order seeking a travel ban from seven Middle Eastern countries. That same day, President Trump rightly fired her for refusing to defend the action.

Judicial Watch immediately began investigating Yates's lawlessness and asked for and then had to sue for Yates's emails for the few weeks she was acting attorney general. We found strong support by top DOJ officials for Yates's refusal to enforce President Trump's Middle East travel ban executive order. In one email, Andrew Weissmann applauds Yates, writing: "I am so proud. And in awe. Thank you so much. All my deepest respects." The other Deep State emails detail the anti-Trump activism at senior levels of the Justice Department:

+ Thomas Delahanty, then the United States attorney for Maine wrote: "You are my hero."

+ Liz Aloi, a career service employee and chief of the Justice Department's Special Financial Investigations Unit, told Yates she was "Inspirational and heroic."

+ Emily Gray Rice, then the U.S. Attorney for New Hampshire and an Obama appointee, said: "AAG Yates, thank you, as always, for making us proud. It is truly an honor to work for you."

+ Obama appointee Barbara McQuade, U.S. attorney for the Eastern District of Michigan, told Yates, "Thank you for your courage and leadership. This is wonderful news."

+ DOJ Civil Division appellate attorney Jeffrey Clair wrote: "Thank you AG Yates. I've been in civil/appellate for 30 years and have never seen an administration with such contempt for democratic values and the rule of law. The President's order is an unconstitutional embarrassment and I applaud you for taking a principled stand against defending it."

These emails from Weissmann and his colleagues helpfully illustrate how the rule of law and legal ethics were of little mind to too many anti-Trump bureaucrats in DOJ.

So, Mr. Weissmann, this pro–Hillary Clinton, vocally anti-Trump activist, was placed in a key leadership slot of the Mueller special counsel operation. How key? Judicial Watch found, through yet another lawsuit, that Weissmann did the hiring for Mueller! Weissmann's calendar shows that he began interviewing people for investigator jobs on the Mueller operation almost immediately after it was announced that he had joined the team in early June.

On June 5, 2017, he interviewed former chief of the Public Corruption Unit of the U.S. Attorney's Office for the Southern District of New York Andrew Goldstein. Goldstein was a *Time* magazine reporter. Goldstein contributed a combined $3,300 to Obama's campaigns in 2008 and 2012. His wife, Julie Rawe, was a reporter and editor for *Time* for thirteen years, until 2013. He became a lead prosecutor for Mueller.

The next day, on June 6, 2017, Weissmann had a meeting with "FARA [Foreign Agents Registration Act] counsel."

Weissmann interviewed another prosecutor, Kyle Freeny, from the DOJ Money Laundering Section for the team on June 7, 2017. She contributed a total of $500 to Obama's presidential campaigns and $250 to Hillary Clinton's. She was later detailed to the Mueller investigation.

He interviewed a trial attorney who worked with him in the

Criminal Fraud Section, Rush Atkinson, on June 9, 2017. Records show that Atkinson donated $200 to Clinton's campaign in 2016. He is a registered Democrat and contributed $200 to Hillary Clinton's 2016 campaign. Atkinson also became part of the Mueller team.

Weissmann interviewed DOJ deputy assistant attorney general Greg Andres for the team on June 13, 2017. Andres donated $2,700 to the campaign for Senator Kirsten Gillibrand (D-NY) in 2018 and $1,000 to the campaign for David Hoffman (D) in 2009. Andres is a registered Democrat. His wife, Ronnie Abrams, a U.S. district judge in Manhattan, was nominated to the bench in 2011 by Obama. He joined the Mueller team in August 2017.

(Our 2018 analysis of Mueller hires found 14 registered Democrats on the Mueller team out of 18 lawyers identified. None could be identified as currently registered Republicans. Nine of the 18 are donors to the Hillary Clinton and/or Obama campaigns! One was a donor to Republicans but none to President Trump.)

These documents show Andrew Weissmann helped lead the hiring of key members of Mueller's team—who also happened to be political opponents of President Trump. No wonder it took us well over a year to get this basic information, and then only after the Mueller operation had largely shut down!

Weissmann retired from the Justice Department after the Mueller operation shut down to become a virulently anti-Trump commentator on cable television's MSNBC. It became known that he would be the star attraction in a "fireside chat" fund-raiser for President Trump's campaign opponent, former Vice President Joe Biden. Evidently, even this was too much for an anti-Trump world desperate to protect the tattered credibility of the Mueller special counsel jihad, and the fund-raiser was canceled.

MEDIA-DEEP STATE ALLIANCE

The anti-Trump media have been active co-conspirators with the Deep State in the attack on the republic. We've uncovered myriad examples of leaks and media management to media friendlies by anti-Trump government officials, but perhaps nothing as shocking as details of the venerable Associated Press's active efforts to get Paul Manafort, the former Trump campaign chairman.

We were generally aware from public reports of an unusual spring 2016 meeting between AP reporters and the Justice Department about Manafort, and we followed up with a freedom-of-information request. Getting the typical runaround from the Justice Department, we sued. And hit pay dirt.

We uncovered about sixty-five pages of FBI documents about an April 11, 2017, "off-the-record" meeting set up by then–chief of the Justice Department's Criminal Fraud Section Andrew Weissmann, between the DOJ, the FBI, and the Associated Press in which AP reporters provided information on former Trump campaign director Paul Manafort, including the actual numeric code to Manafort's storage locker.[22]

You read that correctly. The far-left Associated Press deliberately and openly crossed a number of ethical lines in an attempt to damage the Trump campaign in general and Paul Manafort specifically. It's one thing when political hacks such as Adam Schiff and Nancy Pelosi try to take down a president for partisan and personal reasons. It's quite another when members of the liberal media morph into activist operatives to "get Trump."

Two months later, in early June, Weissmann was hired to work on Robert Mueller's special counsel operation against President Trump. Weissman then reportedly spearheaded the subsequent investigation and prosecution of Manafort.

Included among the documents are two typed write-ups of the meeting's proceedings and handwritten notes taken during the meeting by two FBI special agents.

According to a June 11, 2017, FBI write-up: "The purpose of the meeting, as it was explained to SSA [supervisory special agent, redacted] was to obtain documents from the AP reporters that were related to their investigative reports on Paul Manafort."

No such documents, by the way, were included in the documents released to us.

During the meeting, the AP reporters provided the FBI information about a storage locker Manafort had (the Mueller special counsel operation raided the locker on May 26, 2017):

> The AP reporters advised that they had located a storage facility in Virginia that belonged to Manafort. . . . The code to the lock on the locker is 40944859. The reporters were aware of the Unit number and address, but they declined to share that information.
>
> The reporters shared the information that "payments for the locker were made from the DM Partners account that received money from the [Ukraine] Party of Regions."

The notes suggest the AP reporters actually *pushed* for criminal prosecution of Manafort:

> AP believes Manafort is in violation of the Foreign Agents Registration Act (FARA), in that Manafort send [*sic*] internal U.S. documents to officials in Ukraine AP has documentation proving this, as well as Manafort noting his understanding doing so would get him into trouble.
>
> AP asked about the U.S. government charging Manafort with

violating Title 18, section 1001 for lying to government officials, and have asked if the FBI has interviewed Manafort. FBI and DOJ had no comment on this question.

Also, according to the FBI write-up, "The AP reporters asked about FARA [Foreign Agents Registration Act] violations and they were generally told that they are enforceable."

Although, according to the FBI write-up, "no commitments were made [by DOJ] to assist the reporters," Andrew Weissmann, incredibly, asked the AP to contact foreign authorities to follow up:

[A]fter the meeting was started and it was explained to the reporters that there was nothing that the FBI could provide to them, the reporters opted to ask a series of questions to see if the FBI would provide clarification. No commitments were made to assist the reporters in their further investigation into the life and activities of Paul Manafort and the AP reporters understood that the meeting would be off the record.

They [AP reporters] reiterated what they had written in their article, which was a response from the Cypriot Anti-Money Laundering Authority (MOKAS) that they [MOKAS] had fully responded to Department of Treasury agents in response to [Treasury's] request. The AP reporters were interested in how this arrangement worked and if the U.S. had made a formal request. FBI/DOJ did not respond, but Andrew Weissman [sic] suggested that they ask the Cypriots if they had provided everything to which they had access or if they only provided what they were legally required to provide.

The AP reporters asked if we [DOJ/FBI] would be willing to tell them if they were off based [sic] or on the wrong traack [sic] and they were advised that they appeared to have a good understanding of Manafort's business dealings.

The reporters asked about any DOJ request for the assistance of foreign governments in the U.S. government's investigation of Manafort:

> The AP reporters asked if there had been any official requests to other countries. FBI/DOJ declined to discuss specifics, except to state that the Mutual Legal Assistance Treaty requests are negotiated by diplomats, so they should remain at that level.

AP reporters told the FBI about payments in the "black ledger," a Ukrainian record of allegedly illegal off-the-books payments:

> The reporters advised that their next report, which was scheduled to come out in the next day or so after the meeting, would focus on confirming, to the extent that they could payments in the so called "black ledger" that were allegedly made to Manafort.

The FBI material continues:

> The impression that their sources give is that Manafort was not precise about his finances, specifically as it related to the "black ledger." The AP reporters calculated that he received $60 to $80 million from his work in Ukraine, during the time period the ledger was kept. According to their review of the ledger, it appears that there is a slightly lesser amount documented based on all of the entries. The AP reporters accessed a copy of the ledger online, describing it as "public" document. (Agent's note—the ledger has been published in its entirety

by the National Anti-Corruption Bureau of Ukraine, after it was given to them by Sergei Leshenko, Ukrainian RADA member [Ukrainian parliament] and investigative reporter.)

The AP reporters discussed an extensive list of issues, companies, and individuals that they felt should be investigated for possible criminal activity, including a $50,000 payment to a men's clothing store; a 2007 meeting with Russian oligarch Oleg Deripaska; Loav Ltd., which was possibly incorporated by Manafort; NeoCom, which the AP reporters implied was incorporated solely to cover up money laundering; and other matters.

The reporters also described an "internal U.S. work product that had been sent to Ukraine." The reporters described it as an "internal White House document." The FBI report stated that it "was not clear if the document was classified."

These shocking FBI reports evidence a corrupt collusion between the DOJ and the media, specifically the Associated Press, to target Paul Manafort.

These documents are also further reason for President Trump to pardon Manafort and others caught up in Mueller's abusive web. Remember, under Mueller, Weissmann became known as "the architect of the case against former Trump campaign chairman Paul Manafort," which produced *no* evidence of collusion between Manafort, the Trump campaign, and Russian operatives. The Mueller-Weissmann operation indicted Manafort on unrelated charges . . . but connected to some of the very topics that the AP and Weissmann collaborated on in that April 2017 meeting!

THE LONELY BATTLE

For months, efforts to discredit special counsel Robert S. Mueller III's investigation into Russian meddling in the 2016 campaign flickered at the fringes of political debate.

Now, the allegation that FBI and Justice Department officials are part of a broad conspiracy against President Trump is suddenly center stage. . . .

"Until recently, it has been a lonely battle," said Tom Fitton, whose conservative watchdog group Judicial Watch has helped drive the charges by unearthing internal Justice Department documents. "Our concerns about Mueller are beginning to take hold."—"No Longer a 'Lonely Battle': How the Campaign against the Mueller Probe Has Taken Hold," *Washington Post*, December, 24, 2017

The whole Mueller operation collapsed with the arrival of Attorney General Barr as a replacement for Sessions. Mueller obviously knew Barr would quickly see what Strzok had texted Page in May 2017, that "There's no big there there." Mueller knew his gig was up and quickly ended his investigation with a several-hundred-page report that confirmed what everyone had already known for two years—that no American, let alone Trump, knowingly worked with the Russians to interfere in our elections.

As I look back at this period, I've concluded that President Trump would have been driven out of office but for Judicial Watch.

The *Washington Post* gave us a backhanded compliment in suggesting we were "fringe" on the Mueller attack on our republic. We were indeed virtually alone in our battle, but our leadership saved the republic from a grievous blow.

One must remember that virtually no one in Washington questioned the propriety of the Mueller appointment, except for Judicial Watch. No one in positions of power questioned the constitutionality of the Mueller operation, except Judicial Watch. No one investigated Mueller's operation directly, except Judicial Watch. And few questioned the fundamental basis of the appointment—the notion that there was a Russia conspiracy, that General Flynn did something wrong, and that the other Trump associates were appropriately targeted by Mueller's gang—except for Judicial Watch.

Without our public education efforts highlighting that the Mueller operation was corruptly formed and pursued, one could easily imagine a scenario in which Mueller would have had the political and institutional cover to indict and force out of office President Trump.

As we saw with the Flynn prosecution, President Trump's innocence would have been no impediment to this type of coup operation. But we led the way in exposing that Mueller's probe was an unconstitutional sham. And this allowed Barr to blow down the Mueller house of cards with little effort.

OUR REPUBLIC UNDER ASSAULT . . . FROM THE IMPEACHMENT-COUP ATTACK ON PRESIDENT TRUMP

Adam Schiff Conspires Against the Republic

There has been nothing in American history that compares to the impeachment attack against President Trump. It was nothing but a wild abuse of the Constitution. Frankly, the word *impeachment* should be replaced with the word *coup*, because the president was illicitly targeted for removal from office for doing his job in asking needed questions regarding Ukraine corruption, and Joe Biden trying (and succeeding) to get a prosecutor in the Ukraine removed who was looking into Burisma, which gave Hunter Biden a suspiciously cash-laden seat on its board of directors.

Following the House vote to begin impeachment in the House, I said this:

> Today's vote endorses an abusive process that rolls over the rights of President Trump and undermines the rule of law. This was no impeachment resolution—it was a coup resolution. This coup attack was corruptly formed and corruptly pursued. The U.S. Senate should rule out a trial on any so-called impeachment arising from the Pelosi-Schiff abuse of the U.S. Constitution.

To be clear, our very republic was at stake. Would a president be driven from office over disagreements in policy (over the timing of aid) and for daring to ask questions about the last administration's corruption?

Fortunately, logically, and as it should have done, the Senate, although only after an absurd show trial, then overwhelmingly rejected the Pelosi-Schiff coup.

But what led to this grotesque miscarriage of justice?

"The truth behind House Intelligence Chairman Adam Schiff's role in engineering President Donald Trump's impeachment may soon come out because a nonprofit group promoting government transparency—Judicial Watch—is suing to get the whistleblower's emails."—Betsy McCaughey

A coup attempt indeed, led by shifty Adam Schiff and his collection of equally far-left, Trump-hating Deep State co-conspirators.

Judicial Watch first came across Schiff in 2018 when Representative Devin Nunes (R-CA) became a target of the Left (including Schiff) for exposing the Obama gang's massive unmasking operation against members of Trump world. To take him off the table, the Schiff operation concocted a phony ethics complaint about disclosing classified information against Nunes that resulted in his taking a less prominent role in the important Russiagate investigations.

But when we examined the actual record, it became clear that Schiff and his colleagues were the rule breakers. If the standard for filing a complaint or opening an ethics investigation is that a member has commented publicly on matters that touch on classified information, but the member does not reveal the source of his or her information, then the complaints against Chairman Nunes are incomplete insofar as they target only Nunes. At least two other members of the House Intelligence Committee have made comments about classified material that raise more directly the very same concerns raised against Chairman Nunes because they appear to confirm classified information contained in leaked intelligence community intercepts.

On March 21, 2017, the ranking member of the House Intelligence Committee, Representative Adam Schiff, spoke to an audience at the Brookings Institution in which he commented on an intelligence community intercept of a December 29, 2016, conversation between Russian ambassador Sergey Kislyak and retired U.S. Army general Michael Flynn, who had been selected by then–president elect Donald Trump to serve as national security advisor. Both the fact of the conversation and the conversation's contents were leaked to the news media and reported widely. In his Brookings Institution speech, Schiff stated:

> And then you have leaks that expose malfeasance or illegality. Now, I put that kind of leak, I put the Flynn leak in that category. And what was most disturbing to me, frankly, about that was: here you had a situation where the president is informed that his national security advisor . . . has lied to the vice president, and probably others . . . about a conversation with the Russians over sanctions imposed over hacking in the election to help the president.

Likewise, an April 3, 2017, report in the Daily Caller quotes Representative Jackie Speier as commenting publicly on both the contents of the Kislyak-Flynn conversations and Flynn's subsequent "unmasking" as a U.S. person incidentally intercepted by the intelligence community:

> Now, if in fact, it was unmasked and if it was General Flynn. You have to understand the context in which it was unmasked. *We do know*

that. Ambassador Kislayak [*sic*] and General Flynn were freelancing sanctions relief at the end of December, when he had no portfolio in which to make any kind of negotiations with Ambassador Kislayak [*sic*]. (Emphasis added)

Like Schiff, Representative Speier did not disclose how she knew about the conversation between Ambassador Kislyak and General Flynn or about General Flynn's "unmasking," but the statement attributed to her also appears to confirm the contents of leaked, classified information.

Judicial Watch concludes by asking that the Office of Congressional Ethics conduct a preliminary investigation into whether Rep. Schiff and Rep. Speier disclosed classified information to the public in violation of House ethics rules.

At least two leading Democrats, Representatives Schiff and Speier, on the House Intelligence Committee seem to have improperly disclosed classified information. While the Ethics Committee harassed Representative Nunes over his innocuous statements on Obama's surveillance on the Trump team, we thought it was right that the committee expand its investigation to include the other members of the Intelligence Committee who seem to have flagrantly violated the rules.[1]

Interestingly, the Ethics Committee, which is split evenly between Republicans and Democrats, almost immediately dropped its investigation of Nunes but to this day—two years later—hasn't resolved or made any public comment on our Nunes complaint.

It was clear the rules didn't bother Schiff. And when Mueller dropped his massive nothingburger of a report, Schiff seemed ready to pounce as soon as a Plan B opportunity presented itself.

Who is the so-called whistleblower who tried to topple a president? Reports have settled on Eric Ciaramella, a CIA employee who had been assigned to the Obama White House National Security Council staff to handle Ukraine issues and stayed on for a bit under President Trump. Reports are that he eventually was pushed out of the White House after being tied to anti-Trump leaks.

Ciaramella is also reportedly buddies with Sean Misko—a fellow Obama holdover in the National Security Council who left that position suddenly to go work for Adam Schiff (you really *can't* make this up).

While there is a long list of impeachment cheerleaders who later lined up behind them, Schiff and those two will do for starters.

As was reported by Real Clear Investigations, Ciaramella and Misko were critical of Trump from the outset.[2]

Within the National Security Council of the White House, plots against the president of the United States of America were being hatched.

But, what to do?

A review of House testimony strongly suggest[s] that the infamous Lt. Col. Alexander Vindman was a key source for Ciaramella on the call between President Trump and Ukraine's leader.

Eric Ciaramella, assuming he was the "whistleblower," had no direct, firsthand knowledge of the July 25, 2019, conversation between President Trump and Ukrainian president Volodymyr Zelensky but went ahead and filed a whistleblower complaint. That started the ball rolling for the cabal of Deep State Trump haters within the NSC and the other three-letter U.S. intelligence agencies seeking to have Trump "removed from office."

In his complaint filed with Inspector General for National Intelligence Michael Atkinson, every alleged complaint statement begins with "multiple officials told me," or "I learned from multiple U.S. officials," or "Officials with direct knowledge informed me."

Secondhand information about a call he didn't hear? This is why, on television and on social media, I've repeatedly called the whole absurdity "The Gossip Girl Impeachment." During the impeachment show trial propped up by the hearsay from Ciaramella, Adam Schiff would smash his gavel down anytime a Republican dared to talk about the "whistleblower" whose unreliable hearsay "evidence" was responsible for launching that 2.0 version of the latest invented attack on Trump.

But, as Americans who can actually think for themselves have come to realize, Schiff was not only trying to protect the cowardly whistleblower, but himself most of all.

Why? Because he knows full well he is the ringleader behind the impeachment scam.

Let's look at just a smidge of incriminating evidence.

Again, President Trump placed his call to the Ukrainian president on July 25, 2019. The very next day, Sean Misko—the Obama holdover in the NSC, and Eric Ciaramella's bosom buddy—joined the staff of Adam Schiff.

Are you kidding me? *The very next day?*

They have no shame. None.

As to be expected, right after Misko came on board, Schiff's staff supposedly invited Ciaramella in for a meeting. During that meeting, Schiff's staff reportedly gave Ciaramella "guidance" in how to file a complaint against the president of the United States.

Also not surprising is that Schiff and his staff worked very hard at hiding their coaching of the "whistleblower" from any authorities as well as House of Representative investigators. In fact, Schiff was caught in a bald-faced lie about his office's collusion.

When asked directly if he had heard from the "whistleblower," Schiff told a whopper:

We have not spoken directly with the whistleblower, we would like to. But I'm sure the whistleblower has concerns that he has not been advised, as the law requires, by the inspector general or the director of national intelligence just as to how he is to communicate with Congress, and so the risk for the whistleblower is retaliation.

Even the anti-conservative "fact checkers" at PolitiFact rated Schiff's denial as "False."

Why would the Schiff operation go to such great lengths to lie? The most obvious reason was to hide the fact that the whistleblower was not "independent" but a partisan, get-Trump cutout for Schiff. The other reason, perhaps more significant, is that the whistleblower likely communicated classified information to Schiff's team in violation of law. Recall, the contents of the call between President Trump and Ukraine's leader was classified at the time the whistleblower was colluding with Schiff. Simply put, an executive branch employee can't share classified information with Congress without permission. There is no "whistleblower" exemption to allow the improper dissemination of classified information.

So to the extent there were crimes related to the Ukraine call, they seem to be related to Schiff's collusion with the whistleblower.

After all that coaching and "guidance," the alleged whistleblower Ciaramella filed his formal complaint with Intelligence Community Inspector General Michael Atkinson on August 12, 2019.

The complaint did not inform Atkinson that he had met with, and been coached by, Schiff's staff. Or, so they both say. But then, former inspector general Atkinson seems far from clean in these very dirty dealings.

As the inspector general for the intelligence community, Atkinson knew better than anyone else that regulations stipulated that hearsay and "secondhand or unsubstantiated assertions" are insufficient for a complaint.

Insufficient for a complaint.

Atkinson knew that the "whistleblower's" complaint was *all* hearsay, secondhand, and unsubstantiated, and yet could not wait to process it and spread the gossip.

Why?

After getting the complaint and feedback from Atkinson, the Office of the Legal Counsel's opinion was that "the appropriate action is to refer the matter to the Department of Justice, rather than to report to the intelligence committees."

Atkinson completely ignored that legal advice from the Office of the Legal Counsel and instead sent a letter to . . . drumroll please . . . none other than Adam Schiff, the chairman of the House Intelligence Committee, to inform him of the complaint.

In reality, Atkinson was informing Schiff and his staff about a complaint that Schiff and his staff had set in motion in the first place.

Why would Atkinson violate protocols and run to the most political, most partisan, most anti-Trump member of Congress?

Could it be that Atkinson knew that if he did that, it would be the "justification" Schiff would need to launch the impeachment show trial against Trump?

Inspectors general are supposed to uncover this type of abuses. Not facilitate them.

Had Atkinson done the least part of the professional due diligence required of him, he would have discovered that a number of allegations in the whistleblower complaint were clearly false and that the whistleblower had been coached in the drafting of said complaint.

But . . . such due diligence would have gotten in the way of the *highly orchestrated* coup attempt against Trump. Hence, the documented and disgraceful intrigue that follows below.

DEEP STATE PROTECTS
SCHIFF COCONSPIRATOR

The DC adage is that the "cover-up is often worse than the crime." In my experience, "cover-ups" happen because the underlying crimes and corruption are serious.

As the impeachment/coup against President Trump marched on, Judicial Watch continued to take the lead on exposing the full truth about the various Deep State officials at the center of some of this treasonous behavior.

Naturally, we filed Freedom of Information Act lawsuits against both the DOJ and CIA for CIA analyst Eric Ciaramella's communications. He reportedly worked on Ukraine issues while on detail to both the Obama and Trump White Houses, so whether or not he was the whistleblower, he certainly would have information on the Ukraine issue at the heart of the impeachment/coup attack against President Trump.

We sued the DOJ after it failed to respond to November 2019 FOIA requests seeking communications between Ciaramella and former FBI agent Peter Strzok, former FBI attorney Lisa Page, former FBI deputy director Andrew McCabe, and/or the Special Counsel's Office (*Judicial Watch v. U.S. Department of Justice* [No. 1:19-cv-03809]).

We sued the CIA after it failed to respond to November 2019 FOIA requests seeking all of Ciaramella's emails from June 1, 2016, to November 12, 2019 (*Judicial Watch v. Central Intelligence Agency* [No. 1:19-cv-03807]).

Ciaramella's name appears in Special Counsel Robert Mueller's report on the 2016 presidential election, in reference to two emails Ciaramella sent to then–chief of staff John Kelly and other officials, describing a meeting between President Trump, Russian foreign minister Sergey Lavrov, and Russian ambassador Sergey Kislyak:

> In the morning on May 10, 2017, President Trump met with Russian Foreign Minister Sergey Lavrov and Russian Ambassador Sergey Kislyak in the Oval Office.
>
> . . . (5/9/17 White House Document, "Working Visit with Foreign Minister Sergey Lavrov of Russia") . . . (5/10/17 Email, Ciaramella to Kelly et al.). The meeting had been planned on May 2, 2017, during a telephone call between the President and Russian President Vladimir Putin, and the meeting date was confirmed on May 5, 2017, the same day the President dictated ideas for the Comey termination letter to Stephen Miller. . . . (5/10/17 Email, Ciaramella to Kelly et al.). Information about this phone call was subsequently leaked to *The New York Times.*

Again, in addition to his Ukraine work at the White Houses of Obama and Trump, Ciaramella is widely reported as the person who filed the whistleblower complaint that triggered the impeachment proceedings. His name, as reported by Real Clear Investigations, reportedly was "raised privately in impeachment depositions, according to officials with direct knowledge of the proceedings, as well as in at least one open hearing held by a House committee not involved in the impeachment inquiry."

Our Judicial Watch investigative team took the lead and was the first to compile an extensive list of persons Ciaramella met while in the

Obama-era White House. That list includes, but is not limited to, Daria Kaleniuk, cofounder and executive director of the Soros-funded Anticorruption Action Center (AntAC) in Ukraine (which is also connected to the Biden-Burisma-Ukraine interference scandal); Gina Lentine, formerly the Eurasia program coordinator at the Soros-funded Open Society Foundations; and former assistant secretary of state Victoria Nuland, who had extensive involvement with the Clinton-funded dossier. The logs also reveal that Alexandra Chalupa, a contractor hired by the DNC during the 2016 election who, according to *Politico*, coordinated with Ukrainians to investigate President Trump and his former campaign manager Paul Manafort, and *visited the White House at least twenty-seven times* during the Obama administration.

Some people don't visit their grandmother twenty-seven times . . . in their lifetimes.

Thanks to the Obama Spygate scandal and the related abusive impeachment of President Trump, there is significant public interest in Ciaramella's activities. We know he was involved in the Russia collusion investigation, and he was a key CIA operative on Ukraine in the both the Obama and Trump White Houses. Our lawsuits were designed to break through the unprecedented cover-up of his activities.

Rather than cooperate and expose the full truth about what Ciaramella did, the CIA and Justice Department have attempted to completely shut down our inquiry. They used the shield that is most difficult to overcome—they refused to confirm or deny the existence of any records about him.[3] The CIA response to us states:

> In accordance with section 3.6(a) of Executive Order 13526, the CIA can neither confirm nor deny the existence or nonexistence of records responsive to the requests. The fact of the existence or nonexistence of such records is itself exempt from FOIA under exemption (b)(3) and

Section 6 of the CIA Act of I 949, 50 U.S.C. § 3507, and, to the extent your request could relate to CIA intelligence sources and meth-
ods information, the fact of the existence or nonexistence of such
records is exempt from FOIA under exemption (b)(I) and exemption
(b)(3) in conjunction with Section 102A(i)(l) of the National Security Act of 1947, 50 U.S.C § 3024(i)(I).

The Justice Department also refused to confirm or deny the existence of responsive records, citing, among other justifications, the personal privacy of Ciaramella. The CIA's position is Americans can know
nothing about their operative Ciaramella, who is documented to be involved in the Russia collusion investigation and was a key CIA operative on Ukraine in both the Obama and Trump White Houses. The
incredible secrecy about his activities shows that the DOJ and CIA are
trying to cover up rather than expose any agency abuses that led to unprecedented attacks on President Trump.

So Schiff (and most cowed Republicans) refused to say Ciaramella's
name, even in the most neutral and factual context. And now the CIA
and DOJ want to keep his conduct in a Deep State black hole. On top
of this, major tech companies Google (which also operates YouTube)
and Facebook (which also runs Instagram) decreed that no one could
mention this important government official's name, either. His name is
not protected from disclosure by law, but the tech giants bought into
the Schiff cover-up and did his bidding in censoring Judicial Watch
and millions of other Americans wanting the full truth about this attack on their republic.

Our lawsuits continue but never before has so much government
and private energy been used to cover up the activity of one bureaucrat—
especially one who tried to bring down a president!

SCHIFF SCANDAL EXPOSES ANOTHER DEEP STATE COUP PLOT AGAINST TRUMP

As we are learning with the conduct of Eric Ciaramella and other Deep State operatives—the very hard way—it was all too easy for our intelligence agencies, acting behind their curtains of secrecy, to abuse their power. As outlined earlier, one Deep State player in particular was likely up to no good, and we are on the case.

We filed a FOIA lawsuit against the Justice Department for communications records of Schiff enabler Michael K. Atkinson—former assistant attorney general in DOJ's National Security Division (NSD) from 2016 to 2018 and the past inspector general of the intelligence community (ICIG).

The records we sought were regarding Donald Trump, Hillary Clinton, Anthony Weiner, the Twenty-Fifth Amendment and/or presidential impeachment. We're also seeking all emails and text messages of Representative Adam Schiff (D-CA) and members of Schiff's staff.

We sued after the Justice Department failed to respond to our October 1, 2019, FOIA request (*Judicial Watch vs. U.S. Department of Justice* [No. 1:19-cv-03566]). We asked for:

+ All emails (whether on .gov or non-.gov email accounts) and text messages sent to or from former Senior Counsel to the Assistant Attorney General Michael K. Atkinson regarding Donald Trump, Hillary Clinton, Anthony Weiner, the Twenty-Fifth Amendment, and/or presidential impeachment.

+ All emails and text messages between former Senior Counsel Atkinson and Representative Adam Schiff or any member of Mr. Schiff's staff.

+ All travel requests, travel authorizations, and expense reports of former Senior Counsel Atkinson.

+ All calendar entries of former Senior Counsel Atkinson.

+ All SF50s and SF52s of former Senior Counsel Atkinson.

The NSD falls under the direct supervision of the assistant attorney general.

Atkinson isn't important just because of his improper handling of the so-called whistleblower complaint. During Atkinson's tenure at NSD, he was senior legal counsel, first to NSD head John Carlin (Robert Mueller's former chief of staff when Mueller directed the FBI) and later to acting NSD head Mary McCord. McCord accompanied then–acting attorney general Sally Yates to see White House Counsel Don McGahn regarding Michael Flynn.

During the period Atkinson was legal advisor to Carlin and later McCord, the FISA court found there was "significant non-compliance with the NSA's minimization procedures involving queries of data," otherwise known as spying, under the Obama administration. Additionally, during this period, DOJ-NSD was working in coordination with the FBI Counterintelligence Unit on Operation Crossfire Hurricane, which included former FBI officials Bill Priestap, Peter Strzok, and Lisa Page. Page was the intermediary between FBI Counterintelligence and DOJ-NSD.

Atkinson, as we've highlighted above, also has come under scrutiny for his handling of the so-called whistleblower complaint. He seems to have changed the rules in order to "get Trump."

+ Atkinson changed the standing practice of requiring whistleblowers to present firsthand information in order to have their complaint considered both "credible" and "of urgent concern" for submission under the Intelligence Community Whistleblower Protection Act.

✦ After receiving the complaint and a recommendation from Atkinson that it be referred to Congress, the DNI refused to forward the complaint because, based on an opinion of the Justice Department Office of Legal Counsel, "The complaint submitted to the ICIG does not involve an 'urgent concern.'" In testimony before Congress, Acting Director of National Intelligence Joseph Maguire said the complaint was essentially "hearsay" and not "corroborated by other folks."

✦ After the existence of the whistleblower was leaked to the press, Atkinson told Congress he was unaware the whistleblower had first gone around him to House Intelligence Committee Chairman Adam Schiff and his staff with his complaint before submitting it to the IG's office.

To sum up, under the law, the "whistleblower" wasn't actually a "whistleblower." The complaint against Trump is like a nasty "Letter to the Editor" about the conduct of the president of the United States, whose phone calls with foreign leaders have nothing to do with the whistleblower law covering intelligence operations.

After listening to Atkinson testify about the whistleblower behind closed doors before the House Intelligence Committee on October 4, ranking Republican committee member Republican Devin Nunes (R-CA) said of him:

[The ICIG is] either totally incompetent or part of the deep state, and he's got a lot of questions he needs to answer because he knowingly changed the form and the requirements in order to make sure that this whistleblower complaint got out publicly. So, he's either incompetent or in on it . . . he's either a quack or he's lying . . . and he's going to have more to answer for, I can promise you, because we are not going to let him go; he is going to tell the truth about what happened.

President Trump has already fired Atkinson, citing his lack of confidence in him, but Schiff has yet to release Atkinson's testimony—in fact Atkinson's is the only impeachment testimony that has not been made public. One can only imagine what Schiff is desperate to hide.

As Adam Schiff keeps Atkinson's testimony on the impeachment attack on President Trump secret, we'll keep up the fight in court for transparency under the law.

DEEP STATE DEPARTMENT OFFICIALS JOIN SEDITIOUS CONSPIRACY AGAINST TRUMP

Reports suggest that our embassy in Ukraine was a hotbed of anti-Trump, Deep State activism and tried to promote and protect leftist allies in Ukraine and the United States.

When others—say the DOJ, for instance—ignored these reports, Judicial Watch didn't and jumped into action. We did so by investigating if prominent conservative figures, journalists, and persons with ties to President Donald Trump were unlawfully monitored by the State Department in Ukraine at the request of ousted U.S. ambassador Marie Yovanovitch, an Obama appointee who was held over by President Trump. Yovanovitch testified as a hostile witness against President Trump in Schiff's impeachment show trial.

Judicial Watch obtained information indicating Yovanovitch may have violated laws and government regulations by ordering subordinates to monitor certain U.S. persons using State Department resources. Yovanovitch reportedly ordered monitoring keyed to the following search terms: Biden, Giuliani, Soros, and Yovanovitch. We did what we do best, which is to file a Freedom of Information Act request and then a lawsuit against the State Department.

Prior to being recalled as ambassador to Ukraine in the spring, Yovanovitch and her team apparently created a list of individuals who were to be monitored via social media and other means. Ukraine embassy staff made the request to the Washington, DC, headquarters office of the department's Bureau of European and Eurasian Affairs. After several days, Yovanovitch's staff was informed that the request was illegal and the monitoring either ceased or was concealed via the State Department Global Engagement Center, which has looser restrictions on collecting information.

"This is not an obscure rule, everyone in public diplomacy or public affairs knows they can't make lists and monitor U.S. citizens unless there is a major national security reason," according to a senior State Department official. If the illicit operation occurred, it seems to indicate a clear political bias against the president and his supporters.

Yovanovitch, a career diplomat who has also led American embassies in Kyrgyzstan and Armenia, was appointed ambassador to Ukraine by Obama in 2016. She was recalled by the State Department in May 2019 before leaving the government to . . . wait for it . . . write a book trashing President Trump.

In the public records request to the State Department, Judicial Watch asked for any and all records regarding, concerning, or related to the monitoring of any U.S.-based journalist, reporter, or media commentator by any employee or office of the Department of State between January 1, 2019, and the present. That includes all records pertaining to the scope of the monitoring to be conducted and individuals subject to it as well as records documenting the information collected pursuant to the monitoring. The FOIA request also asks for all records of communication between any official, employee, or representative of the State Department and any other individual or entity.

The prominent conservative figures—journalists and persons with ties to President Donald Trump—allegedly unlawfully monitored by the State Department in Ukraine at the request of ousted U.S. ambassador Marie Yovanovitch include: Jack Posobiec, Donald Trump Jr., Laura Ingraham, Sean Hannity, Michael McFaul (Obama's ambassador to Russia), Dan Bongino, Ryan Saavedra, Rudy Giuliani, Sebastian Gorka, John Solomon, Lou Dobbs, Pamela Geller, and Sara Carter.

On October 10, 2019, Congressman Devin Nunes backed our reporting up, telling Sean Hannity on his program, "What I've heard is that there were strange requests, irregular requests to monitor not just one journalist, but multiple journalists. . . ." Hannity followed this statement by adding that multiple sources also told him they "believe there is evidence that government resources were used to monitor communications" of U.S. journalists and that Yovanovitch may have been involved. Yovanovitch was questioned on the issue during the impeachment proceeding in the House and seemed to deny any illegal monitoring took place. She denied being directly involved, but her answers seem to confirm a monitoring op was run out of her embassy:

Q: "Could you help us understand how the embassy and the State Department back in Washington collects information on social media?"

A: "I can't really answer the question, because I don't know all the inner details of how the press section works to gather information. But they provide us with a press summary, or they used to provide me, I mean. They provide the embassy with a press summary and it goes out to other people at the State Department as well."

Q: "And is part of that monitoring social media accounts from . . ."

A: "Yeah. I mean, in today's age, yeah, social media is really important."

So, was the Ukraine embassy illegally monitoring American critics of Ambassador Yovanovitch? It certainly is disturbing that the State Department stonewalled Judicial Watch's requests for information on this controversy until after the impeachment of President Trump. In fact, we're still waiting for the documents.

Also, in November 2019, our Judicial Watch lawyers filed a lawsuit against the State Department seeking documents related to a reported "untouchables list" given in late 2016 by Yovanovitch to Ukraine prosecutor general Yuriy Lutsenko. Lutsenko told the *New York Times* that Yovanovitch "pressed him not to prosecute anti-corruption activists." Lutsenko reportedly said earlier the do-not-prosecute list included a founder of the Ukraine group Anti-Corruption Action Centre (AntAC, the group who visited Ciaramella in the White House!), which was funded by Soros foundations, the U.S. government, and two members of the Ukrainian Parliament who vocally supported the Soros group's agenda.

The State Department has stonewalled all our requests on Ukraine and the coup against President Trump, using the coronavirus as an excuse to further ignore our nation's transparency laws, but our sources tell us the truth is out there—and we won't relent.

SCHIFF SPIES ON TRUMP WORLD

If a police officer took your phone records without court permission *and* published them, they'd face prosecution. You'll see below that Schiff and Pelosi did exactly this—in the least, abusing the civil rights of President Trump, his attorney Rudy Giuliani, Representative Devin Nunes (R-CA), and journalist John Solomon (among others).

Precisely because of Schiff's outrageous abuse of power, we filed a lawsuit against him and the House Intelligence Committee for the controversial subpoenas issued for phone records, including those of Rudy Giuliani. The phone records led to Schiff's publication of the private phone records of Giuliani, Nunes, John Solomon, Trump attorney Jay Sekulow, attorney Victoria Toensing, and other American citizens.

We sued under the public's common-law right of public access to examine government records after we received no response to a December 6, 2019, records request (*Judicial Watch v. Adam Schiff and U.S. House Permanent Select Committee on Intelligence* [No. 1:19-cv-03790]). It was a simple request for:

1. All subpoenas issued by the House Permanent Select Committee on Intelligence on or about September 30, 2019, to any telecommunications provider including, but not limited to, AT&T, Inc., for records of telephone calls of any individuals;

2. All responses received to the above-referenced subpoenas.

Schiff remains a member of the U.S. House of Representatives, currently serving as chairman of the United States House Permanent Select Committee on Intelligence. We sued Schiff in his capacity as chairman of that committee. This lawsuit states the simple basis for our claim:

> The records are of critical public importance as the subpoenas were issued without any lawful basis and violated the rights of numerous private citizens. Disclosure of the requested records would serve the public interest by providing information about the unlawful issuance of the subpoenas.
>
> The requested records fall within the scope of the public's right of access to governmental records as a matter of federal common law.

What else is Mr. Schiff hiding? Everything.

He and his committee ran roughshod over the rule of law in pursuit of the abusive impeachment of President Trump. This lawsuit serves as reminder that Congressman Schiff and Congress are not above the law.

Schiff, with the full support of the Pelosi-run House, responded to our lawsuit with incredible assertions of privilege.

In just one fourteen-page motion opposing our suit, Schiff and the committee claim "sovereign immunity"; "Speech or Debate Clause" privilege; immunity from FOIA and transparency law; that the records are secret; and that Judicial Watch and the public do not need to see them.

Schiff's filing to try to avoid disclosing his abusive subpoenas of confidential phone records suggests he and Congress can secretly subpoena and publish the phone records of any American with zero accountability under law to the people. Speaker Pelosi and every House member should be asked if they agree that they are above the law and can spy on any American.

This case raises very serious questions about your constitutional rights and the power of Congress to violate them. One might think this abuse is about President Trump, but it is broader than that—it is about whether Congress has the right to spy on any American without a warrant approved by a court.

The "coup" isn't just against President Trump, fellow American, the coup is against you.

OUR REPUBLIC (STILL) UNDER ASSAULT . . . FROM HILLARY CLINTON

Hillary Clinton did it.

When it comes to pursuing the origins of the spying abuse and seditious conspiracy against President Trump, all roads lead to Hillary.

The abusive Mueller investigation in particular had the side-benefit of freezing the Justice Department from doing the necessary audit and review of the corrupted pretend investigation of the Clinton email and other scandals by the Obama administration. Surely, Mueller and the DOJ Deep State weren't going to investigate its partner in crime in the targeting of Trump. Clinton world was a central source of the smears that were ginned up to help create the Mueller special counsel operation—an operation run by Hillary Clinton's political supporters.

Confucius supposedly said: "Study the past if you would define the future."

Judicial Watch studies the past to *protect* our future.

We must never forget one of the most shameful episodes in our recent past: that being former president of the United States Barack

Obama and his secretary of state Hillary Clinton, with mourning family members present, staring into TV cameras and *lying* to the American people about the slaughter at Benghazi.

Because of those lies, because of that past, and because of the subject of this section, is timely to remember the role Judicial Watch played in uncovering the truth about Benghazi. It was our lawsuit on Clinton's handling of Benghazi that *directly* led to the discovery of her illicit email system.

That illicit email system and the attempts to deny its existence and then delete the emails and destroy the servers and hard drives holding them precipitated—and *activated*—successive scandals. Scandals involving highly corrupt elements of the FBI and Department of Justice that not only refused to investigate Clinton and her illicit emails, but were *part of the cover-up*.

It is for that reason and more why the Hillary Clinton email scandal and its subsequent cover-up is still so incredibly relevant today. The Obama/Clinton machine's desperate concern about the legal and political consequences of the Clinton email corruption issue, as I've suggested, helps explain their motive for the distraction of the Russiagate smears against President Trump. The fact is—and always will be—that some operatives associated with Barack Obama were desperate to protect Hillary Clinton's 2016 candidacy—and cover up for her—for a variety of self-serving and nefarious reasons.

These Obama operatives—as well as Hillary loyalists—knew beyond a shadow of a doubt that Hillary Clinton's email scandal was pure kryptonite to her and her presidential campaign. So, in order to stave off any further investigations and distract from that scandal, a number of these operatives jumped at the chance to smear candidate Donald J. Trump with false allegations regarding his campaign and Russia.

They did so knowing full well they had the mainstream media and the Deep State in the bag.

They just didn't count on Judicial Watch and its millions of supporters working as one to drag the scandal and its many participants into the light of day.

HILLARY CLINTON—CORRUPTION MATTERS

Hillary Clinton lost the election to Donald Trump in 2016 in part as a consequence of the nonstop, diligent work of Judicial Watch. It is fair to say she could be sitting in the Oval Office if we hadn't caught her in her email cover-up. We had begun our investigations years earlier not because she was a candidate but because we knew she was corrupt, and our long experience with her and her husband's corruption taught us that they would continue their scheming at the State Department.

In 2015, Judicial Watch broke the Clinton email scandal wide open. For years previous, we had been pushing the Clinton (and the Kerry) State Department for material tied to the infamous Benghazi terrorist attack and Hillary Clinton's conflicts of interest that resulted from her husband's well-paying "speaker" racket and the infamous Clinton Foundation. Thanks to Judicial Watch's relentless pressure, the Obama administration fessed up to the Clinton emails and had to begin an accounting to the courts and the American people.

It quickly became apparent that Mrs. Clinton set up and used a private server to hide her emails from Judicial Watch and other investigators. This meant that classified information was improperly stored and transferred. When she left office, she took tens of thousands of government emails, including classified information, and attempted to destroy or hide half of the emails (33,000) even after they were all subpoenaed by Congress (and subject to review under FOIA for Judicial Watch!).

Her unprecedented subversion of the Freedom of Information Act led to two courts reopening Judicial Watch FOIA cases. I am aware of no precedent for this—that's how extraordinary Hillary Clinton's email misconduct was. One of these courts was led by none other than Judge Emmet Sullivan, the same judge who would later be assigned the General Flynn prosecution, which we all now know to be a frame job set in motion by the Obama administration and pursued by a corrupt FBI and Justice Department. In 2016, Judge Sullivan granted Judicial Watch discovery on the Clinton email issue. Discovery is the ability to gather evidence (including testimony under oath, either in writing [by "interrogatories"] or in-person testimony, known as "depositions"). This resulted in senior Clinton-era State Department officials having to answer, under oath, questions from attorneys about the Clinton email scheme.

The Comey-run FBI seemed to be in a conundrum. Senior Obama administration officials, including President Obama, corresponded with Hillary Clinton via her nongovernmental emails. In fact, we confirmed at least nineteen email communications between Hillary Clinton and then-president Obama, all of which are being withheld, ironically, by the Trump State Department.

Barack Obama signaled where the "investigation" was going early on. As the DOJ inspector general June 2018 report states about its investigation of the FBI's handling of the Clinton investigation documents:

> On Sunday, October 11, 2015, an interview of then President Barack Obama was aired on the CBS show 60 Minutes. During this interview, Obama characterized former Secretary Clinton's use of a private

email server as a "mistake," but stated that it did not "pose a national security problem" and was "not a situation in which America's national security was endangered." Obama also stated that the issue had been "ginned up" because of the presidential race. Two days later, on October 13, 2015, Obama's Press Secretary, Josh Earnest, was asked whether Obama's comments "should be read as an attempt to steer the direction of the FBI investigation." Earnest replied that Obama made his comments based on public information, and they were not intended to influence an independent investigation.

Former President Obama's comments caused concern among FBI officials about the potential impact on the investigation. Former EAD John Giacalone told the OIG, "[W]e open up criminal investigations. And you have the President of the United States saying this is just a mistake. . . . That's a problem, right?" Former AD Randy Coleman expressed the same concern, stating, "[The FBI had] a group of guys in here, professionals, that are conducting an investigation. And the . . . President of the United States just came out and said there's no there there."

President Obama's involvement in the campaign for his successor was also unusual and must have added to the pressure (to not only put the Clinton email aside but to target then-candidate Trump). One would have to go back nearly a century to find an incumbent president involve himself as directly in the campaign for his successor as President Obama did in 2016. When you consider the direct partnership we uncovered between Clinton campaign operatives (and lawyers) and the Obama FBI/DOJ/State Department in the effort to get Trump, it would be fair to conclude that the Obama administration had effectively become an arm of the Clinton presidential campaign.

And then there was the secret tarmac meeting between Bill Clinton and then attorney general Loretta Lynch. On June 27, 2016, Lynch met with former president Bill Clinton on board a parked plane at Sky Harbor International Airport in Phoenix, Arizona. The private meeting only became public thanks to the reporting of local Phoenix reporter Christopher Sign. The meeting occurred during the then-ongoing investigation of Mrs. Clinton's email server, and only a few days before she was interviewed by the Justice Department and FBI.

The tarmac meeting also came just days before Comey held the July 5, 2016, press conference in which he announced that no charges would be filed against Mrs. Clinton. Judicial Watch launched an immediate investigation and lawsuit that exposed and ended a FBI cover-up of key Clinton tarmac meeting records.

The FBI originally informed Judicial Watch they could not locate any records related to the tarmac meeting. However, in a related FOIA lawsuit, the Justice Department located emails in which DOJ officials communicated with the FBI and wrote that they had communicated with the FBI. As a result, by letter dated August 10, 2017, the FBI stated, "Upon further review, we subsequently determined potentially responsive documents may exist. As a result, your [FOIA] request has been reopened. . . ."

Cover-up exposed.

The FBI then gave us two batches of documents they originally said they never had.

The new FBI documents show FBI officials were concerned about a leak that Bill Clinton delayed his aircraft taking off in order to "maneuver" a meeting with the attorney general. A resulting story in the *Observer* causes a flurry of emails about the source of the article. FBI official(s) write "we need to find that guy" and that the Phoenix FBI office was contacted "in an attempt to stem any further damage." Another FBI official, working on Lynch's security detail, suggests instituting nondisclosure agreements. The names of the emails authors are redacted. There are zero documents showing concern about the propriety of the meeting itself.[1]

Another batch of FBI docs we were told never existed included emails by notorious FBI official Peter Strzok. In a *previously unseen email*, on July 1, 2016, Strzok forwarded to Bill Priestap, assistant director of FBI counterintelligence, and other FBI officials an article in the *New York Times* titled "Lynch to Remove Herself from Decision Over Clinton Emails, Official Says." Priestap comments on it, saying: "The meeting in PX is all over CNN TV news this morning . . ." Strzok replies: "Timing's not ideal in that it falsely adds to those seeking the 'this is all choreographed' narrative. But I don't think it's worth changing . . . later won't be better." Priestap responds, "Agreed."

What were they discussing "changing"? The context suggests Comey's pending announcement a few days later that Hillary Clinton wouldn't be recommended for prosecution by the FBI.

When was the decision made to let her off? Long before July. Incredibly, our lawsuit for tarmac documents backed into an email from Strzok that suggests the decision on how to end the Clinton email matter has been under discussion since *April 2016*—three months before then–FBI director James Comey announced he would recommend no prosecution.

Another July 1, 2016, email from an unidentified official in the FBI Security Division sent to his colleagues bears the subject line "Media Reports***Not for Dissemination***." It was sent in the wake of the tarmac meeting. An FBI official warns his colleagues, "Our job is to protect the boss from harm and <u>embarrassment</u>" (emphasis in original). He emphasizes that FBI officials should ask themselves "What issues are currently being reported in the media? And what actions/interactions/situations that the Director may be in could impact them." The official then cites an example of a public relations disaster near-miss when Comey's plane "literally just missed Clinton's plane" when they flew into White Plains [New York] Airport a few months earlier, and saying, "Imagine the optics and the awkward situation we would have put the Director in [if] we would have been at the FBO at the same time as Secretary Clinton."

This is all incredible.

These emails are astonishing, and it's no wonder the FBI hid them from Judicial Watch and the court. They suggest anti-Trump, pro-Clinton FBI agent Peter Strzok admitting the decision not to prosecute the Clinton email issue was made back in April 2016—long before even Hillary Clinton was interviewed. And the emails show that the FBI security had the political objective of protecting then-director Comey from "embarrassment"—which is, frankly, disturbing.

Also disturbing was the Justice Department's decision to withhold from us the details of the "talking points" used by the Lynch Justice Department to respond to inquiries about the Bill Clinton–Lynch meeting. I found it jaw-dropping that the Trump administration blacked out key information about how the Obama Justice Department tried to spin Loretta Lynch's scandalous meeting with Bill Clinton.

In subsequent, May 3, 2017, testimony before the Senate Judiciary Committee, Comey stated that the Lynch-Clinton tarmac meeting was the "capper" among "a number of things" that had caused him to determine that Department of Justice leadership "could not credibly complete the investigation and decline prosecution without grievous damage to the American people's confidence in the justice system." So because he couldn't trust Lynch, Comey decided to be FBI director, attorney general, and public scold all at once!

The IG concluded this was inappropriate. I think Hillary Clinton "got away" with serious crimes. But she also is an American citizen who has rights to be treated fairly under law. So for Comey to hold a press conference attacking her, based on a FBI investigation that recommended no prosecutions, was an absolute abuse. Comey wanted to have his cake and eat it, too. Protect his and the FBI's reputation by attacking Clinton while dishonestly advocating to let her skate on rather obvious violations of law. As the IG concluded in a mild reprimand:

> We concluded that Comey's unilateral announcement was inconsistent with Department policy and violated long-standing Department practice and protocol by, among other things, criticizing Clinton's uncharged conduct. We also found that Comey usurped the authority of the Attorney General, and inadequately and incompletely described the legal position of Department prosecutors.

The Clinton email investigation was also irredeemably compromised by two FBI officials who will surely be known as among the most notorious couples in modern American history: Lisa Page and Peter Strzok.

PAGE-STRZOK: THE FBI'S COMPROMISED LOVEBIRDS

Lisa Page was a senior attorney in the FBI who worked for Deputy Director Andrew McCabe. Peter Strzok was a senior FBI agent who had risen to be the lead counterintelligence agent who ran both the Clinton email and Trump Russiagate investigations.

They were reportedly having an affair while running these investigations and exchanging text messages that detailed anti-Trump and pro–Hillary Clinton sentiments.

The anti-Trump animus in the text messages is overwhelming:

+ August 16, 2015, Strzok: "[Bernie Sanders is] an idiot like
  Trump. Figure they cancel each other out."

+ February 12, 2016, Strzok: "Oh, [Trump's] abysmal.
  I keep hoping the charade will end and people will just
  dump him. The problem, then, is Rubio will likely lose to
  Cruz. The Republican party is in utter shambles. When
  was the last competitive ticket they offered?"

+ March 3, 2016, Page: "God trump is a loathsome human."

+ March 3, 2016, Strzok: "Omg [Trump's] an idiot."

+ March 3, 2016, Page: "He's awful."

+ March 3, 2016, Strzok: "God Hillary should win
  100,000,000–0."

+ August 26, 2016, Strzok: "Just went to a southern Virginia
  Walmart. I could SMELL the Trump support. . . ."

They go on and on like this. When it came to Hillary Clinton,
who was then under criminal investigation, they were much more sensitive. As the DOJ inspector general recounts:

February 24, 2016: In connection with a discussion about how many
people from the FBI and Department should be present during a potential interview of former Secretary Clinton, Page stated in a February 24, 2016 text message to Strzok, "One more thing: she might be
our next president. The last thing you need us going in there loaded
for bear. You think she's going to remember or care that it was more
doj than fbi?" Strzok replied, "Agreed. . . ."

But when it came to investigating Trump, the duo was loaded for bear. Again, from the IG:

+ July 31, 2016: In connection with formal opening of the FBI's Russia investigation, Strzok texted Page: "And damn this feels momentous. Because this matters. The other one did, too, but that was to ensure we didn't F something up. This matters because this MATTERS. So super glad to be on this voyage with you."

+ August 8, 2016: In a text message on August 8, 2016, Page stated, "[Trump's] not ever going to become president, right? Right?!" Strzok responded, "No. No he's not. We'll stop it."

+ August 15, 2016: In a text message exchange on August 15, 2016, Strzok told Page, "I want to believe the path you threw out for consideration in Andy's office—that there's no way he gets elected—but I'm afraid we can't take that risk. It's like an insurance policy in the unlikely event you die before you're 40. . . ." The "Andy" referred to in the text message appears to be FBI deputy director Andrew McCabe.

The IG pretends that all this is *not* evidence that the Clinton and Trump investigations were compromised by political bias. The rest of us will believe our own eyes.

But even the IG couldn't rule out bias in the handling of the infamous "Weiner laptop." Anthony Weiner, Huma Abedin's then-husband who was convicted on sex charges, had a laptop that was found by local and New York FBI law enforcement to contain a trove of emails from the Clinton email server. How? Because Huma Abedin was the only other

State Department employee to have an account on the Clinton email server and she evidently used her husband's laptop to access the server.

Despite being alerted to this new trove in September 2016, Strzok, who was by then full into the fabulist Russia allegations against Trump, couldn't be bothered to subpoena and investigate the issue until a month later. Comey then alerted Congress only after leaks of the find were threatened!

Judicial Watch seems to be the only entity seriously investigating the Page-Strzok issue and is in court now seeking (and slowly getting) all their releasable emails and texts. The FBI has been slow-rolling the release of these documents in an unconscionable way and is *still* withholding all text messages (protesting they are not covered by FOIA). The emails show the corruption infecting the upper levels at the FBI and help explain why the agency has been slowing their release (so slow that we may not get everything due to us until 2022!). One of the many remarkable finds from the Page-Strzok emails include Strzok's "weiner timeline."[2]

On November 3, 2016, Strzok sends an email to Page with a "Weiner timeline." The document shows that on September 28, 2016, the assistant director in charge (ADIC) of the New York Office of the FBI reported "potential MYE-related material," referring to Midyear Exam, which was the code name of the FBI's Clinton email investigation. The timeline shows that not until October 30, almost a month after the discovery, was a search warrant for the emails obtained:

09/26/2016 NYO [New York Office] obtains SW [search warrant] for Weiner laptop

09/28/2016 ADIC NY **notes potential MYE-related material** following weekly SAC [Special Agent in Charge] SVTC [Secure Video Teleconference]

09/29/2016 Conference call between NYO and MYE team

NYO notes processing is crashing system and not complete, but during troubleshooting **observes material potentially related to MYE (clintonemail.com and state.gov domains) seen during course of review**

No numbers/volume available

Discussion about ability to search for material determines such activity would be outside scope of warrant

Request to NYO to gather basic facts (numbers, domains, etc.) based on their review

Approx. 10/19/2016 NYO completes carving

NYO observes SBU [Sensitive but Unclassified] attachment

10/21/2016 6:00 PM DOJ/NSD advises MYE leadership that SDNY informed them of **MYE-related media on Weiner media**

10/25/2016 **DOJ-DD conversation re material**

10/26/2016 **DOJ-MYE-NYO conference call**

DD advised of results of call with MYE team conclusion material should be looked at; DD directs briefing to D

10/27/2016 Briefing to D; D concurs with conducting investigation to obtain data

10/30/2016 **SW** [search warrant] **sworn out at SDNY**

Copy of media obtained by MYE SAs [Special Agents], entered into evidence, and provided to OTD [Operational Technology Division] for processing

(Emphasis added)

Again, the IG report suggested possible bias by Strzok: "[W]e did not have confidence that Strzok's decision to prioritize the Russia investigation over following up on the Midyear-related investigative lead discovered on the Weiner laptop was free from bias."

These new records show how Hillary Clinton was protected from investigation over the Weiner laptop by the FBI for a full month during the presidential campaign.

We also know from separate Judicial Watch litigation that the Weiner laptop contained emails and classified material that Hillary Clinton had destroyed or otherwise withheld from government investigators and the American people.

Reportedly, only 3,077 of the more than 300,000 emails found on the Weiner laptop "were directly reviewed[3] for classified or incriminating information. Three FBI officials completed that work in a single 12-hour spurt the day before Comey again cleared Clinton of criminal charges" on November 6, 2016.[4]

The numbers of emails alleged to be on the laptop has been hard to pin down, though a top FBI official recently testified in writing to Judicial Watch that the FBI reviewed 48,982 emails as a result of the delayed warrant for Clinton email account information from the laptop of Anthony Weiner. (Though other information suggest the emails could have been in the hundreds of thousands. We've been unable to resolve the discrepancy.)

Throughout litigation, we forced the State Department and FBI to turn over to us government-related emails from the Clinton emails found on the Weiner laptop.

What we uncovered is shocking. There were at least eighteen classified emails on Weiner's laptop and the State Department was forced to turn over numerous emails that Hillary Clinton had tried to delete or hide from the American people. In other words, many emails she tried to delete or hide were on Anthony Weiner's laptop!

The classified material includes discussions about Saudi Arabia, The Hague, Egypt, South Africa, Zimbabwe, the identity of a CIA official, Malawi, the war in Syria, Lebanon, Hamas, and the PLO.[5]

On two occasions, classified material was sent by Abedin on her clintonemail.com account to Weiner's laptop (sent to "Anthony Campaign") on November 25, 2010. The email discusses an upcoming call with Prince Saud of "expected WikiLeaks leaks." Abedin sent classified information the following day to Weiner's laptop concerning a call that "Jeff" (presumably then–U.S. assistant secretary of state for Near Eastern affairs Jeffrey Feltman) had with United Arab Emirates prime minister Abdullah bin Zayed.

The Weiner laptop also contains classified material from Abedin's BlackBerry. A July 9, 2011, email contained classified information regarding a then-upcoming call between Clinton and Israeli prime minister Benjamin Netanyahu. On November 25, 2011, classified information was sent regarding Feltman's notes on the Egyptian Ministry of Foreign Affairs impression of the Hamas–Palestine Liberation Organization talks.

The classified information on Weiner's laptop is part of a pattern of mishandling national security material by Clinton and her aides. The Weiner emails emphasize the need for the Justice Department to conduct a fresh, serious investigation of Hillary Clinton's and Huma Abedin's obvious violations of law.

The Strzok-Page material also has a surfeit of information on cover-ups and corruption:

The emails show that Clinton apologized to the FBI over her email abuses, but that apology was not in the FBI 302 report documenting her interview.[6] Strzok's August 2016 email says:

> Though not in the 302, at the end of the interview she apologized
> for the work and effort it created for the FBI. She said words to the

effect of, I'm sorry this has caused so much work and expenditure of resources by the FBI. I chose to use my own server out of convenience; it proved to be anything but.

So now we have confirmation that the FBI report of Clinton's "interview" is incomplete—incomplete in a way, of course, that inured to her benefit? What else did Strzok leave out of the Clinton interview? Other finds include:

Strzok-Page emails that confirm what many suspected—that special accommodations were given to the lawyers of Clinton and her aides during the investigation of her email controversy. Additionally, in November 2019, Judicial Watch uncovered Strzok-Page emails[7] showing the attorney representing three of Clinton's aides met with senior FBI officials.

DOJ records showing that, after Clinton's statement[8] denying the transmission of classified information over her unsecure email system, Strzok sent an email to FBI officials citing "three [Clinton email] chains" containing (C) [classified] portion marks in front of paragraphs.[9]

Records that show that then–FBI general counsel James Baker instructed FBI officials to expedite the release[10] of FBI investigative material to Hillary Clinton's lawyer, David Kendall, in August 2016. Kendall and the FBI's top lawyer discussed specifically quickly obtaining the FBI's 302 report of its interview with Clinton.[11]

CLINTON FOUNDATION
PAY-TO-PLAY SCHEME EXPOSED—
AT THE CLINTON STATE DEPARTMENT

Huma Abedin, who, in 2016, along with many other top Clinton State officials who testified to my Judicial Watch attorney colleagues as part of one of our FOIA lawsuits, admitted it was Clinton's decision to use her non-state.gov email; that to her knowledge only Hillary Clinton, Abedin, and Chelsea Clinton had accounts on the clintonemail.com system; and that the clintonemail.com system may have interfered with Mrs. Clinton's ability to do her job. Abedin also testified that the reason she had an email account on the Clinton server was so that she could use it for Clinton family matters. Well, it turns out that Abedin's idea of family matters was to use the Clinton email system for government work (which meant more classified info mishandling) and to allow her to facilitate the pay-to-play operation involving the Clinton Foundation.

Once again, it was your friendly neighborhood Judicial Watch that had to do the legwork to ask for and then sue for the Abedin email cache. What we found may have been the death knell for Clinton's presidential ambitions.

The Obama State Department had accessed the Abedin emails in 2015 but slow-rolled the release of the material to us in the late summer of 2016.

The Clinton obstruction, designed to hide from us her every email about her conduct at State, collapsed against Judicial Watch's relentless litigation at the worst possible moment—just a few months before Election Day.

In August 2016, we uncovered emails that showed cash for favors at the Clinton State Department. They were simply extraordinary. We knew that Hillary Clinton and Bill Clinton had already leveraged State, lining their pockets with up to $48 million in personal speaking fees. But now we had evidence that she used the State Department to take care of donors to the Clinton Foundation, their personal and political platform used to support her aspirations to the presidency. I testified for Judicial Watch to Congress in one of the last major hearings the House Republicans held before they turned over the keys to Democrats in 2019:

> It is no secret Judicial Watch has had longstanding concerns with the Clintons' ethics and respect for the rule of law. So, it was with some skepticism that we greeted Hillary Clinton's promises ten years ago to avoid conflicts of interest with her Foundation and her husband's business activities as Secretary of State.
>
> At the time,[12] even CNN reported that Bill Clinton's "complicated global business interests could present future conflicts of interest that result in unneeded headaches for the incoming commander-in-chief."

To reassure President Obama and senators of both parties that she would be above reproach, Mrs. Clinton sent a January 5, 2009, letter[13] to State Department designated agency ethics official James H. Thessin, stating:

> For the duration of my appointment as Secretary if I am confirmed, I will not participate personally and substantially in any particular matter involving specific parties in which The William J. Clinton Foundation (or the Clinton Global Initiative) is a party or represents a party. . . .

What a crock that promise turned out to be.[14]

Our headline-making disclosures in August 2016 included documents showing that in April 2009 controversial Clinton Foundation official Doug Band pushed for a job for an associate. In the email Band tells Hillary Clinton's former aides at the State Department, Cheryl Mills and Huma Abedin, that it is "important to take care of [Redacted]. Band is reassured by Abedin that "Personnel has been sending him options." Band was cofounder of Teneo Strategy[15] with Bill Clinton and a top official of the Clinton Foundation, including its Clinton Global Initiative.

Included in that document production was a 2009 email in which Band directs Abedin and Mills to put Lebanese-Nigerian billionaire and Clinton Foundation donor Gilbert Chagoury in touch with the State Department's "substance person" on Lebanon. Band notes that Chagoury is a "key guy there [Lebanon] and to us," and insists that Abedin call Ambassador Jeffrey Feltman to connect him to Chagoury.

Chagoury[16] is a close friend of former president Bill Clinton and a top donor to the Clinton Foundation. He has appeared near the top of the foundation's donor list as a $1 million to $5 million contributor, according to foundation documents.[17] He also pledged[18] $1 billion to the Clinton Global Initiative.[19] According to a 2010 investigation[20] by PBS's *Frontline*, Chagoury was convicted[21] in 2000 in Switzerland for laundering money from Nigeria, but agreed to a plea deal and repaid $66 million to the Nigerian government.

You can see that the Clinton Foundation and the Clinton State Department almost immediately broke promises to President Obama and the Senate to maintain a wall of separation between the foundation and State.

Judicial Watch has since uncovered many other instances of seeming pay-to-play and favoritism for the Clinton Foundation at the Clinton State Department.

Steve Bing/Shangri-La Entertainment: On July 16, 2009, Shangri-La Entertainment executive Zachary Schwartz asked Clinton Foundation official Doug Band for help reversing the State Department's denial of a travel visa to Cuba. Band sent the request to Huma Abedin, writing, "please call [Schwartz] asap on this . . . Important." Abedin responded that she would call him. Media reports indicate that two weeks later, Shangri-La owner Steve Bing's team was in Cuba. Bing is a longtime Clinton friend and donor and is listed as having donated between $10 million and $25 million to the foundation. His construction company, Shangri-La Industries, paid Bill Clinton $2.5 million from 2009 to 2010 to serve as an advisor.

Crown Prince Salman of Bahrain: A Judicial Watch–obtained Huma Abedin–Doug Band email exchange from 2009 revealed that Crown Prince Salman of Bahrain requested a meeting with Secretary of State Clinton but was forced to go through the Clinton Foundation for an appointment. Abedin advised Band that when she went through "normal channels" at State, Clinton declined to meet. After Band intervened, however, the meeting was set up within forty-eight hours. According to the Clinton Foundation website, in 2005 Salman committed to establishing the Crown Prince's International Scholarship Program (CPISP) for the Clinton Global Initiative. And by 2010, it had spent $32 million in conjunction with CGI. The Kingdom of Bahrain reportedly gave between $50,000 and $100,000 to the Clinton Foundation. And Bahrain Petroleum also gave an additional $25,000 to $50,000."

Wolverhampton Football Club: In another Judicial Watch–obtained an Abedin-Band email exchange from May 2009, Band urged Abedin to get the Clinton State Department to intervene in order to obtain a visa for members of the Wolverhampton (UK) Football Club, one of whose members was apparently having difficulty because of a "criminal charge." Band was acting at the behest of Casey Wasserman, a millionaire Hollywood sports entertainment executive and president of the Wasserman Foundation. Wasserman had donated between $5 million and $10 million to the Clinton Foundation through the Wasserman Foundation.

Slimfast founder Danny Abraham: A May 2009 Abedin-Band email reveals that Slimfast tycoon S. Daniel Abraham was granted almost immediate access to then–secretary of state Clinton, with Abedin serving as the facilitator. According to the Clinton Foundation website, Abraham, like the Wasserman Foundation, has given between $5 million and $10 million to the Clinton Foundation. The emails indicate that Abraham was granted almost immediate access to Clinton upon request.

Coal industry lobbyist Joyce Aboussie: Another record reveals that in June 2009, prominent St. Louis political power broker Joyce Aboussie exchanged a series of insistent emails with Abedin concerning Aboussie's efforts to set up a meeting between Clinton and Peabody Energy vice president Cartan Sumner. Aboussie wrote, "Huma, I need your help now to intervene please. We need this meeting with Secretary Clinton, who has been there now for nearly six months. This is, by the way, my first request. I really would appreciate your help on this. It should go without saying that the Peabody folks came to Dick [Gephardt] and I because of our relationship with the Clinton's. [*sic*]" After further notes from Aboussie, Abedin responded, "We are working on it and I hope we can make something work . . . we have to work through the beauracracy [*sic*] here." Aboussie donated between $100,000 and $250,000 to the Clinton Foundation.

It was hard to tell, in light of all this evidence, where the Clinton State Department ended and where the Clinton Foundation began.

I recall reporters asking how and if we timed the disclosures. I explained that the timing of the disclosures was a consequence of Hillary Clinton's cover-up! If the emails had been disclosed as required under law and not hidden by her, these emails could have emerged years earlier. And, again, the Obama State Department had the emails for a year but only turned them over to us just before the elections.

Our work on the Clinton email and her foundation corruption issues led to another FBI investigation/non-investigation of Clinton Inc. And it also led to the exposure of yet more corruption at the top levels of the Obama FBI.

ANDREW MCCABE—CLINTON'S ACE IN THE HOLE?

Judicial Watch, once again, did the heavy lifting to expose the truth about Obama deputy FBI director McCabe's conflicts of interest on the Clinton and Trump investigations with a series of FOIA lawsuits to get the truth. McCabe's conflicts and related leaks and lies were the subject of yet another DOJ inspector general report that, once again, seemed to follow our lead!

The documents we uncovered include an email showing McCabe's wife, Jill McCabe, was recruited for a Virginia state senate race in February 2015 by then–Virginia lieutenant governor Ralph Northam's office.

The news that Clinton used a private email server broke five days later, on March 2, 2015. Five days after that, former Clinton Foundation board member and Democrat Party fund-raiser Virginia governor

Terry McAuliffe met with the McCabes. She announced her candidacy on March 12. Soon afterward, Clinton/McAuliffe-aligned political groups donated nearly $700,000 (40 percent of the campaign's total funds) to McCabe's wife for her campaign. My colleague Micah Morrison detailed the devastating timeline after the initial campaign recruitment call:

> Less than two weeks later, in March 2015, McCabe and his wife drive to Richmond for what they thought was a meeting with a Virginia state senator to discuss Dr. McCabe's possible run for office.
>
> In Richmond, according to the OIG report, they are told there had been "a change of plans" and that "Governor McAuliffe wanted to speak to Dr. McCabe at the Governor's mansion." It's around this time that a veteran FBI agent's radar might start blinking.
>
> McCabe and his wife meet with McAuliffe for 30 to 45 minutes, according to the OIG report. Fundraising was discussed. "Governor McAuliffe said that he and the Democratic Party would support Dr. McCabe's candidacy." McAuliffe asked McCabe about his occupation and "McCabe told him he worked for the FBI but they did not discuss McCabe's work or any FBI business." McCabe later described it to an FBI official as a "surreal meeting."
>
> After the meeting, the couple rode to a local event with the governor, then returned to the mansion with the governor to retrieve their car.
>
> McCabe informed FBI ethics officials and lawyers about the meeting and consulted with them about his wife's plans. No one raised strong objections. McCabe recused himself from all public corruption cases in Virginia and Dr. McCabe jumped into the race.
>
> On July 2015, the FBI opened an investigation into Mrs. Clinton's email practices.

Let's pause to note here that while the official FBI investigation was opened in July 2015, Mrs. Clinton was known to be in hot water as far back as March 2015, when the State Department inspector general revealed her widespread use of a private, nongovernment email server.

Swamp cats will notice that March 2015 is also when Andrew and Jill McCabe got their surprise audience with McAuliffe, the long-time Clinton moneyman.

The McCabe fortunes rose in the autumn of 2015. Mr. McCabe was promoted to associate deputy director of the FBI. Dr. McCabe received $675,000 from two McAuliffe-connected entities for her state senate race. They were by far the biggest donations to her campaign.

In November 2015, Dr. McCabe lost her race.

In January 2016, the FBI opened an investigation into the Clinton Foundation.

On February 1, Mr. McCabe was promoted again, to deputy director of the FBI.

Despite the McAuliffe connection, the OIG report notes, there was no FBI re-evaluation of McCabe's recusals following his promotions. Although recused from Virginia public corruption investigations, he retained a senior role in Clinton-related matters.

In May 2016, news broke that McAuliffe was under FBI investigation for campaign finance violations. CNN reported that investigators were scrutinizing "McAuliffe's time as a board member of the Clinton Global Initiative" and Chinese businessman Wang Wenliang, a U.S. permanent resident who made large donations to both the McAuliffe 2013 gubernatorial campaign and to the Clinton Foundation.

On October 23, the Wall Street Journal revealed the McAuliffe-linked donations to Dr. McCabe's campaign. At FBI headquarters, McCabe resists pressure from senior executives to recuse himself from all Clinton-related matters.

Finally, on November 1—a week before the presidential election—McCabe recused himself from the Clinton email and Clinton Foundation investigations.

Per usual, it wasn't the IG that first exposed McCabe's conflicts but Judicial Watch through its FOIA litigation.

Again, in January 2016, the FBI had reportedly begun investigating the Clinton Foundation, as it expanded from the email probe launched in response to our forcing the disclosure of the Clinton email cache. In October 2016, FBI agents were told they did not have "enough evidence to move forward" with their investigation of the foundation.

Things went off the rails when the *Wall Street Journal* published an article detailing McCabe's links to Clinton world. An October 23, 2016, email we uncovered shows McCabe running the response effort to the *Wall Street Journal* article published that day, titled "Clinton Ally Aided Campaign of FBI Official's Wife." McCabe provides Michael Kortan, the assistant director of public affairs, his version of a timeline of events surrounding the Clinton investigation and his wife's campaign. McCabe said he contacted then–FBI chief of staff Chuck Roseburg about Jill McCabe's candidacy and was told that "the D [Comey] has no issue with it."

Internally, the *Wall Street Journal* article started a flurry of emails among Mrs. McCabe's campaign, Kortan, Director McCabe, and the FBI's general counsel. Part of that exchange is an email from McCabe to someone in the General Counsel's Office: "Sucks pretty much. Buckle in. It's going to get rough." The colleague responds, "I know.

It's awful. I shouldn't be shocked by now, but I really am appalled." McCabe also forwarded the article to Comey who responded, "Copy."

On October 24, 2016, a memo was sent to all Special Agents in Charge, assistant directors, executive directors, and the General Counsel's Office regarding the *Wall Street Journal* article discussing campaign activities concerning Mrs. McCabe. Kortan suggested that questions could be referred to his office and he attached an "Overview of Deputy Director McCabe's Recusal Related to Dr. McCabe's Campaign for Political Office." One of the "Overview" talking points confirms that McCabe was involved in the Clinton email investigation while he was running the FBI's Washington Field Office before being promoted to DAD. The following question and answer is provided in the talking points:

> While at [Washington Field Office] did Mr. McCabe provide assistance to the Clinton investigation?

> After the referral was made, FBI Headquarters asked the Washington Field Office for personnel to conduct a special investigation. McCabe was serving as [assistant director] and provided personnel resources. However, he was not told what the investigation was about. In February 2016 McCabe became Deputy Director and began overseeing the Clinton investigation.

The Overview also shows, if asked whether McCabe played any role in his wife's campaign, the scripted response was: "No. Then–[assistant director] McCabe played no role, attended no events and did not participate in fundraising or support of any kind."

This was false.

In June 2017, Circa reported that social media photos showed "McCabe wearing a T-shirt supporting his wife's campaign during a public event and then posting a photo on social media urging voters to join him in voting for his wife."

And we uncovered docs that show repeated use of the official FBI email system in connection with Mrs. McCabe's political campaign. For example:

+ On March 13, 2015, Mrs. McCabe emails to her husband's official FBI email account a draft press release announcing her run for state senate.

+ In August 2015, McCabe uses his official FBI email account to advise a redacted recipient to visit his wife's campaign website: "Jill has been busy as hell since she decided to run for VA state senate (long story). Check her out on Facebook as Dr. Jill McCabe for Senate."

+ On November 2, 2015, Mrs. McCabe forwards an email to her husband—then the assistant director in charge of the FBI's Washington office—that accuses her opponent of extorting local businessmen. The email was sent to her husband's official FBI account.

(The McCabe documents also show that FBI leadership was sensitive to reports of FBI internal dissent with then-director Comey's handling of the Clinton investigation. On October 24, 2016, Mrs. McCabe forwarded to Director McCabe a True Pundit article titled, "FBI Director Lobbied Against Criminal Charges for Hillary After Clinton Insider Paid His Wife $700,000." The story reported that former FBI executive assistant director John Giacalone resigned in the middle of the Clinton email investigation because he saw it going "sideways" and that Jill McCabe received money from a PAC headed by McAuliffe, who was under investigation by the FBI for campaign finance law violations.

McCabe forwarded the article to Comey, noting "FYI. Heavyweight source." Comey replied to McCabe, copying Chief of Staff James Rybicki, saying, "This still reads to me like someone not involved in the investigation at all, maybe somebody who heard rumors. . . .")

So as the FBI pursued a baseless investigation against Trump, the DOJ inspector general report detailed evidence that the Obama DOJ sought to shut down the FBI investigation of Clinton Foundation in August 2016 (just as we were finally exposing the Clinton pay-to-play scandal docs to the world):

> McCabe [fired former deputy director of the FBI] told the OIG that on August 12, 2016, he received a telephone call from PADAG [Principal Associate Deputy Attorney General, likely Matthew Axelrod] regarding the FBI's handling of the CF [Clinton Foundation] Investigation (the "PADAG call"). McCabe said that PADAG expressed concerns about FBI agents taking overt steps in the CF Investigation during the presidential campaign. According to McCabe, he pushed back, asking "are you telling me that I need to shut down a validly predicated investigation?" McCabe told us that the conversation was "very dramatic" and he never had a similar confrontation like the PADAG call with a high-level Department official in his entire FBI career.

So the irony is that McCabe actually pushed back against DOJ efforts to help protect Hillary Clinton. And after it became known about his Clinton conflicts, McCabe then tried to rescue his reputation (and the FBI's) by improperly leaking confirmation of the Clinton Foundation investigation to the *Wall Street Journal*. It was this leak and associated lies that resulted in McCabe's firing and an IG referral for prosecution (which was not pursued by DOJ, of course).

CLINTON NOT OUT OF THE WOODS YET

That email scandal is far from over. Secrets are still being hidden. The rule of law is still being flaunted. Because of that, we have never stopped our investigations and never stopped digging.

In 2016, Judge Sullivan allowed Judicial Watch to depose many top State Department officials and members of the Clinton inner circle—Huma Abedin and Cheryl Mills, in particular—about the Clinton email scheme. As Judge Sullivan remarked during one hearing, "We wouldn't be here today if this employee [Hillary Clinton] had followed government policy." But Judge Sullivan allowed only limited discovery and there was more to be uncovered.

Judge Royce Lamberth, the federal judge handling the Judicial Watch lawsuit that uncovered the Clinton email scandal, saw there was more information the court needed to resolve the case and authorized discovery with an initial ruling in March 2016:

> Where there is evidence of government wrong-doing and bad faith, as here, limited discovery is appropriate, even though it is exceedingly rare in FOIA cases.

> [Judicial Watch] is certainly entitled to dispute the State Department's position that it has no obligation to produce these documents because it did not "possess" or "control" them at the time the FOIA request was made. The State Department's willingness to now search documents voluntarily turned over to the Department by Secretary Clinton and other officials hardly transforms such a search into an "adequate" or "reasonable one. [Judicial Watch] is not relying on "speculation" or "surmise" as the State Department claims. [Judicial

Watch] is relying on constantly shifting admissions by the Government and the former government officials.

The court then moved the ball forward at an extraordinary October 2018 hearing, stating, "The information that I was provided was clearly false regarding the adequacy of the [Clinton email] search and . . . what we now know turned out to be the Secretary's email system."

Turning his attention to the Department of Justice, Judge Lamberth said that he was "dumbfounded" by the agency's inspector general report revealing that Cheryl Mills had been given immunity and was allowed to accompany former secretary of state Hillary Clinton to her FBI interview:

> I had myself found that Cheryl Mills had committed perjury and lied under oath in a published opinion I had issued in a Judicial Watch case where I found her unworthy of belief, and I was quite shocked to find out she had been given immunity—by the Justice Department in the Hillary Clinton email case. So I did not know that until I read the IG report and learned that and that she had accompanied the Secretary to her interview.

(In an April 28, 2008, ruling relating to Mills's conduct as a White House official in responding to concerns about lost White House email records, Judge Lamberth called Mills's participation in the matter "loathsome." He further stated Mills was responsible for "the most critical error made in this entire fiasco . . . Mills' actions were totally inadequate to address the problem.")

Lamberth also complained that the Justice Department attorney representing the State Department was using "doublespeak," and playing "word games." The back-and-forth with the DOJ lawyer representing the State Department (Mr. Prince) follows:

THE COURT: The State Department told me that it had produced all records when it moved for summary judgment and you filed that motion. That was not true when that motion was filed.

MR. PRINCE: At that time, we had produced all—

THE COURT: It was not true.

MR. PRINCE: Yes, it was—well, Your Honor, it might be that our search could be found to be inadequate, but that declaration was absolutely true.

THE COURT: It was not true. It was a lie.

MR. PRINCE: It was not a lie, Your Honor.

THE COURT: What—that's doublespeak.

MR. PRINCE: There's strong precedent saying that items not in the State's possession do not need to be searched. . . .

THE COURT: And that's because the Secretary was doing this on a private server? So it wasn't in the State's possession? . . . So you're playing the same word game she played?

Judge Lamberth said he was relieved that he did not allow the case to be shut down prematurely, as the State Department had requested:

The case started with a motion for summary judgment [seeking to close the case] here and which I denied and allowed limited discovery because it was clear to me that at the time that I ruled initially, that false statements were made to me by career State Department officials

and it became more clear through discovery that the information that
I was provided was clearly false regarding the adequacy of the search
and this—what we now know turned out to be the Secretary's email
system.

I don't know the details of what kind of IG inquiry there was into
why these career officials at the State Department would have filed
false affidavits with me. I don't know the details of why the Justice Department lawyers did not know false affidavits were being filed with
me, but I was very relieved that I did not accept them and that I allowed limited discovery into what had happened.

Judge Lamberth then followed up with a ruling in December
2018:

[T]he Court ORDERS the parties to meet and confer to plan discovery into (a) whether Hillary Clinton's use of a private email while
Secretary of State was an intentional attempt to evade FOIA; (b)
whether the State Department's attempts to settle this case in late
2014 and early 2015 amounted to bad faith; and (c) whether State
has adequately searched for records responsive to Judicial Watch's
requests.

Terming Clinton's use of her private email system "one of the gravest modern offenses to government transparency," Lamberth wrote in
his memorandum opinion:

[H]is [President Barack Obama's] State and Justice Departments fell
far short. So far short that the court questions, even now, whether they
are acting in good faith. Did Hillary Clinton use her private email as
Secretary of State to thwart this lofty goal [the Obama-announced
standard for transparency]? Was the State Department's attempt
to settle this FOIA case in 2014 an effort to avoid searching—and

disclosing the existence of—Clinton's missing emails? And has State ever adequately searched for records in this case?

At best, State's attempt to pass off its deficient search as legally adequate during settlement negotiations was negligence born out of incompetence. At worst, career employees in the State and Justice Departments colluded to scuttle public scrutiny of Clinton, skirt FOIA, and hoodwink this Court.

Turning his attention to the Department of Justice, Lamberth wrote:

The current Justice Department [AG Barr's!] made things worse. When the government last appeared before the Court, counsel claimed, "it is not true to say we misled either Judicial Watch or the Court." When accused of "doublespeak," counsel denied vehemently, feigned offense, and averred complete candor. When asked why State masked the inadequacy of its initial search, counsel claimed that the officials who initially responded to Judicial Watch's request didn't realize Clinton's emails were missing, and that it took them two months to "figure out what was going on." . . . Counsel's responses strain credulity.

Citing an email (uncovered as a result of Judicial Watch's lawsuit) in which Hillary Clinton acknowledged that Benghazi was a terrorist attack immediately after it happened, Judge Lamberth asked:

Did State know Clinton deemed the Benghazi attack terrorism hours after it happened, contradicting the Obama Administration's subsequent claim of a protest-gone-awry?

Did the Department merely fear what might be found? Or was State's bungling just the unfortunate result of bureaucratic red-tape and a failure to communicate? To preserve the Department's integrity, and to reassure the American people their government remains committed to transparency and the rule of law, this suspicion cannot be allowed to fester.

This is the sort of concern about the rule of law we should have been hearing from the Justice Department and State Department after President Trump came to power. But as you can see, nothing changed with the end of the Obama presidency. In fact, the agencies continued to mislead the court and defend Hillary Clinton's emails misconduct!

Even after Judge Lamberth's tongue-lashings, the DOJ and State still fought us—objecting to our asking any more questions about the Clinton emails and the outrageous Benghazi scandal. Nonetheless, we proceeded to discovery gathering new blockbuster documents and important and shocking testimony:

- Justin Cooper, former aide to President Bill Clinton and Clinton Foundation employee who registered the domain name of the unsecure clintonemail.com server that Clinton used while serving as Secretary of State, testified he worked with Huma Abedin, Clinton's deputy chief of staff, to create the nongovernment email system.

- In the interrogatory responses of E. W. (Bill) Priestap, assistant director of the FBI Counterintelligence Division, he stated that the agency found Clinton email records in the Obama White House, specifically the Executive Office of the President.

- Jacob "Jake" Sullivan, Clinton's senior advisor and deputy chief of staff when she was secretary of state, testified that both he and Clinton used her unsecure nongovernment email system to conduct official State Department business.

+ Eric Boswell, former assistant secretary of state for diplomatic security during Clinton's tenure as secretary of state, testified that Clinton was warned twice against using unsecure BlackBerrys and personal emails to transmit classified material.

+ Lauren Jiloty, former special assistant to then–secretary of state Hillary Clinton, admitted in written responses under oath to loading contacts on Clinton's unsecure BlackBerry. Jiloty also said that she conducted official State Department business from her own personal email account.

+ Obama national security advisor and U.S. ambassador to the United Nations Susan Rice admitted in written responses given under oath that she emailed with former secretary of state Clinton on Clinton's nongovernment email account and that she received emails related to government business on her own personal email account.

+ John Hackett, former director of Information Programs and Services (IPS), testified under oath that he had raised concerns that former secretary of state Hillary Clinton's staff may have "culled out 30,000" of the secretary's "personal" emails without following strict National Archives standards. He also revealed that he believed there was interference with the formal FOIA review process related to the classification of Clinton's Benghazi-related emails. (More on Hackett's testimony below.)

✦ We deposed Clarence Finney, the deputy director of the Executive Secretariat staff, who was the principal advisor and records management expert in the Office of the Secretary responsible for control of all correspondence and records for Clinton and other State Department officials.

✦ Jonathon Wasser, the State Department employee who conducted FOIA searches during part of Hillary Clinton's tenure as secretary of state, testified that he did not clearly recollect whether he had any knowledge of potential email addresses for Secretary Clinton.

✦ Ben Rhodes, former Obama White House deputy strategic communications advisor, who continued to blame an online video for the Benghazi attacks, claims he doesn't remember using personal email for official business, and says that he wasn't aware of Hillary Clinton using her non-government email for official State Department business before press reports made the fact public.

✦ Heather Samuelson, Clinton's White House liaison at the State Department, and later Clinton's personal lawyer, admitted under oath that she was granted immunity by the Department of Justice in June 2016.

✦ Former State Department director of the Office of Information Programs and Services Sheryl Walter stated that she did not recall a call from the Obama White House asking for "quick turnaround" of information concerning a FOIA request on former Secretary Clinton's use of personal email to conduct official business.

✦ We deposed Elissa Pitterle, the corporate representative assigned by the State Department to address questions concerning the processing of FOIA requests.

✦ We deposed Tasha Marie Thian, former records officer of the Records and Archives Management Division in the State Department, who testified: "I had been told repeatedly that [Clinton] did not use email for work" and therefore the records-management office "operated as if she did not use [email]." She said that a key FOIA official informed her Clinton used her personal email about Benghazi when she told him she was leaving in April 2014.

✦ We deposed Jamie Bair, an attorney in the Office of the Legal Adviser who was assigned to our FOIA request and lawsuit. Bair testified that he first learned about Clinton's email address shortly after joining the State Department in April 2014 and that he saw it while reviewing documents for congressional requests regarding Benghazi. Bair said he informed his supervisor, Matt Burton. Bair testified that he told DOJ attorney Rob Prince about Clinton's email address but would not provide a time frame. He also testified that his normal practice was to be in close touch with DOJ attorneys on any given case.

You can see that our work here was as comprehensive as possible and certainly much more honest than the conflicted, corrupted, and compromised Obama DOJ/FBI "investigation" of the Clinton email issue. In fact, we kept finding evidence that the DOJ and State Department were neck-deep in the cover-up.

NEW BENGHAZI DOCUMENTS
CONFIRM CLINTON EMAIL COVER-UP

Just last year, more than four years after we first uncovered Clinton's email scheme, we forced the release of new Clinton emails on the Benghazi controversy that had been covered up for years and would have exposed Hillary Clinton's email account in 2014 if the emails had been released when the State Department first uncovered them. The Clinton email in question was first identified by the State Department in September 2014, but was withheld from us despite its specific reference to Benghazi talking points—the very issue we had sued about! Even after a court had ordered its production. It was only after we informed the State Department we were prepared to file a motion with the court to compel production of the records that the agency relented and produced the email in question.

In September 2019, the State Department provided us a previously hidden email, which shows top State Department officials used and were aware of Hillary Clinton's email account, and that "she guards it pretty closely."

The September 2012 email chain begins with an email to Clinton at her private email address, "hdr22@clintonemail.com," from Jacob Sullivan, Clinton's then senior advisor and deputy chief of staff. The email was copied to Cheryl Mills, Clinton's then chief of staff, and forwarded to then–deputy assistant secretary of state for strategic communications and Clinton advisor Philippe Reines:

From: Sullivan, Jacob J
Sent: Saturday, September 29, 2012 11 :09 AM
To: 'hdr22@clintonemail.com'
Cc: Mills, Cheryl D

Subject: Key points

HRC, Cheryl –

Below is my stab at tp's for the Senator call. Cheryl, I've left the last point blank for you. These are rough but you get the point.

I look forward to sitting down and having a Hillary-to-John conversation about what we know. I know you were frustrated by the briefing we did and I'm sorry our hands were tied in that setting.

It's important we see each other in person, but over the phone today I just wanted to make a few points.

First, we have been taking this deadly seriously, as we should. I set up the ARB in record time, with serious people on it. I will get to the bottom of all the security questions. We are also in overdrive working to track down the killers, and not just through the FBI. We will get this right.

Second, the White House and Susan were not making things up. They were going with what they were told by the IC [intelligence community].

The real story may have been obvious to you from the start (and indeed I called it an assault by heavily armed militants in my first statement), but the IC gave us very different information. They were unanimous about it.

Let me read you an email from the day before Susan went on the shows. It provides the talking points for HPSCI [House Permanent Select Committee on Intelligence] and for her public appearance. It's from a very senior official at CIA, copying his counterparts at DNI [Director of National Intelligence], NCTC [National Counterterrorism Center], and FBI:

Here are the talking points . . .

+ The currently available information suggests that the demonstrations in Benghazi were spontaneously inspired by the protests at the US Embassy in Cairo and evolved into a direct assault against the US Consulate and subsequently its annex. There are indications that extremists participated in the violent demonstrations.

+ This assessment may change as additional information is collected and analyzed and as currently available information continues to be evaluated.

+ The investigation is on-going, and the US Government is working with Libyan authorities to bring to justice those responsible for the deaths of US citizens.

That is exactly what Susan said, following the guidance from the IC. She obviously got bad advice. But she was not shading the truth.

Third, you have to remember that the video WAS important. We had four embassies breached because of protests inspired by it. Cairo, Tunis, Khartoum, and Sanaa. We had serious security challenges in Pakistan and Chennai and some other places. All this was happening at the same time. So many of the contemporaneous comments about the video weren't referring in any way to Benghazi. Now of course even in those countries it was about much much more than the video, but the video was certainly a piece of it one we felt we had to speak to so that our allies in those countries would back us up.

(In fact, as Judicial Watch famously uncovered in 2014, the "talking points" that provided the basis for Susan Rice's false statements were created by the Obama White House.)

Again, Judicial Watch requested records related to the Benghazi talking points in May 2014. In July 2014, it filed suit. The Clinton email finally released was first identified by the State Department in September 2014 *but was withheld from* Judicial Watch despite it specifically referencing talking points. So both the State Department and DOJ had been covering up a smoking gun for years. This is not just a Clinton scandal, it is a government corruption scandal of the first order. They hid evidence about who knew what and when about one of the most significant terrorist attacks in American history!

BLOCKBUSTER TESTIMONY
ABOUT THOSE MISSING EMAILS

The missing Clinton emails case was like a thread you pull at from a suit and it just keeps unraveling, and unraveling, and unraveling with no end in sight.

But, to get it started, someone has to pull at the thread in the first place. That was us.

No matter what the State Department or any other government agency or individual under suspicion said or says, Judicial Watch investigates and verifies everything.

Roadblocks and obstacles put in our path encourage us to do more. With exactly that strategy and mission in mind, Judicial Watch attorneys grabbed a significant portion of that thread when they obtained blockbuster testimony from former State Department official John Hackett, who was director for Information Programs and Services (IPS), which handles records management at the State Department. Hackett testified under oath that he had raised concerns about former secretary of state Hillary Clinton's missing emails.

Her staff had "culled out 30,000" of the secretary's "personal" emails without following strict National Archives standards, he said in his deposition.

His testimony came as part of the series of Judge Lamberth–ordered depositions and questions under oath of senior Obama-era State Department officials, lawyers, and Clinton aides.

Hackett also revealed that he believed there was interference with the formal FOIA review process related to the classification of Clinton's Benghazi-related emails.

Hackett served first as deputy director then as director for Information Programs and Services, which handles the FOIA request program and the retirement of and declassification of documents at the State Department. He was at the department from April 2013 to March 2016.

In March 2015, Clinton told reporters that she and her staff had deleted more than 30,000 emails "because they were personal and private about matters that I believed were within the scope of my personal privacy." ABC News reported: "However, after a year-long investigation, the FBI recovered more than 17,000 emails that had been deleted or otherwise not turned over to the State Department, and many of them were work-related, the FBI has said." Hackett recalled a conversation about requesting rules or parameters from Secretary Clinton or her attorneys that they used to segregate her personal and official work emails.

Hackett: I recall it wasn't much of a conversation. I—I was—I mean, I have to say, it was emphatic to the Under Secretary of Management—and I didn't speak in tones like that very often to him—you know, that we needed these—you know, the guidelines.

Judicial Watch: And when you said, the Under Secretary, are you referring to Patrick Kennedy [then–Under Secretary of State for Management]?

Hackett: Yes.

Hackett: I think I might have raised it to Rich Visek, the acting office of Legal Advisor, or Peggy—or Margaret Grafeld [an executive-level State Department FOIA official] raised it to Rich, as well.

Judicial Watch: Why did you feel so strongly that this was necessary, that they provide this information?

Hackett: Well, we heard that there were 50,000 or 60,000 emails, and that they had—"they" being the secretary's team—had culled out 30,000 of these. And which is—so we wanted to know what criteria they used. The standard from the National Archives is very strict. If there was—if there were mixed records, that would be considered a federal record. If it was mixed personal and mentioned a discussion, that would be—under the narrow National Archives rules, it would be considered a federal record.

Judicial Watch: And do you know if the emails that were returned by Secretary Clinton and her attorneys, if they followed that guideline to include an email that would include mixed information, personal and official?

Hackett: I don't know.

Judicial Watch: Was a request ever made by Patrick Kennedy or anybody else who you raised this to?

Hackett: Ambassador Kennedy told me he would ask for the— the guidelines.

Judicial Watch: Do you know if the guidelines were ever provided to Patrick Kennedy?

Hackett: Not during my tenure at the State Department.

In August 2014 the State Department sent some documents to the Benghazi Select Committee that included a small number of Clinton emails. Hackett was alerted about this. Hackett was asked if the State Department attorney who gave him the heads-up asked why he was providing the information. Hackett answered: "I think only because he knew that there was going to be publicity involved relating to this."

We also asked Hackett about his concerns over 296 of Secretary Clinton's Benghazi-related emails that were made available to Congress. Hackett testified that he had concerns regarding Catherine Duval, an attorney who worked for the Office of Legislative affairs (and who was also involved in the Obama-era IRS scandal):

Judicial Watch: And what was—what was your concern there, if you can elaborate?

Hackett: The concern was, in the 296 that there were other agencies' equities in those documents, you know, potentially classified information. But any release decisions—and doing a FOIA review, we would normally make a referral back to that home agency. And Ms. Duval seemed to imply that she had already done that kind of coordination. But when we asked who she had coordinated with, they were people not familiar in our regular FOIA process.

Judicial Watch: And that's people, when you—the people you are referring to, that's—is it within just one agency, or is that dispersed through different agencies?

Hackett: It would be different agencies.

Hackett: Again, I mean, we were familiar with the—our—our parallel shops, you know, in other agencies, similar to IPS; we knew all the players there, the other directors of the office. And, so, we contacted them, and they have not received any referrals from her. So we wondered who she was working with.

We also asked Hackett if, as he had previously stated, he "believed there was interference with the formal FOIA review process" in 2014? Hackett said he believed "that some bureaus were convinced, or—and analysts were convinced, once it was explained to them, to redact something but use a B5 exemption [which applies to deliberative process and allows government officials to discuss policy without the discussions being made public, or attorney-client privilege] versus a B1 [national security] exemption."

When we asked if he thought that was appropriate, Hackett responded, "No, I didn't," and said he voiced that concern to his boss, Margaret Grafeld.

Hackett testified that his initial concern over Secretary Clinton's email use arose in June 2013 when he said he viewed a photograph on the WTOP website of Clinton "sitting on a plane with a BlackBerry. "And that got me thinking that, well, what—what was that Black-

Berry? Was it a government BlackBerry? And if so, where were the emails relating to that BlackBerry?" Hackett said.

Hackett testified he went to then-IPS director Sheryl Walter "after seeing that photograph and suggested that we had to be careful about what sort of responses we made relating to Hillary Clinton's emails, when it—if there was a No Record Located response that was being given out. In fact, I advised Sheryl that we should stop giving No Record Located responses until we come to—kind of come, you know—find out what that BlackBerry meant, come to ground about what was known about the former Secretary's emailing habits."

Asked how Walter responded, Hackett said, "My recollection is, she agreed with me."

"The other thing that we did, or I did at that time, was, we wanted to find out what this BlackBerry meant," Hackett testified. "So we tasked—my recollection is, we verbally tasked Tasha Thian, the department's Records Manager at that time, to look into the BlackBerry. And I believe Tasha contacted Clarence Finney in the Secretary's office to ask him what he knew about the former Secretary's emailing habits."

Asked what Thian found out, Hackett responded: "I don't recall exactly what she found out, but she didn't find out much. Tasha also contacted the part of the State Department that's part of the intelligence community, and Intelligence and Research Bureau, to ask to see if there were any classified emails on—in the classified systems that the Secretary might have produced. And I do recall that I think Tasha came back with the answer that they did not have any."

Hackett went on to say, "There was a lot of confusion about exactly what that BlackBerry, you know, meant at that time. You had a concern as to how the department was responding to FOIA requests that related to Secretary Clinton's emails after you saw the photograph of the Secretary holding a BlackBerry. . . . My recollection is—and I

had only been there two months—that someone had told me that—
and I can't remember—that she did not have an email account, a government email account. So there was obviously a contradiction here
when, you know, there's that photograph. So we were just trying to
find out what was the ground truth. So that's why I had a concern
about issuing responses that said no records had been located."

Hackett also said he knew of other employees in the State Department who were using their personal email accounts for government
business and that "some were senior officials, too."

Asked who the senior officials were, Hackett responded: "I can't remember the time frame, but the IG did a couple of studies, reviews. I
think the ambassador to Japan, Caroline Kennedy, was cited as using
her personal email account. That's one that comes to my mind."

Hackett said: "We knew that some employees at times had a personal email address for Hillary Clinton, and that they might forward
something to her at times. That's the only thing that we knew. At that
time I did not know who those employees were. I mean, the—the gist
of that email I remember was one person saying to the other person,
don't use that—remember, you're not supposed to use that email. But I
don't remember who those people were. I think one of them might
have been in Public Affairs."

Here's my take on his testimony: It's disturbing. It points to an
Obama administration conspiracy to hide and destroy Hillary Clinton
emails. Even worse, the testimony suggests Clinton's Benghazi emails
were underclassified in order to protect Hillary Clinton (and mislead
Congress). Attorney General Barr needs to prioritize reopening the
Clinton email investigation. We've heard much about "whistleblowers" these days. Most of the anti-Trump whistleblowers were nothing
of the sort—they were government employees who simply had policy
disagreements or thinly disguised hatred for President Trump. In

Hackett's case, he described actual government misconduct. Remember, his testimony happened over the objections of the Justice and State Departments!

OUR DIGGING PAYS OFF:
COURT GRANTS SIGNIFICANT NEW
DISCOVERY IN CLINTON EMAIL CASE

All of that investigative work with State Department official John Hackett and many others ultimately only had one goal in mind: to get to the truth and paint Hillary Clinton into a corner and force her to directly answer questions from Judicial Watch.

Precisely because of the work of Judicial Watch, Judge Lamberth granted us the right to question more witnesses and gather some more documents about the Clinton email abuses. The judge held a hearing on the issue about a year ago and again spanked the government over its gamesmanship.

"There is no FOIA [Freedom of Information Act] exemption for political expedience, nor is there one for bureaucratic incompetence," noted Judge Lamberth, after reviewing the evidence Judicial Watch had already gathered that shot down the Justice/State attempts to argue we had no "Good cause" for more discovery. He stated: "Today the good cause continues from whether or not State was acting in good faith, and I'll tell you everything they've discovered in this period raises serious questions about what the hell the State Department's doing here."

Judge Lamberth went to call the government's arguments "preposterous" and cited a prior Judicial Watch FOIA case in which he ordered U.S. marshals to seize records from a Clinton administration official:

I'll tell you another thing I didn't like in your brief. I'll tell you right now upfront. You put in your brief the most preposterous thing, I thought, in your brief was the very idea that—let me read you the line. "*Competitive Enterprise Institute* was a case of first impression." . . . Now, that wasn't a case of first impression at all. The first impression with me was a case I had involving Ron Brown and the travel records of whether or not, in the Commerce Department—and it was a Judicial Watch case—whether or not the Commerce Department was selling seats on trade missions, and I had a Deputy Under Secretary of Commerce who took a box of records home and then they gave a no-records response and, in the course of that, I found out he had taken the records home and they said they had no records. I sent marshals over and they got the box at his house, and I ordered them—the marshals—to seize the records. That was the first case.

The court also stated that the government has mishandled this case and the discovery of information including former Secretary Clinton's emails so poorly that Judicial Watch may have the ability to prove the they acted in "bad faith," which would entitle us to attorney's fees.

Judge Lamberth detailed how the State Department "spent three months from November 2014 trying to make this case disappear," and that after discovering the State Department's actions and omissions, "Now we know more, but we have even more questions than answers. So I won't hold it against Judicial Watch for expanding their initial discovery request now."

Judge Lamberth stated his goal was to restore the public's faith in their government, which may have been damaged because of the Clinton email investigation.

Below is the court's ruling from the bench granting Judicial Watch's significant new discovery. It is worth your close reading:

First, let me clarify the Government's misunderstanding. We're not reopening discovery here. Discovery never closed. Back in January, I said, quote, The Government will—the Court will hold a post-discovery hearing to ascertain the adequacy of State's searches; to determine if Judicial Watch needs to depose additional witnesses, including Hillary Clinton or her former Chief of Staff, Cheryl Mills; and to schedule dispositive motions, unquote. So June 19th was a checkpoint, not a finish line. And whether Judicial Watch previously knew about some of the other individuals it now wants to depose is beside the point. They tailored their initial discovery request to the facts and questions then before the Court.

Now we know more, but we have even more questions than answers. So I won't hold it against Judicial Watch for expanding their initial discovery request now.

Remember what got us started down this path in the first place. In late 2014 and early 2015, at least some State Department officials knew Secretary Clinton's emails were missing; they knew Judicial Watch didn't know that; they knew the Court didn't know that, but the Department pressed forward trying to settle this case. So I authorized discovery into whether these settlement efforts amounted to bad faith.

Now, the Government says, quote, there is simply no factual basis to justify any further discovery on that subject, unquote, but Judicial Watch's most recent submission lays out the following:

It appears that in the middle of 2013, State's Office of Information and Program Services launched an inquiry into Clinton's email practices.

It appears that in August 2013, that office directed FOIA responders to stop issuing, quote, no record located, unquote, responses to FOIA requests for Clinton's emails.

It appears that by the summer of 2014, State knew a large volume of Clinton's emails had never been searched, potentially violating FOIA and record management obligations. It turns out State had a standing meeting every Wednesday afternoon during the summer of 2014 to discuss Clinton-related FOIA inquiries. Attendees included Secretary Kerry's Chief of Staff; his Deputy Chief of Staff; the Deputy Secretary for Management and Resources; the Assistant Secretary for Legislative Affairs; several attorneys; and Patrick Kennedy, the Under Secretary for Management. That's every Wednesday afternoon.

It appears that in August 2014, State began planning for media investigations into Clinton's emails.

It appears that in November 2014, State told Judicial Watch it performed a legally adequate search and tried to settle. In fact, I think, in my original opinion on authorizing discovery, I noted that State had given a draft Vaughn index to Judicial Watch at that time. I don't think I have ever seen that, but I think it was given to I think, in my opinion, I said that it had been given to Judicial Watch. Indeed, State spent the next three months from November 2014 trying to make this case disappear. They kept doing it even after they came into the possession of Clinton's emails.

Judicial Watch wants to follow up with the State attorney assigned to this FOIA request to participate in settlement discussions and negotiations. That seems reasonable to me.

[Judicial Watch] wants to ask the Department official responsible for overseeing FOIA requests more about why he directed his office to stop using "no record located" responses to FOIA requests relating to Clinton's emails if that, in fact, is what happened. I'm curious, too.

They want to ask the current Department FOIA overseer more about what went on in those weekly 2014 meetings. I look forward to hearing what he says.

They want to ask the Justice Department attorney who led the settlement negotiations to divulge when he learned Clinton's emails were missing. He must answer.

Another reason we had this initial discovery was to see if Secretary Clinton intentionally attempted to evade FOIA by using a private email. When Judicial Watch deposed the Deputy Director who oversaw State's FOIA responses, he recalled an instance when in—his office found an email from Clinton's private account and the Public Affairs team said, Remember, you're not supposed to use that email. How can you spin that?

I agree with Judicial Watch that it's worth deposing the State Department records officer who personally reviewed archiving procedures with Secretary Clinton and her departing staff to see what they discussed.

I also think Judicial Watch is justified to seek more information about how Secretary Clinton ultimately determined which emails were public records and which were private.

The final reason I authorized discovery was to determine whether State adequately searched for records responsive to Judicial Watch's FOIA request. Now the Government seeks to duck behind an unpublished D.C. Circuit opinion from 2018 holding the Government has already taken every reasonable action under the Federal Records Act to retrieve Clinton's 30,000 missing emails and no imaginable enforcement action could recover any more.

But just last week, the Senate's—Senate Finance and Homeland Security Committees released documents revealing Clinton IT aide Paul Combetta copied all but four of the missing emails to a Gmail account that does not appear to have ever been reconstructed and searched. The Court thinks Judicial Watch ought to shake this tree.

And the Court agrees with Judicial Watch that it should talk to three never-before-deposed State officials who raised concerns about Clinton's private email use all the way back to 2009.

There is no FOIA exemption for political expedience, nor is there one for bureaucratic incompetence.

The Government also tries to say this Court is—no longer—or no longer presents a live controversy. This is wrong. Judicial Watch can still obtain fees if they prove agency bad faith.

I'll close with this. When I authorized discovery back in December, I described my goal: to rule out egregious government misconduct and vindicate the public's faith in the State and Justice Departments. That's still my goal today. This isn't a case I relish, but it's the case before me now, and it's a case of the government's making.

The Court authorizes Judicial Watch to take the additional discovery described in its status report, except for deposing Secretary Clinton and her Chief of Staff, Cheryl Mills. I will give their attorneys 30 days to file any additional opposition to their depositions and 10 days thereafter for Judicial Watch to file any reply. . . .

JUDICIAL WATCH "SEARCHES" GOOGLE FOR CLINTON EMAILS

As referenced above, Judge Lamberth raised concerns about a potential Clinton "Gmail" cache and ordered Judicial Watch to "shake this tree" on the issue. Judge Lamberth noted that Senator Grassley released

a report in which he had some very troubling information about a guy named Combetta who had been one of the contract employees on the Clinton emails, and he and the Senator who Chairs the

Homeland Security Committee released in the Senate this report Friday, and the gist of it was that Combetta had said, I guess, that he had created a dummy email account with all of the Hillary Clinton emails in it in a different name, and the FBI had investigated that to see whether or not the Chinese had ever hacked into it. They have determined that the Chinese hadn't, but that the FBI never told the State Department about that account and that the emails that were not given over to State could have been obtained from that account, but the FBI never told State about it. So it leaves out in the open whether there are these other emails that State could have obtained but nobody ever bothered to tell State about them. I don't know the status of that and I'm sure you don't either, but that did occur to me that would be a problem for me as to whether an adequate examination of that circumstance occurred and, assuming that Combetta deleted them, as he said he did before he took the Fifth, I guess, whether or not the server that they were on or the—or whoever maintained the server, whether they can be reconstructed from—by that . . .

[J]ust last week, the Senate's—Senate Finance and Homeland Security Committees released documents revealing that Clinton IT aide Paul Combetta copied all but four of the missing emails to a Gmail account that does not appear to have ever been reconstructed and searched. The court thinks Judicial Watch ought to shake this tree.

Shaking the tree meant, for the Court, allowing us to issue a subpoena to Google for the Clinton emails:

Judicial Watch seeks to subpoena Google for relevant documents and records associated with Secretary Clinton's emails during her tenure at State. . . . The subpoena seeks to discover new emails, so it certainly relates to whether State conducted an adequate search.

———————

The Court is not confident that State currently possesses every Clinton email recovered by the FBI; even years after the FBI investigation, the slow trickle of new emails has yet to be explained. For this reason, the Court believes the subpoena would be worthwhile and may even uncover additional previously undisclosed emails. Accordingly, the Court GRANTS this request.

Once again, a federal court, tired of the government's stonewalling and games, authorized Judicial Watch to do the basic legwork on the Clinton email issue. DOJ and State are AWOL and covering up for Hillary Clinton, so it again is up to Judicial Watch to do the basic investigative heavy lifting to get at the truth.

Google did pony up illuminating evidence about never-before-seen Clinton emails. After a painstaking review of the data, our preliminary analysis suggests there seems to be 260 Clinton emails that appear to be work-related and appear to not have been previously identified either in the emails that Secretary Clinton provided to State in 2014 or among the emails that the FBI recovered and turned over to the State Department. So what is in these emails? We don't have that data yet. But this whole episode shows that Judicial Watch is able to uncover leads and basic information missed by the vaunted FBI!

FBI MAGICALLY "FINDS" CLINTON EMAILS

Remember when Hillary Clinton repeatedly stated that the 55,000 pages she turned over to the State Department in December 2014 included all of her work-related emails?

As the joke goes: "How do you know a politician is lying? Their lips are moving."

Well . . . Hillary's lips were surely moving then.

In response to a court order in a Judicial Watch case, she declared under penalty of perjury that she had "directed that all my emails on clintonemail.com in my custody that were or are potentially federal records be provided to the Department of State, and on information and belief, this has been done."

We've known for a while that this was not the case.

Now there's more proof. The State Department turned over to us thirty-seven pages of new Clinton emails recently "found" by the FBI that provide more evidence of how the former secretary of state used her unsecure, nongovernment email to transmit classified information. The new emails also show Clinton used text messages for government business.

Here's how poorly these emails were handled. The State Department did not provide information about where they were found, why they were not previously produced, or if additional records are anticipated. In fact, the Justice Department attorney could not tell Judge Lamberth how and where the FBI discovered the new cache of Clinton emails.

The State Department previously claimed it had produced *all* responsive Clinton emails, including emails recovered by the FBI that Hillary Clinton tried to destroy or withhold. The State Department initially claimed all responsive emails had been produced in 2018, but then found more emails, which were produced, for the first time, early last year. Then in November 2019, the State Department first disclosed to the court that the FBI had found this latest batch of emails.

In an email to Clinton's personal email account, dated January 23, 2012, former British prime minister Tony Blair sent details that were redacted as classified.

In an email containing classified information dated August 30, 2011, Jeffrey Feltman, then assistant secretary for the Bureau of Near Eastern Affairs, suggested Clinton meet Lebanese prime minister Najib Mikati in Paris to talk about Syria and other issues.

In an email exchange on August 31, 2011, Clinton top aide Huma Abedin says she sent Clinton "a couple text messages," and offers to "send Monica [Hanley] to hamptons to help you get organized."

What does all this mean? Magically, after years, the FBI finds more Clinton emails that show Clinton used text messages for government work, not to mention the continuing flow of classified information transmitted over her unsecure email system. These documents further underscore the need for a fresh, unbiased, and thorough criminal investigation into Clinton's blatant malfeasance—and the related DOJ, FBI, and State Department cover-up. AG Barr?

The production of documents in this case was to have been concluded with the FBI's recovery of approximately 5,000 of the 33,000 government emails Clinton took and tried to destroy, but, as you see, this case is still in progress.

IT IS TIME TO HEAR FROM HILLARY CLINTON!

Hillary Clinton's "convenience" explanation for her private email system was one of the worst whoppers of modern presidential politics. As you can see from the breadth and scope of the emails we uncovered, we have the answer to the question many ask, "What was Hillary Clinton trying to hide?" My answer: Everything!

The Clinton email scandal is bipartisan, as she received email advice on how to avoid transparency at the beginning of her term at State from former Bush secretary of state Colin Powell. The emails are devastating—as they expose Clinton mendaciousness and Powell's utter contempt for accountable government.

Less than forty-eight hours after taking the oath of office, Clinton emailed Colin Powell with a "pressing question." The question did not concern the global economic crises or how to deal with a foreign power. It was about her email. She wrote, "What were the restrictions on your use of your blackberry? Did you use it in your personal office? I've been told that DSS [Diplomatic Security] personnel knew you had one and used it but no one fesses up to knowing how you used it! President Obama has struck a blow for berry addicts like us. I just have to figure out how to bring along the State Dept. Any and all advice is welcome." She wanted advice about how to do what she and her staff had been told not to do. And how to get away with it.

And she received it. Powell provided her with "written guidance on why and how [he] had been doing it."

He first described his practice: "I didn't have a BlackBerry. What I did do was have a personal computer that was hooked up to a private phone like (sounds ancient). So I could communicate with a wide range of friends directly without it going through the State Department servers. I even used it to do business with some foreign leaders and some of the senior folks in the Department on their personal email accounts. I did the same thing on the road and in hotels." He then explained the drawback: "However, there is a real danger. If it is public that you have a BlackBerry and it [is] government and you are using it, government or not, to do business, it may become an official record and subject to the law." And he concluded with a warning: "Be very careful. I got around it all by not saying much and not using systems that captured the data." Clinton thanked Powell for his advice. Little did he know that Clinton and her team would use his guidance as a blueprint for how Clinton would communicate by email for the next four years.

In spite of all their efforts to avoid the issue as advised by Powell, Clinton and her staff were definitely told not to use personal Black-Berrys on March 6, 2009. In an Information Memorandum to Mills, Eric Boswell, then–assistant secretary of state for diplomatic security, wrote:

> We have worked closely . . . to review all options that would allow Secretary Clinton, you, and a small number of staff [to] use Black-berries. . . . Our review reaffirms our belief that the vulnerabilities and risks associated with the use of Blackberries in the Mahogany Row . . . considerably outweigh the convenience their use can add to staff that have access to the unclassified OpenNet system on their desktops. . . . We also worry about the example using Blackberries in Mahogany Row might set as we strive to promote crucial security practices and enforcement [of] important security standards among State Department staff.
>
> As an alternative, we suggest that DS work with S/ES-IRM to make access to the Secretary's OpenNet account on her desktop workstation as easy and convenient as possible. For example, we are happy to work with IRM to lengthen or even eliminate the time-out function to allow the Secretary's Special Assistant to log-on to review her emails and schedules.
>
> While we cannot recommend using Blackberries inside the

Mahogany Row . . . we do not want to stand in the way of issuing Department Blackberries to the Secretary and her senior staff for use outside Mahogany Row. These Blackberries can be synchronized with your OpenNet Microsoft Outlook accounts, provide full cellular, e-mail, and internet functionality, and provide unclassified mobile technology when you are away from Mahogany Row.

I cannot stress too strongly, however, that any unclassified Blackberry is highly vulnerable in any setting to remotely and covertly monitoring conversations, retrieving e-mails, and exploiting calendars. I am attaching reports from DS's Office of Computer Security's Cyber Threat & Analysis Division that give further background of those risks.

Diplomatic security could not be clearer. The vulnerabilities and risks associated with using a personal BlackBerry were too great. And, it appeared that Clinton understood that and would comply with the recommendations, after a March 11, 2009, meeting, only five days after Boswell delivered the memorandum to Mills. As we told the Court "Clinton approached Boswell and mentioned that she had read the [Information Memorandum] and that she 'gets it.'" However, Clinton's perceived understanding and compliance were nothing more than an appearance. No less than two days after the memorandum was provided and three days before she said she "got it," Clinton emailed a colleague, "Against the advice of the security hawks, I still do carry my berry."

Despite evidence of purposeful violations of law, rules, and ethical norms, Hillary Clinton has never been seriously or competently questioned about her email usage, especially as it relates to the law she obviously was trying to subvert—the Freedom of Information Act. She testified to Judicial Watch under oath, but in writing. And she tried to argue with the collusive support (!) of this Justice Department and State Department that she not have to testify in person to Judicial Watch. She essentially argued "What difference" would her testimony make! After all, she answered some questions under oath, albeit in writing, and had to sit through "11 hours" of hapless questioning by congressmen!

Judge Lamberth rejected her arguments.

"As extensive as the existing record is, it does not sufficiently explain Secretary Clinton's state of mind when she decided it would be an acceptable practice to set up and use a private server to conduct State Department business," Lamberth said.

The judge went on to recognize that while Clinton responded to written questions in a separate Judicial Watch case, "those responses were either incomplete, unhelpful, or cursory at best. Simply put her responses left many more questions than answers." Lamberth said that using written questions this time "will only muddle any understanding of Secretary Clinton's state of mind and fail to capture the full picture, thus delaying the final disposition of this case even further."

Lamberth even gave some examples of lingering questions about Clinton's emails, such as how did she come to believe that her private emails would be preserved under normal State Department processes, who told her this and when, at what point did she learn department records management officials did not know about the server, "[a]nd why did she think that using a private server to conduct State Department business was permissible under the law in the first place?"

And so Judge Lamberth ordered Mrs. Clinton's testimony:

The Court has considered the numerous times in which Secretary Clinton said she could not recall or remember certain details in her prior interrogatory answers. In a deposition, it is more likely that plaintiff's counsel could use documents and other testimony to attempt to refresh her recollection. And so, to avoid the unsatisfying and inefficient outcome of multiple rounds of fruitless interrogatories and move this almost six-year-old case closer to its conclusion, Judicial Watch will be permitted to clarify and further explore Secretary Clinton's answers in person and immediately after she gives them. The Court agrees with Judicial Watch—it is time to hear directly from Secretary Clinton.

The court also ordered the deposition testimony of her top aide, Cheryl Mills. Rather than sit for the questioning, Mrs. Clinton and Mills made a desperate appeal to overturn Judge Lamberth's well-reasoned order. They filed a *writ of mandamus*, which is generally reserved for the most extraordinary circumstances. Mrs. Clinton argued that, as a former government official, she simply is too important to testify. Sure enough, as this book went to print, a liberal-controlled appellate court issued a politicized ruling that protected Mrs. Clinton from having to testify. The decision deviated from precedent and created the appearance of favoritism toward Clinton—further undermining the public's confidence in the fair administration of justice.

OBAMA KNEW?

Before I move on from the Clinton email issue, I must highlight how we uncovered the likely reason for the Obama and continued Deep State effort to disrupt our probe. We already describe how there are nearly twenty emails between Obama and Clinton still being withheld from us. But the discovery authorized by Judge Lamberth shows the Obama-Clinton email connection goes much deeper than those communications (which by the way, seem to curiously center around the time of the infamous Benghazi attack!).

First, we had the revelation from a senior FBI official that the Obama White House was a "repository" for Clinton emails. E. W. (Bill) Priestap, assistant director of the FBI Counterintelligence Division, made the disclosure to Judicial Watch as part of the court-ordered discovery into the Clinton email issue. Priestap was the senior FBI official who supervised the Clinton email investigation.

Priestap was asked by Judicial Watch to identify representatives of Hillary Clinton, her former staff, and government agencies from which "email repositories were obtained." Priestap responded with the following non-exhaustive list:

> Bryan Pagliano [Clinton tech aide at State]
>
> Cheryl Mills [Clinton State chief of staff, Clinton campaign official, and lawyer]
>
> **Executive Office of the President** [Emphasis added]
>
> Heather Samuelson [Clinton State official, Clinton lawyer]
>
> Jacob Sullivan [Clinton State Spokesman]
>
> Justin Cooper [Clinton Foundation official]
>
> United States Department of State
>
> United States Secret Service
>
> Williams & Connolly LLP [Clintons' personal legal firm]

This astonishing confirmation, made under oath by the FBI, shows that the Obama FBI had to go to President Obama's White

House office to find emails that Hillary Clinton tried to destroy or hide from the American people!

No wonder Hillary Clinton has thus far skated—Barack Obama is implicated in her email scheme.

But it got worse. Other documents turned over to us because of Judge Lamberth's court orders directly implicate the Obama White House in the Clinton email cover-up.[22]

The cover-up happened in 2012. It turns out the Obama White House was tracking a December 2012 FOIA request for records about Clinton use of nongovernment emails for government business. Months after the Obama White House involvement, the State Department responded to the requestor, the left-wing Citizens for Responsibility and Ethics in Washington (CREW), falsely stating that no such records existed.

The State Department's Office of Inspector General issued a report in January 2016 saying, "At the time the request was received, dozens of senior officials throughout the Department, including members of Secretary Clinton's immediate staff, exchanged emails with the Secretary using the personal accounts she used to conduct official business." Also, the IG "found evidence that [Clinton chief of staff Cheryl Mills] was informed of the request at the time it was received. . . ."

In a December 20, 2012, email with the subject line "Need to track down a FOIA request from CREW," Sheryl L. Walter, director of the State Department's Office of Information Programs and Services (A/GIS/IPS), writes to IPS officials Rosemary D. Reid and Patrick D. Scholl and their assistants:

> WH called—have we received a FOIA request from CREW
> (Citizens for Responsible Ethics in Washington) on the topic
> of personal use of email by senior officials? Apparently other

agencies have. If we have it, can you give me the details so I can call the WH back? I think they'd like it on quick turnaround. Thanks! Sheryl

In the same email chain, Walter on December 20, 2012, also emailed Heather Samuelson, Clinton's White House liaison, describing the CREW FOIA request:

Hi Heather—Copy attached, it was in our significant weekly FOIA report that we send to L and S/ES also. Do you want us to add you to that list? It's a subset of things like this that we think likely to be of broader Department interest. More detail below re this request. As a practical matter given our workload, it won't be processed for some months. Let me know if there are any particular sensitivities. If we don't talk later, happy holidays! All the best, Sheryl

Sheryl: The request is assigned Case #F-2012-40981. It was received on 12/6/2012 and acknowledged on 12/10/2012. The request is assigned for processing.

On January 10, 2013, Walter writes to Samuelson that she is not including "personal" accounts in the FOIA request search:

Hi Heather—did you ever get any intel re what other agencies are doing re this FOIA request that seeks records about the number of email accounts associated with the Secretary (but isn't specifying "personal" email accounts so we are interpreting as official accounts only). We are considering contacting the requester to find out exactly what it is they are looking for. Do you have any concerns about that approach?

Soon afterward, Samuelson responds, "White House Counsel was looking into this for me. I will circle back with them now to see if they have further guidance."

CREW's general counsel, Anne Weismann, submitted a FOIA request to the State Department on December 6, 2012, seeking "records sufficient to show the number of email accounts of or associated with Secretary Hillary Rodham Clinton, and the extent to which those email accounts are identifiable as those of or associated with Secretary Clinton."

On May 10, 2013, IPS replied to CREW, stating that "no records responsive to your request were located."

Again, Samuelson became Secretary Clinton's personal lawyer and in 2014 led the review of Clinton's emails to determine which ones were work-related and which were personal. She was also one of five close Clinton associates granted immunity by the Department of Justice in the Clinton email investigation.

The new documents also include a January 2013 email exchange discussing Clinton's departure from the State Department in which Agency Records Officer Tasha M. Thian specifically states that Secretary Clinton "does not use email."

This was directly contradicted by an email exchange between Secretary Clinton and General David Petraeus dating back to January 2009—the very first days of Clinton's State Department tenure—in which she tells Petraeus that she "had to change her email address."

Interestingly, this email exchange between Petraeus and Clinton was not produced in a related FOIA lawsuit[23] seeking "all emails" of Hillary Clinton. The bottom portion of the email chain was produced, but not the beginning[24] emails.

In a January 2013 email under the subject "RE: Sec Clinton's papers," Thian writes:

> Just so you know, Secretary Clinton—she brought with her a
> lot of material as Senator and First Lady—47 boxes. In case
> you hear there are many boxes I wanted you to know what they
> are. She is taking her copies of photos, public speeches, press
> statements, contacts, templates (some of these are both hard
> copy and electronic), reimbursements, etc. . . .
>
> Although Sec. Clinton **does not use email** [emphasis added]
> her staffers do—I have agreed that the emails of the three
> staffers will be electronically captured (and not printed out).

These smoking gun documents suggest the Obama White House knew about the Clinton email lies being told to the public at least as early as December 2012! If you want to know why DOJ, FBI, and State had zero interest in prosecuting Clinton, it is because Obama and his White House team were not only witnesses to any Clinton email crimes, but also coconspirators.

BIDEN, INC.

The assault on our republic has included the rise of a kleptocracy that has too often monetized public service for private fortune. The issue with Clinton Inc. was their brazenness. But the Biden Inc. operation seemed to show that the Biden clan could use public office to shake down foreign potentates as well as smooth-talking Bill and conspiratorial Hillary could.

Let's examine the cases of former vice president Joe Biden and his family. To be sure, Joe Biden was involved in a number of curious and suspect activities during his very long career as a senator from the state of Delaware.

But those days of murky dealings most certainly pale in comparison to what was about to come. For in the summer of 2008, when Democratic nominee Barack Obama picked him to be his running mate, Biden stumbled his way into the epicenter of political and wealth-creating corruption.

Not only was Biden able to watch the Chicago machine behind Barack Obama in action, but he was given a free ringside seat to observe the decades-long, incredibly corrupt Clinton machine—via Hillary Clinton and her cast of cronies—wheeling, dealing, cashing in, and, most important of all, covering up.

If one was looking for ways to perfect the art of corruption, then Joe Biden—and certain members of his family—truly hit the jackpot when he became the vice president of the United States of America.

Beyond the former vice president, you have his son Hunter, who is becoming a rising star in the never-ending Corruption Chronicles. After Hunter, and trailing much further behind, comes the vice president's brother, James.

But, in terms of outright slimy and highly questionable dealings and curious business partnerships, it is Hunter Biden who takes the cake. Be it in his home state of Delaware, in the Ukraine, in China, or during his very brief stint in the navy, Hunter Biden has raised eyebrows and suspicions wherever he has gone.

What follows is but a very brief recap:

In Delaware in the mid-to-late 1990s, Hunter Biden got a sweetheart job, and then consulting contract, with Delaware based financial services company MBNA. Not by coincidence, this came during the time his father represented the state of Delaware as its senior senator.

Also, not by coincidence, and for good reason, Senator Joe Biden's nickname in his home state of Delaware was "Senator MBNA."

This father-son, giant-bank, too-good-to-be-legitimate arrangement soon caught the attention of famous NBC News journalist Tom Brokaw. In 2008, Brokaw said to Senator, soon-to-be Vice President Joe Biden: "Wasn't it inappropriate for someone like you in the middle of all this [the banking collapse of 2008] to have your son collecting money from this big credit card company while you were on the floor [of the Senate] protecting its interests?"

Next, we have Hunter Biden's connection to Amtrak. Apparently, because he actually *rode* on Amtrak trains from time to time, he was appointed—and then confirmed by the Senate—for a very lucrative seat on the Amtrak board.

Come 2014, and we find that Hunter Biden was kicked out of the navy after less than a year from a part-time position as a public affairs officer. The reason given was that he tested positive for cocaine.

While still in 2014, we find that Hunter Biden has magically been appointed to the board of the Ukrainian gas company Burisma Holdings. This in spite of the fact that not only did Hunter Biden not speak Ukrainian, but he had no relevant natural gas experience.

As that was the case, why, oh, why would this Ukrainian gas company put Hunter Biden on its board? Could it be that Joe Biden was *vice president of the United States at the time* and that the Ukrainian gas company needed Hunter Biden so they could curry favor with his father?

The next question: How could Hunter Biden be getting $50,000 per month from this company? Could that have been his going price to sell access to his father? Curious minds most certainly want to know.

Next, we come to quite possibly the most troubling corruption connection involving Hunter Biden. That being his position as one of nine directors on the board of BHR—a private-equity company controlled by *Chinese government*-backed stakeholders.

Among many others who found this business connection with a

Chinese-controlled company very disturbing were Senate Finance Committee chairman Chuck Grassley (R-IA) and Senate Homeland Security and Governmental Affairs Committee chairman Ron Johnson (R-WS). Said Grassley and Johnson in part: "In December of 2013, one month after Rosemont Seneca's joint venture with Bohai Capital to form BHR, Hunter Biden reportedly flew *aboard Air Force Two with then Vice President Biden to China. . . .*"

Hello.

Does anyone plan to connect *those* dots?

Aside from some in the Senate, you can bet Judicial Watch has been working overtime to connect those dots and many others. In fact, we just uncovered Secret Service records showing that Hunter Biden was quite the world traveler while his father was serving as vice president. During the first five and a half years of the Obama administration, Hunter Biden traveled extensively while receiving a Secret Service protective detail. During the time period of the records provided, Hunter took 411 separate domestic and international flights, including to 29 different foreign countries.[25] He visited China five times!

Judicial Watch's February 7, 2020, Freedom of Information Act request sought:

> Records reflecting the dates and locations of travel, international and domestic, for Hunter Biden while he received a U.S. Secret Service protective detail; please note whether his travel was on Air Force One or Two, or other government aircraft, as applicable and whether additional family members were present for each trip; time frame is 2001 to present.

The Secret Service did not indicate, as was requested, whether Biden's travel was on Air Force One, Air Force Two, or other government aircraft, or whether additional family members were present.

The Secret Service records show that countries and territories visited by Hunter Biden, between June 2009 and May 2014, included:

+ Ethiopia and India on June 14–22, 2009

+ Argentina on September 14–17, 2009

+ France and Spain on November 9–13, 2009

+ Canada on February 12–15, 2010

+ Dominican Republic on February 18–22, 2010

+ Puerto Rico on March 20–27, 2010

+ China on April 6–9, 2010

+ Belgium, Spain, and the United Kingdom on May 5–8, 2010

+ UK, Egypt, Kenya, South Africa, Ascension Island, U.S. Virgin Islands on June 6–13, 2010

+ Denmark and South Africa on August 9–24, 2010

+ Hong Kong, Taiwan, and China on April 16–22, 2011

+ Mexico on May 15–17, 2011

+ Colombia, France, United Arab Emirates, and France again on November 1–11, 2011

+ UK and Russia on February 15–18, 2012

+ Germany, France, and UK on February 1–5, 2013

+ UK and Ireland on March 20–22, 2013

+ China on June 13–15, 2013

+ Switzerland and Italy on July 26–August 7, 2013

+ Japan, China, South Korea, and the Philippines on December 2–9, 2013

+ China and Qatar on May 7–14, 2014

The records were also provided, but were not made public, to Senate Finance Committee chairman Chuck Grassley and Senate Homeland Security and Governmental Affairs Committee chairman Ron Johnson in a request the senators sent to Secret Service director James Murray on February 5, 2020.

In its cover letter to Grassley and Johnson, which was included in the records produced to Judicial Watch, the Secret Service said that the senators' request was time- and labor-intensive, and they could only provide a limited amount of information by the senators' imposed turnaround time of February 19.

(This is an example of Congress getting and then sitting on records of intense public interest. If we hadn't released them, who knows when the Senate would have publicized them!)

Again, we know that Vice President Biden and Hunter Biden flew on Air Force Two for the official trip to Beijing in December 2013. The records obtained by Judicial Watch from the Secret Service show Hunter Biden arrived in Tokyo on December 2, 2013, and departed for Beijing two days later. While it is typical for the families of the president and vice president to travel with them, questions have been raised about whether Hunter Biden used the government trip to further his business interests.

NBC reporter Josh Lederman, who was one of four reporters on the December 2013 trip, noted in an October 2, 2019, report,[26] "What wasn't known then was that as he accompanied his father to China, Hunter Biden was forming a Chinese private equity fund that associates said at the time was planning to raise big money, including from China."

But even more important than any possible corruption involving the Biden family is the role Vice President Joe Biden and his son Hunter played in changing American history . . . for the worse.

For, as discussed earlier, the impeachment of President Donald J. Trump in the House of Representatives—which quickly led to a landslide acquittal in the United States Senate—came about because President Trump legally and quite naturally asked Ukrainian president Volodymyr Zelensky to look into the investigation regarding then Vice President Joe Biden's *admitted* role on videotape in ousting a Ukrainian prosecutor who also had been investigating the Ukrainian energy company, Burisma Holdings, where Hunter Biden held a very lucrative board position.

The Democrats were so unnerved by President Trump's focus they conspired to undo our republic by trying to drive him out of office for daring to ask a question about Biden's very real corruption issue.

Once again, it has been left to Judicial Watch to do the basic investigative work that the Department of Justice should also be doing as well, given the strong evidence of criminal misconduct by at least Hunter Biden.

With regard to Hunter Biden, there is no evidence it was a legitimate business relationship with Burisma—the background or capability to serve on the board . . . The payments were out of the ordinary and extraordinary suggesting some other improprieties.

Judicial Watch will continue to press for information to get to the bottom of this influence-peddling scandal involving Joe Biden and his son.

What follows is a quick rundown on some of that work:

THE BIDEN-UKRAINE
WHISTLEBLOWER CONNECTION

Somebody has to try to categorize the various Biden misdeeds. We are happy to assume that role.

With that goal in mind, Judicial Watch filed two FOIA lawsuits against the United States Department of State relating to Burisma Holdings. The first lawsuit seeks records of communications from the U.S. embassy in Kyiv related to Burisma. The second lawsuit seeks records related to a January 19, 2016, meeting at the White House that included Ukrainian prosecutors, embassy officials, and CIA employee Eric Ciaramella, who reportedly worked on Ukraine issues while on detail to both the Obama and Trump White Houses (*Judicial Watch v. U.S. Department of State* [No. 1:20-cv-000229]) and (*Judicial Watch v. U.S. Department of State* [No. 1:20-cv-000239]). Again, Ciaramella is widely reported as the person who filed the whistleblower complaint that triggered the impeachment proceedings. His name reportedly was "raised privately in impeachment depositions, according to officials with direct knowledge of the proceedings, as well as in at least one open hearing held by a House committee not involved in the impeachment inquiry."

The lawsuits were filed after the State Department failed to respond to separate FOIA requests for:

+ All cables/teletypes or emails sent or addressed to any official, employee, or representative of the Department of State stationed at the U.S. embassy in Kyiv containing the term "Burisma."

+ All records regarding the January 19, 2016, meeting at the White House that included State Department Ukrainian resident legal advisor Jeff Cole and U.S. Embassy Kyiv employee Svitlana Pardus.

✦ All records of communication between State Department resident legal advisor Jeff Cole and National Security Council staffer Eric Ciaramella.

✦ All records of communication between U.S. embassy Kyiv employee Svitlana Pardus and National Security Council staffer Eric Ciaramella.

✦ All emails sent by or addressed to State Department resident legal advisor Jeff Cole and/or U.S. embassy Kyiv employee Svitlana Pardus between January 10, 2016, and January 30, 2016.

In April 2014, Hunter Biden joined the board of Burisma Holdings, one of Ukraine's largest natural gas companies. Hunter was reportedly paid $50,000 a month to, in the words of a Burisma news release, "provide support for the Company among international organizations." Biden has denied that was his role. Biden had no previous energy experience.

In 2015, Viktor Shokin, Ukraine's prosecutor general, launched an investigation into allegedly corrupt practices by Burisma. Shokin was ousted in 2016. And in a widely distributed 2018 video from a Council on Foreign Relations meeting, Joe Biden confirmed that he had successfully pressured the Ukrainian government, under threat of withholding $1 billion in U.S. government aid, to fire Shokin. Said Biden in part: "I said, I'm telling you, you're not getting the billion dollars. I said, you're not getting the billion. I looked at them and said, 'I'm leaving in six hours. If the prosecutor is not fired, you're not getting the money.' Well, son of a bitch. He got fired."

On January 22, 2020, Fox News' Laura Ingraham reported that *New York Times* journalist Ken Vogel was investigating the January 19, 2016, meeting at the White House. Vogel had contacted the State Department via email for comment, specifically mentioning concerns about Hunter Biden's position with Burisma:

> We are going to report that [State Department official] Elizabeth Zentos attended a meeting at the White House on 1/19/2016 with Ukrainian prosecutors and embassy officials as well as . . . [redacted] from the NSC. . . . The subjects discussed included efforts within the United States government to support prosecutions, in Ukraine and the United Kingdom, of Burisma Holdings . . . and concerns that Hunter Biden's position with the company could complicate such efforts.

These lawsuits could confirm that President Trump had every right to be concerned about Ukraine and Biden corruption—and that the impeachment against him was a shameful attempt to cover up these scandals. The anti-Trump bureaucracy knows this. So, sure enough, the Deep State Department has stalled the release of any documents, most recently using the coronavirus as an excuse to completely halt producing of any information.

BIDEN'S CHINAGATE SCANDAL

President Trump was well within his rights to be curious about the dealings of Hunter Biden, period.

We say that because Hunter Biden cast a very wide net in some shady places, looking to haul in some cash.

Knowing that, Judicial Watch filed Freedom of Information Act lawsuits against the State and Treasury Departments seeking documents related to consideration by the Committee on Foreign Investment in the United States (CFIUS) of investments in the United States by two companies tied to Joe Biden's son, Hunter Biden—Ukraine's Burisma Holdings and China's Bohai Harvest RST (BHR).

The Judicial Watch lawsuits were filed in the U.S. District Court for the District of Columbia after the State and Treasury Departments failed to respond to June 24, 2019, FOIA requests for CFIUS records related to investments by the Ukrainian company Burisma Holdings Ltd. or any of its affiliated entities and records related to investments by the Chinese company Bohai Harvest RST or any of its affiliated entities (*Judicial Watch v. U.S. Department of State* [No. 1:19-cv-02960]), (*Judicial Watch v. U.S. Department of Treasury* [No. 1:19-cv-02961]).

CFIUS is supposed to review "transactions involving foreign investment in the U.S. in order to determine the effect of such transactions on the national security of the United States." This is the same entity on which Hillary Clinton served that blessed the controversial Uranium One deal. A deal seemingly greased with millions of foreign funds to Clinton Inc.

Hunter Biden is reported to be one of nine directors of BHR Partners, which was registered twelve days after the vice president's son, in December 2013, flew to Beijing aboard Air Force Two, while his father made an official visit as vice president. Hunter Biden, then chairman of the private equity firm Rosemont Seneca, reportedly signed a deal with the Chinese government-owned Bank of China to set up the BHR $1 billion joint venture investment fund.

In 2015, BHR Partners participated in a $60 million buyout of Michigan automotive suspension systems maker Henniges Automotive. Henniges produces anti-vibration technologies that have important military uses, particularly in military aircraft.

The Commerce Department recently barred more than two dozen

Chinese companies from doing business in the United States, one of which is reported to be Megvii Technology, an artificial intelligence company focused on developing facial recognition technology. BHR Partners owns a stake in Megvii.

Even though we had an impeachment that had at its center questions about the misconduct of Biden, that has gone down the DC memory hole.

Hillary Clinton, by comparison, was treated like Nixon by her party's own Justice Department. She must be shaking her head to see this Justice Department, Congress, and the legacy media virtually ignore these Biden scandals. At least Hillary Clinton faced an investigation and questioning, however rigged. Biden? Nothing, but for Judicial Watch.

As we did with Clinton, it will be up to Judicial Watch to do the heavy lifting on these Biden scandals—no matter what happens on Election Day. In fact, we just sued the University of Delaware on our behalf and for the Daily Caller News Foundation for both his Senate document collection housed there and documents about the university's machinations to keep them secret.[27] Judicial Watch filed the lawsuit after the university denied its April 30, 2020, FOIA request for:

- All records regarding the proposed release of the records pertaining to former vice president Joe Biden's tenure as a senator that have been housed at the University of Delaware Library since 2012. This request includes all related records of communication between the University of Delaware and any other records created pertaining to any meeting of the board of trustees during which the proposed release of the records was discussed.

- All records of communication between any representative of the University of Delaware and former vice president

Biden or any other individual acting on his behalf between January 1, 2018, and the present.

On April 30, 2020, the Daily Caller News Foundation submitted its FOIA request to the university for:

+ All agreements concerning the storage of more than 1,850 boxes of archival records and 415 gigabytes of electronic records from Joe Biden's Senate career from 1973 through 2009.

+ Communications between the staff of the University of Delaware Library and Joe Biden or his senatorial, vice presidential, or political campaign staff, or for anyone representing any of those entities between 2010 and [April 30, 2020] about Joe Biden's Senate records.

+ Any logs or sign-in sheets recording any individuals who have visited the special-collections department where records from Joe Biden's Senate career are stored between 2010 to the date of this request.

+ All records from Joe Biden's Senate career that have been submitted to the University of Delaware Library.

The university denied our requests, parsing, without corroboration, that "public funds" are not used to support the Joseph R. Biden, Jr., Senatorial Papers.

We want the records.

Tara Reade, who has accused Biden of sexually assaulting her in 1993 when she worked as a staff assistant to the then senator, has said[28] that she believes a workplace discrimination and harassment complaint she filed against Biden at the time may be in the records housed at the

University of Delaware. Biden also admitted to communicating with Vladimir Putin[29] and other foreign leaders when he was a United States senator.

"The University of Delaware should do the right thing and turn over Joe Biden's public records as required by law," Daily Caller News Foundation cofounder and president Neil Patel said. "Partisan games-manship by a public university is unseemly and unlawful. If they don't want to do the right thing, we will force them in court."

The University of Delaware should stop protecting Joe Biden and provide the public access to his public records, as Delaware law requires.

OUR REPUBLIC UNDER ASSAULT . . . AT THE BALLOT BOX

Soros, Soros, Everywhere

With regard to this section and the next—*Our Republic Under Assault at Our Border*—there is one name that, time and again, plays the leading role in both of those escalating assaults upon our very liberty.

That name: *George Soros.*

For those of you still not aware of Mr. Soros, what follows is a brief description of his background:

George Soros was born in Hungary and became a naturalized citizen of the United States in 1961. He made his fortune managing hedge funds and investments worldwide. In the February 2017 issue of *Forbes* magazine his net worth was estimated at $25.2 billion, ranking him—at the time—as the nineteenth wealthiest individual in the world.

Over the course of the past several years much of our research, investigations, and litigation have been involved in the closely interrelated issues of enforcing our immigration laws and protecting the honesty of our elections. During this time, we have observed aggressive efforts by the Organized Left to break down existing laws and regulations at the federal, state, and local levels that are designed to block

voter fraud and help ensure that only eligible U.S. citizens are allowed
to vote.

As we dug deeper, we found that almost every single time, these
hyperaggressive efforts by the organized Left to destroy our rule of law
were being well funded by one man:

George Soros.

In 1979, George Soros created his Open Society Foundations
(OSF). According to the group's website, OSF has contributed $1.5
billion to groups in the United States alone.

DiscoveringtheNetworks.org has stated that the OSF has funded
199 organizations in the United States, and an additional seven American groups have been funded indirectly by contributions from other
Soros-funded groups. In late 2017, Soros transferred $18 billion . . .
the bulk of his personal wealth . . . to OSF. In one fell swoop, the
George Soros machine's financial assets not only dwarfed those of
America's two major political parties, but was second only to the Bill
and Melinda Gates Foundation in the value of its U.S. assets.

That is the far-left mega-billions monster we at Judicial Watch have
had to face repeatedly the last number of years in court.

The Soros operation hates us and has tried to smear and suppress
Judicial Watch but we won't be cowed. Facing negative publicity over
his radical activism here and abroad, he's falsely and outrageously accused us and most anyone critical of him of anti-Semitism. This malicious lie is especially rich coming from a inveterate critic of Israel.
Reuters reported, for instance that the Israeli Foreign Ministry said that
Soros "continuously undermines Israel's democratically elected governments" and that Soros-funded organizations defame the Jewish state
and seek to deny it the right to defend itself.

WHERE DOES SOROS'S MONEY GO?

Groups receiving funds from OSF are universally "progressive" in their philosophy. Some recipients cover the full range of radical and progressive causes, including:

- ✦ The American Civil Liberties Union (ACLU)

- ✦ The Brookings Institution

- ✦ The Center for American Progress

- ✦ Common Cause

- ✦ Planned Parenthood

At this point we should once again stress that Judicial Watch is nonpartisan and does not endorse or oppose candidates for public office. We have routinely sued corrupt Republican and Democratic politicians. We firmly believe that our elections should be conducted honestly and free of corruption, and that only eligible voters should be allowed to cast votes. We are the national leader in forcing states to clean voter rolls between elections as required by federal law, and we've supported and defended in court a number of state efforts to enact commonsense election integrity measures like voter ID.

That stated, Judicial Watch does fully support George Soros's right to spend his money in any lawful way. And he can surely contribute his wealth to any organization (however radical) as he pleases.

But in fact he is giving his billions away to organizations trying to undermine the rule of law and values.

As such, we strongly oppose his agenda to:

- ✦ Promote an open U.S. border with Mexico, amnesty, and voting rights for illegal aliens;

- ✦ Weaken the integrity of our elections in ways that make vote fraud easier and more likely.

The Soros operation has either founded or funded dozens of radical groups dedicated to effectively erasing America's borders and any legal distinctions between citizens and noncitizens in our country.

A key component of these groups' strategy is to enact amnesty for illegal aliens, inevitably leading to illegal aliens voting in American elections. Here is a partial list of open-border and pro-amnesty groups that his network of groups has funded:

- ✦ America's Voice (pro–comprehensive immigration reform);

- ✦ American Bar Association Commission on Immigration Policy ("opposes laws that require employers and persons providing education, health care or other social services to verify citizenship or immigration status");

- ✦ American Immigration Council (pro-amnesty);

- ✦ American Immigration Law Foundation (legal actions in support of amnesty);

- ✦ Brennan Center for Justice (legal actions, pro bono support to activists, media campaigns);

- ✦ Center for Constitutional Rights (pro–open borders);

- ✦ National Council of La Raza;

- ✦ National Immigration Forum (pro-amnesty for illegal

aliens and more visas for individuals wishing to immigrate legally to the United States);

+ National Immigration Law Center.

And so it is no surprise that Soros and his OSF are also major supporters of "sanctuary" policies in cities, counties, and states across America. Most sanctuary policies undermine and violate federal immigration law by forbidding local police from cooperating with federal immigration authorities.

Beyond that is the fact that Soros-funded groups continually seek to weaken ballot integrity and open voting in U.S. elections to ineligible voters.

As just one example, George Soros made national headlines in 2016 when it was revealed he was funding legal challenges across the country to state efforts to ensure honest elections.

What do George Soros and the radical Far Left have against honest elections? Everything.

Here is but a partial list of "voting rights" groups—which really are anti–election integrity groups—that the Open Society Foundations has funded:

+ The Advancement Project (which advertises itself as "the next generation, multi-racial civil rights organization");

+ Bend the Arc Jewish Action (condemns voter ID laws as barriers that make it harder for minorities to vote);

+ Demos (whose board is now chaired by the daughter of radical presidential candidate U.S. senator Elizabeth Warren);

+ Project Vote (the voter-mobilization arm of the discredited ACORN organization, which also received Soros
  support);

+ Southern Coalition for Social Justice (involved in several
  challenges to voter ID and redistricting legal challenges in
  the South).

Ultimately, the George Soros radical network of advocacy groups
and the Left's weakening ballot integrity and establishing amnesty for
illegal aliens as important keys to ensuring victories for leftist allies far
into the future.

─────────────

Now, understanding the Soros hand in all of this, imagine if you will
that all the investigations, all the hard work, and all the good we are
doing together to protect our nation was . . . a complete and total waste
of time.

All of it. Every second, every hour, and every effort, all for nothing.

But, once again, we won't have to imagine that liberty and hope-
destroying scenario for much longer if the Left gets its way.

We won't have to imagine it because they are doing all in their
power—even as you read these words—to make that nightmare for us
a triumphant reality for them.

The Left understands better than anyone that if they can steal our
elections, they can dramatically increase their corrupt power centers in
every city, county, and state in our nation.

And if they can pull that off—and if we *allow* them to pull that off—
then they can make *all* the work we are doing to protect our republic and
our freedoms totally irrelevant.

All the debates about borders, taxes, abortion, foreign aid, big government, policing, etc. All that is for naught if our elections can be stolen out from under us.

Knowing that is one of the Left's most desperate goals is precisely why Judicial Watch does have a massive project in place to force the counties and states across our nation to monitor and clear up their voter rolls.

Why is the Left so desperate to muddy the election rolls, oppose voter ID and citizen verification laws, and promote highly suspect and truly dangerous practices like ballot harvesting?

Again, the answer is obvious to all. It gives them the means and advantages needed to steal elections when needed.

Judicial Watch has been relentless in trying to stop this, but it would be nice if the Department of Justice actually did its job and joined all of us in this fight.

Totally on our own, and without the help of the Department of Justice, in 2019, we did find at least 2.5 million extra names on the voting rolls—2.5 million!

Which as mentioned, is actually good news in the sense that our prior efforts identified 3.5 million extra names on the voting rolls. Our work and our lawsuits resulted in a process that could remove up to 1 million "inactive" voters from Los Angeles County alone.

If Judicial Watch can do that, why can't our own Department of Justice?

When it does pay attention to the laws of our land, the DOJ knows as well as we do that the Left is being funded with hundreds of millions of dollars with the express purpose of weakening our clean election process, our voter ID laws, and now even the sanctity of our Electoral College. The Soros-funded Left and other far-left, antidemocratic groups are pouring in endless money and thousands of man-hours to upend our election systems with policy proposals that undermine clean elections, subvert federal laws, and place the core civil rights of millions at risk—the right *not* to have one's vote stolen or negated by voter fraud. Yet the DOJ has largely failed to take any steps to enforce the rule of law on election integrity.

As we talked about at the beginning of this book, the Left rarely, if ever, lets a crisis go to waste. That was particularly true of the Wuhan COVID-19 pandemic that is now burdening our nation.

As mentioned, the organized Left and its politician allies instantly called for the need for "mail-in" ballots in the face of the pandemic. Of course, they've already supported this—as it was a part of their number one priority, literally HR1 (House Resolution 1), the *first* bill introduced after the Democrats gained control of the House in 2018.

Why? Because mail-in votes can be easily manipulated, or . . . conveniently lost.

To that exact point, according to our own federal government as well as reporting in the media, since 2012 more than 28 million "mail-in" ballots have gone missing—meaning they were neither returned by voters nor returned as undeliverable in the mail.

Yes, 28 million! That is the population of several states.

As an example, according to the reports, in 2012, more than 33 million mail-in ballots were sent out to registered voters. Almost 4 million were not returned.

During the 2014 election cycle, approximately 30 million mail-in ballots were sent out. Just over 8 million went missing.

During the 2016 and 2018 election cycles, approximately 84 million mail-in ballots were sent to registered voters. Of that number, more than 16 million were not returned.

As our friend J. Christian Adams, the president of the Public Legal Interest Foundation, who produced this "lost ballot" data, said to Breitbart News: "Vote by mail is a disaster. People who think it works haven't studied the failures. The facts show mail voting doesn't work."

But, maybe the Left *has* studied those "failures," and is in fact counting on them.

It is entirely because of those failures and irregularities that the Democratic Party and its ultraliberal allies—including and especially the George Soros money machine—are lobbying nonstop for mail-in voting for the 2020 presidential election most of all. They are well aware that if they get their way, *millions of ineligible and illegal voters* may get those mail-in ballots.

As to be expected, many high-profile powerful leftist politicians and Hollywood celebrities are pushing hard for these mail-in ballots. The likes of former vice president Joe Biden, First Lady Michelle Obama, former Obama White House advisor Valerie Jarrett, and liberal Hollywood couple Tom Hanks and Rita Wilson, just to name a few.

No surprise that Valerie Jarrett also instantly dials up the vote by mail-in ballot scam to online voting. Insisted Ms. Jarrett: "Every single American should be able to register to vote online."

Gee. Aren't these the exact same people who were insisting those mean Russians were trying to hack our voting system during the 2016 presidential election?

It's also quite predictable that those who want mail-in ballots for the safety of the people during a time of pandemic have no problem whatsoever with what is called "ballot harvesting."

For those not familiar with that tactic from the liberal playbook, it goes like this: "Ballot harvesting" allows campaign workers, union members, and various other volunteers to go door-to-door—*even during the height of a pandemic*—to personally collect mail-in ballots and then hand-deliver them to election officials to be tabulated.

Again, what could possibly go wrong with that process? Everything.

Such as the high number of documented cases of these "ballot harvesters" actually going into the homes of the voters to "help" them find and fill out their ballots.

This is a recipe for voter fraud, intimidation, and lost votes for countless Americans.

But Judicial Watch isn't sitting idly by—as we are the most significant force for cleaner elections in America.

———

There is a plan. Not to do good. But to do harm to basic American concepts of free and fair elections.

The Left's reform agenda is actually regressive, as it would erase the progress made toward cleaner elections over the last three decades.

1. *Ignore the National Voter Registration Act (NVRA)*
   Section 8 of the NVRA (passed by a Democratic Congress and signed into law by President Bill Clinton in 1993) requires states to make "*a reasonable effort to remove the names of ineligible voters*" from voter rolls . . . proof that less than twenty years ago Democrats and Republicans recognized that dirty voter rolls are an open invitation to voter fraud!

   But in the years since, many state and local election officials, Republicans and Democrats, have failed to clean their voter rolls, usually citing the costs. And the organized Left has determined that keeping voter lists "dirty" leaves the door open for them to engage in ACORN-style voter fraud. Judicial Watch aggressively and successively challenged states to clean their voter rolls. We have also done what the Obama and Trump Justice Departments have failed to do . . . we sued states not complying with the NVRA.

2. *"All Mail-In Ballots" voting*
"All mail-in ballots" voting is a system where ballots are both distributed and returned by mail. In the 2016 presidential election it is estimated that roughly 25 percent of the votes cast were cast by mail. Leftists say that postal voting saves money . . . but what they don't say is that postal voting enhances the chance of voter fraud.

3. *"Ballot harvesting"*
"Ballot harvesting" allows individuals to collect and return ballots from other individuals and turn those ballots in to be counted. Judicial Watch believes ballot harvesting is an irresistible invitation for bad actors to engage in voter fraud . . . Indeed, in North Carolina, a Republican congressional campaign operative used ballot harvesting to eke out a "victory" for his client . . . while apparently throwing away some of the ballots he collected. The state elections board launched an investigation, refused to certify the Republican "winner," and forced a new special election in September 2019. This type of fraud is why ballot harvesting is illegal virtually everywhere, with California being the worst exception. Of course, the Pelosi House wants to impose unbridled ballot harvesting *nationally.*

4. *"Opt-out" Automatic Voter Registration (AVR)*
For many years, states have used citizen interactions with local government agencies, especially departments of

motor vehicles, as a place to register voters. But in 2016, Oregon instituted a new wrinkle in this process, automatic voter registration . . . which is now on the books in seventeen states and the District of Columbia.

If you live in an AVR state and register your car at the local DMV, you will automatically be registered to vote. You will have to "opt out" if you don't want to or are ineligible to vote. AVR's threat to election integrity is its inability to adequately filter noncitizens from registering to vote, since so many states issue driver's licenses with minimal or no validation of citizenship. The Left is an expert at exploiting failings in governmental systems to their political benefit.

5. *Abolition of Voter ID Requirements*
The Left does all it can to help noncitizens vote in our elections, which is why they have declared all-out war on states that attempt to require a photo voter ID to vote. Next to clean voter rolls, voter ID is the best way to block voter fraud, but the Left's legal attacks on voter ID laws, frequently spearheaded by Soros-funded groups, are unremitting. Judicial Watch believes that only eligible U.S. citizens should vote, which is why we have defended voter ID laws in the courts.

6. *Abolition of Voter Residency Requirements*
North Dakota requires voters to produce identification showing a name, birth date, and residential address. The Left is fighting the residential address requirement, falsely

charging that it discriminates against the homeless and Native Americans. Judicial Watch is monitoring this situation very closely, because we believe North Dakota is just the tip of the iceberg when it comes to attacks on residency requirements . . . because eliminating residency requirements will enhance opportunities for more illegal, multiple voting!

7. *Abolition of the Electoral College*

Under the Electoral College, the president is elected by "the most votes in the most states." This system allows for the possibility that a candidate may win the Electoral College vote, and the presidency, while losing the popular vote . . . as happened in 2016, 2000, 1888, and 1876. Not surprisingly, considering the 2016 and 2000 results, the Left is all in for abolishing the Electoral College.

Some liberals are going the lawful route (a constitutional amendment to abolish the Electoral College was introduced in the U.S. Senate by four senators, including former presidential candidate Kirsten Gillibrand of New York). Far more insidiously, some groups are pushing states to pledge—by state law—to follow the national popular vote results when casting their Electoral College votes. Too many states (including blue states like California, Illinois, and New York), plus the District of Columbia, have signed on to this scheme to bypass the Constitution in order to increase their chances of winning the White House. Not surprisingly, it has been reported that a George Soros foundation gave $1 million to one of these groups, National

Popular Vote Inc. Judicial Watch stands firmly for the Constitution, and opposes tampering with the Electoral College.

8. *Same-Day Voter Registration*

Liberals say same-day voter registration makes it easier for people to vote and increases voter turnout. In fact, same-day voter registration is just one more effort to corrupt honest elections, as it opens the door to allowing ineligible individuals to vote (because inadequate time is allowed to determine eligibility), as well as permitting unscrupulous individuals to vote in more than one place on Election Day. As of today, seventeen states and the District of Columbia permit same-day registration . . . and the Left is pushing hard to increase those numbers. Judicial Watch is looking for appropriate ways to intervene in opposition to the expansion of what is nothing more than an open invitation to increased voter fraud.

9. *Out-of-Precinct Voting*

This is a variation of same-day voter registration . . . and again, the Left's argument is that it will make it easier for people to vote and will increase voter turnout. There is no proof to substantiate their claims, but for sure this scheme will make it impossible for local precinct officials to identify voters they know by sight! Out-of-precinct voting is a priority for Soros-funded groups . . . and Judicial Watch is exploring legal strategies to challenge it!

This agenda is a serious threat to honest elections not only this year but beyond, and as the Left aggressively pushes these under-the-radar fronts to make it easier for voter fraud—including noncitizen voting—to tilt the electoral playing field permanently in its favor.

As you will see by what follows, we are doing all in our power to protect the security of the franchise and elections.

DIRTY VOTER ROLLS
CAN MEAN DIRTY ELECTIONS

Judicial Watch is the nation's leaders in enforcing the National Voter Registration Act's (NVRA) requirements that states take reasonable steps to clean their voter registration rolls by removing ineligible registrations.

The law allows private, aggrieved parties to sue to enforce the cleanup provision. Judicial Watch brought the first such lawsuits in history against Indiana and Ohio. Indiana, in response to our lawsuit, got its act together and fixed a key state law tied to voter list maintenance. In Ohio, we were able to settle our case. And the Left went crazy. They challenged the simple resulting process of Ohio's sending one mailing to voters who hadn't voted in an election. If the voter then didn't respond to the card *and* didn't vote in the next two federal elections—only then could the voters be cleaned from the rolls.

This leftist challenge went all the way to the Supreme Court, and we won!

Specifically, the Supreme Court decision known as *Husted* upheld the Ohio law providing that the state had to send address confirmation notices to all registered voters who had not voted in the previous two years. This ruling has the effect of also upholding our 2014 settlement agreement with Ohio, which required Ohio to use that same procedure as part of a regular Supplemental Mailing designed to identify whether registered Ohio voters had moved away—one of many steps intended to fulfill Ohio's obligations under the National Voter Registration Act (NVRA) to maintain the integrity of its voter list.

Judicial Watch filed several amicus briefs supporting Ohio's efforts at every level of the federal court system as the case progressed from the trial court all the way up to the Supreme Court. The case was on appeal from the United States Court of Appeals for the Sixth Circuit, which held Ohio's process was in violation of the National Voter Registration Act of 1993 (NVRA) (*Jon Husted, Ohio Secretary of State v. Philip Randolph Institute*, et al. [No. 16-980]).

Judicial Watch's amicus brief argued that the Sixth Circuit ruling would adversely affect its settlement agreement with Ohio were it allowed to stand. Judicial Watch also pointed out that failing to respond to an address confirmation notice does not mean that a registration is removed from the voter rolls. It merely triggers another waiting period, which can last up to four more years, during which the registrant still has the right to vote. In all, it can take up to six years before a registration is canceled under the process.

This Supreme Court win was a historic victory for cleaner elections. And it meant states with dirty voting rolls had less legal room to maneuver when Judicial Watch came knocking with evidence of problems.

In 2018, after the *Husted* Supreme Court decision, a federal court judge issued a historic consent decree directing the commonwealth of Kentucky to remove the names of ineligible voters no longer in residence from its official voter registration lists. U.S. District Judge Gregory F. Van Tatenhove of the Eastern District of Kentucky, Central Division, signed the consent decree between Judicial Watch, Kentucky, and the U.S. Department of Justice (DOJ). (This was one of the rare DOJ sightings in election integrity cases!)

Kentucky consented to clean its voter rolls:

> The Kentucky State Board of Elections shall develop and implement a general program of statewide voter list maintenance that makes a reasonable effort to remove from the statewide voter registration list the names of registrants who have become ineligible due to a change in residence in accord with section 8 of the NVRA.

> Kentucky State Board of Elections shall create a Comprehensive Plan and implement and adhere to its terms.

The decree was comprehensive, and required:

+ Procedures for a general program of list maintenance

+ Sources of information used regularly

+ Procedures for sending a non-forwardable canvass mailing

+ Procedures for using the data that is successfully matched to the statewide voter registration list

+ Timing of notices and updates

+ List of registrants to whom notices have been sent

+ Procedures for removing from the statewide voter registration list any registrant who is mailed a notice

+ A description of databases to be used in list maintenance activities and a plan to consult with relevant database

managers, assess the quality of data to be used in list maintenance activities, and develop sound and reliable match-
ing criteria

✦ Procedures for maintaining and making available for
   inspection and copying the records concerning implemen-
   tation of the general program activities

✦ A detailed description of any role that local election officials
   may play in list maintenance activities

✦ Public outreach

Our battle began in November 2017, when Judicial Watch sued
Kentucky over its failure to take reasonable steps to maintain accurate
voter registration lists (*Judicial Watch, Inc. v. Alison Lundergan Grimes
et al.* [No. 3:17-cv-00094]). In June 2018, with Judicial Watch's consent, the Justice Department moved to intervene in the lawsuit
against Kentucky.

Our lawsuit argued that forty-eight Kentucky counties had more
registered voters than citizens over the age of eighteen. The suit noted
that Kentucky was one of only three states in which the statewide
active registration rate is greater than 100 percent of the age-eligible
citizen population.

The Kentucky win is the first statewide consent decree (and still
the only one!) ever issued in a "clean voter rolls" lawsuit started by private litigants. This consent decree was a big victory for the voters of
Kentucky and across America that want clean elections. But something
even bigger was coming—in California!

CALIFORNIA CLEANS UP

Never would I have imagined that our most significant clean elections success would be in California—and arise as a result of a settlement with the notoriously leftist political leadership of that state.

Kentucky had dirty voting rolls but California, given its size, had a list maintenance problem of epic proportions.

In 2018, Judicial Watch and our clients/fellow co-plaintiffs sued California and Los Angeles County over the election rolls issue. California had the highest rate of inactive registrations of any state in the country. Los Angeles County has the highest number of inactive registrations of any single county in the country. Judicial Watch argued that the state of California and a number of its counties, including the county of Los Angeles, have registration rates exceeding 100 percent:

+ Eleven of California's 58 counties have registration rates exceeding 100% of the age-eligible citizenry.

+ Los Angeles County has more voter registrations on its voter rolls than it has citizens who are old enough to register. Specifically, according to data provided to and published by the EAC, Los Angeles County has a registration rate of 112% of its adult citizen population.

+ The entire State of California has a registration rate of about 101% of its age-eligible citizenry.

Judicial Watch pointed out that this is due in part to the high numbers of inactive registrations that are still carried on California's voter rolls:

+ About 21% of all of California's voter registrations, or more than one in five, are designated as inactive.

+ California has the highest rate of inactive registrations of any state in the country. . . . Los Angeles County has the highest number of inactive registrations of any single county in the country.

Although these inactive registrations should be removed after a statutory waiting period consisting of two general federal elections, California officials are simply refusing to do so.

Even though a registration was officially designated as "inactive," it may still be voted on Election Day and is still on the official voter registration list. The inactive registrations of voters who have moved to a different state "are particularly vulnerable to fraudulent abuse by a third party" because the voter who has moved "is unlikely to monitor the use of or communications concerning an old registration." Inactive registrations "are also inherently vulnerable to abuse by voters who plan to fraudulently double-vote in two different jurisdictions on the same election day."

In essence, we were talking about millions of potentially dirty names in a state that hasn't had a proper voter list maintenance procedure for twenty years. This was setting up to be a giant legal battle. But our election law legal team, led by Robert Popper, a former DOJ Civil Rights Division senior official, plowed ahead and took testimony and gathered documentary evidence.

Armed with helpful evidence we had gathered, and with the *Husted* Supreme Court decision at our back, we had a strong case to make. But even getting to trial and then winning would be still be tough slough against a massive state legal apparatus and leftist cohorts whose groups had sought to intervene against us and our coplaintiffs in the federal court case.

But then we settled!

As a result, the state of California and the county of Los Angeles have begun the process of removing from their voter registration rolls as many as 1.6 million inactive registered names. Huge!

Los Angeles County has over 10 million residents, more than the populations of forty-one of the fifty United States. California is America's largest state, with almost 40 million residents.

The new settlement required all of the 1.6 million potentially ineligible registrants on Lost Angeles County's rolls to be notified and asked to respond. If there is no response and they don't vote in the next two federal elections, those names are to be removed as required by the NVRA. The county sent the mailing as promised, which could and should result in the immediate removal of ineligible names.

California secretary of state Alex Padilla also agreed, which he did, to update the State's online NVRA manual to make clear that ineligible names must be removed and to notify each California county that they are obligated to do this. This should lead to cleaner voter rolls statewide.

This settlement vindicated Judicial Watch's groundbreaking lawsuits to clean up state voter rolls to help ensure cleaner elections. We were obviously thrilled with this historic settlement that will clean up election rolls in Los Angeles County and California—as it also set a nationwide precedent to ensure that states take reasonable steps to ensure that dead and other ineligible voters are removed from the rolls.

The massive settlement received national notice and caught the attention of President Trump, who repeatedly referenced the numbers as indications of voter fraud.

As president of a national organization, I sign a lot of documents.

I would daresay that one of my most important signatures to date was on behalf of Judicial Watch and our millions of supporters on that settlement agreement with California and Los Angeles County.

Despite our successful litigation to bring counties and states into compliance with the NVRA, voter registration lists across the country remain significantly out of date. According to our analysis of data released by the U.S. Election Assistance Commission (EAC) in 2019, 378 counties nationwide have more voter registrations than citizens old enough to vote, that is, counties where registration rates exceed 100 percent.

These 378 counties combined had about 2.5 million registrations over the 100 percent–registered mark, which is a drop of about one million from our previous analysis of voter registration data. Although San Diego County removed 500,000 inactive names from voter rolls following our settlement with Los Angeles County, San Diego still had a registration rate of 117 percent and has one of the highest registration rates in the county.

In the latest round of warning letters, we explain that implausibly high registration rates raise legal concerns.

> An unusually high registration rate suggests that a jurisdiction is not removing voters who have died or who have moved elsewhere, as required by [federal law].
>
> Judicial Watch also considers how many registrations were ultimately removed from the voter rolls because a registrant [had moved]. If few or no voters were removed . . . the jurisdiction is obviously failing to comply. . . . States must report the number of such removals to the EAC.

We found major voting list issues in California, Pennsylvania, North Carolina, Virginia, and Colorado. The following counties have excessive registration rates or have failed to cancel sufficient numbers of ineligible registrations:

- ✦ Colorado
  - ✦ Jefferson County

- ✦ California
  - ✦ Imperial County
  - ✦ Monterey County
  - ✦ Orange County
  - ✦ Riverside County
  - ✦ San Diego County
  - ✦ San Francisco County
  - ✦ San Mateo County
  - ✦ Santa Clara County
  - ✦ Solano County
  - ✦ Stanislaus County
  - ✦ Yolo County
  - ✦ North Carolina
  - ✦ Guilford County
  - ✦ Mecklenburg County

- ✦ Virginia
  - ✦ Fairfax County

- ✦ Pennsylvania
  - ✦ Allegheny County
  - ✦ Bucks County
  - ✦ Chester County
  - ✦ Delaware County

We don't make idle threats and have followed up with two new federal lawsuits against North Carolina and Pennsylvania.

In North Carolina, we sued the state and Mecklenburg County and Guilford County to make reasonable efforts to remove ineligible voters from their registration rolls as required by the federal law. On top of that, they couldn't be bothered to provide us with basic records we requested under the law.

In June 2019, the U.S. Election Assistance Commission released data showing that voter registration rates in a significant proportion of North Carolina's one hundred counties are close to, at, or above 100 percent of their age-eligible citizenry—statistics considered by the courts to be a strong indication that a jurisdiction is not taking the steps required by law to remove ineligible registrants. Judicial Watch's analysis also showed that at the time of the EAC report the entire state of North Carolina had a registration rate close to 100 percent of its age-eligible citizenry.

As of March 2020, North Carolina's own data shows it has nearly one million inactive registrations!

Pennsylvania wasn't much better.

We sued Pennsylvania and three of its counties for failing to make reasonable efforts to remove ineligible voters. According to Judicial Watch's analysis of voter registration data, these counties removed almost no names under NVRA procedures for identifying and updating the registrations of those who have moved. In some good news, one Pennsylvania county almost immediately removed 69,000 inactive names earlier this year in response to a Judicial Watch letter.

In its complaint, Judicial Watch points out that the state's abnormally low number of removals under NVRA procedures designed to identify voters who have changed residence indicates that it is not removing inactive registrations as the law requires. According to data the state certified for the Election Assistance Commission (EAC), in the most recent two-year reporting period:

> Bucks County, with about 457,000 registrations, removed a total of eight names under the relevant NVRA procedures;

> Chester County, with about 357,000 registrations, removed five names under those procedures; and

> Delaware County, with about 403,000 registrations, removed four names under those procedures.

As of April 2020, Pennsylvania's own data shows it has more than 800,000 inactive registrations!

Thankfully, at least one Pennsylvania county acted to avoid being sued by Judicial Watch. On January 14, 2020, CBS Pittsburgh reported that because of the threat of a lawsuit from Judicial Watch, Allegheny County removed 69,000 inactive voters. David Voye, elections manager for the county, told CBS, "I would concede that we are behind on culling our rolls," and that this had "been put on the backburner."

Nearly 2 million "extra" names in just two states. You can see, especially as the Left pushes for unsecure vote by mail mass mailing, why it is urgent that we get the work done to clean up the rolls.

CAN CONGRESS HANDLE THE TRUTH?

Our battles aren't limited to the courtroom. We were invited to testify in a major House hearing on elections and the coronavirus threat. The Left is pushing for national registration that would mandate vote by mail, undo voter ID, and push ballot harvesting across the nation (all under the pretext of the coronavirus emergency). Well, I was honored to testify (even if the hearing was stacked against us!). As you'll see below from much of my prepared testimony, we confronted the Left head-on:

> For years, Americans have been losing faith in the integrity of our electoral system. Many polls have been taken on this subject and they reach the same conclusion. The Gallup organization conducts a particularly interesting poll, which compares American attitudes with those of other countries. The poll simply asks respondents if they "have confidence" in the "honesty of elections." Last year, only 40% of Americans answered yes, while an astonishing 59% said no. According to Gallup, the United States has "one of the worst ratings across the world's wealthiest democracies," with only Chile and Mexico reporting statistically lower ratings. This phenomenon long predates the COVID-19 pandemic. Gallup reports that "[m]ajorities of Americans have consistently lacked confidence in the honesty of elections every year since 2012."

Among the explanations for this loss of faith, we must include the public's impatience with the politicization of electoral procedure, and, in particular, with dubious objections to what are widely perceived to be commonsense election integrity measures. The most obvious example to date concerns the heated, partisan fight against voter ID laws. A Pew Research Center study after the 2018 elections found strong, bipartisan support for voter ID, which was favored overall by 76 percent of those polled and even by a considerable majority of those identifying as Democrats (63 percent). This support is understandable in a society where one must produce identification for so many different reasons, from getting on a plane to buying prescription drugs to working out in a gym.

That voter ID laws are so often opposed, and with significant success, by political operators is a sad sign of our times. This opposition often relies on unsupported claims that voter ID will depress minority turnout, but this effect is never seen in actual elections. Opponents also try to flip the burden of proof, arguing in effect that, unless those favoring voter ID can prove that voter fraud is a common occurrence that costs elections, there is no justification for requiring an ID. This argument is bogus. As the Supreme Court has noted, regardless of the prevalence of fraud, states have an obvious, legitimate "interest in counting only the votes of eligible voters" and in "carefully identifying all voters participating in the election process." This interest is justified by the nature of voter fraud, which is hard to detect or punish after the fact. On a more practical note, those expressing doubt about the existence of voter fraud reveal an unrealistic, if touching, view of human nature. People cheat at more or less everything. They cheat at baseball. They cheat at sumo wrestling. They cheat when it doesn't matter, for example at online gaming or internet chess. Indeed, they cheat at solitaire. I cannot understand why voting, which is so tied up with intense partisan feeling and enthusiasm, would be exempt from cheating.

I could easily multiply examples of commonsense election integrity laws that partisans have made the subject of unnecessary and manufactured opposition. By far the silliest example I have found was a 2017 Virginia state bill that would have required electronic poll books to contain the photograph taken by the Department of Motor Vehicles for each registered voter who has a driver's license. Note that the actual photograph of a voter taken by the DMV cannot possibly discriminate against that voter. Yet Governor McAuliffe vetoed that bill.

My point here is that the American people see what they conclude are disingenuous fights over electoral procedures and lose faith in the honesty of our elections. With this background in mind I turn to measures proposed in response to the COVID-19 pandemic. One of the more common suggestions now is to require greater reliance on mail-in ballots. For example, last month Governor Newsom issued an executive order requiring that county elections officials transmit mail ballots to every registered voter in the state. I view this as a real threat to the integrity of American elections.

In 2005, the bipartisan Carter-Baker Commission noted the particular risks associated with absentee (mail-in) ballots:

> Absentee ballots remain the largest source of potential voter fraud. . . .
> Absentee balloting is vulnerable to abuse in several ways: Blank ballots
> mailed to the wrong address or to large residential buildings might
> get intercepted. Citizens who vote at home, at nursing homes, at the
> workplace, or in church are more susceptible to pressure, overt and
> subtle, or to intimidation. Vote buying schemes are far more difficult
> to detect when citizens vote by mail.

While I share all of these concerns, I would like to focus on the problem of ballots mailed to the wrong address. Voter registration lists throughout the country are routinely out of date, containing registrations for voters who no longer live at the stated address, who have died, or who are ineligible under the law for some other reason. This has been a problem for years. A Pew Research Center report issued during the Obama years noted that "[a]pproximately 2.75 million people have active registrations in more than one state," that "24 million—one of every eight—active voter registrations in the United States are no longer valid or are significantly inaccurate," and that "[m]ore than 1.8 million deceased individuals are listed as active voters." We know about this problem at Judicial Watch because of our work in enforcing the NVRA. Data states provided to the Election Assistance Commission in 2019 showed hundreds of U.S. counties with voter lists containing more registered voters than there were citizens over the age of eighteen—meaning a registration rate of more than 100 percent. Considering just the part of counties' voter rolls in excess of 100 percent shows that there are 2.5 million "extra" registrants on our nations' voter rolls.

In particular, counties throughout the country have high numbers of "inactive" registrations that have not yet been canceled. A registration becomes inactive when a registrant is sent, and fails to respond to, an address confirmation notice. If that registrant does not vote or otherwise contact election officials for the next two general federal elections (from two to four years), that registration is canceled pursuant to the NVRA. During that statutory waiting period the voter is called inactive.

It is crucial to note that an inactive registration can still be voted on Election Day. This does not even require the voter to use a provisional ballot. The voter need only affirm his or her address, and in many states this can be done orally. To be clear, the poll worker asks a voter if he or she lives at the listed address, and the voter says "yes." At that point, the voter can vote.

Now consider our experience in Los Angeles County, which we sued for noncompliance with the NVRA in 2017. We learned that the state of California had not been removing inactive registrations for *twenty years*, pursuant to a misguided accommodation reached with Janet Reno's Justice Department. As a result, Los Angeles County by 2018 had about 1,565,000 inactive registrations—almost one-fourth of all the registrations in the county. Stated differently, the county of Los Angeles alone had more *inactive* voter registrations than the state of Hawaii has people of every age. And this is not just Judicial Watch's calculation. These inactive registrations were tallied by Los Angeles County and were openly admitted in the agreement it signed settling the lawsuit. Most had moved long ago. Tens of thousands of these inactive registrants had died. But all currently remain "registered voters."

Until all of these registrations are formally processed under the NVRA, however, which will not be completed until 2022, they still can be voted in Los Angeles County. But Governor Newsom's executive order requires county officials to "transmit vote-by-mail ballots for the November 3, 2020 General Election to all voters who are . . . registered to vote in that election," making clear that "every Californian who is eligible to vote in the November 3, 2020 General Election shall receive a vote-by-mail ballot."[1] Under the plain terms of Governor Newsom's order, these 1.6 million inactive registrations, the vast majority of whom no longer reside in Los Angeles County, should receive ballots. Circulating all of those live ballots, unmonitored by their original owners who have moved or died, is a threat to the integrity of California's elections. (Governor Newsom [and the California state legislature] later backed off this scheme to mail ballots to dead and voters who had moved away in response to Judicial Watch's lawsuit on behalf of aggrieved California voters and a congressional candidate.)

Many other counties have lists containing old, inactive registrations. Our 2018 consent decree with the commonwealth of Kentucky addressed the hundreds of thousands of outdated registrations in that state. A few months ago, Allegheny County, Pennsylvania, admitted that it had nearly 70,000 inactive registrations that it had failed to remove for longer than the NVRA's statutory waiting period of two general federal elections. It only removed them after receiving a warning letter from Judicial Watch. North Carolina's own published data shows it has nearly a million inactive registrants. Pennsylvania admits to about 800,000 inactive registrants. Judicial Watch recently commenced lawsuits against both of those states over their failures to clean their voter rolls. If mail-in ballots are sent to the addresses of such inactive voters, there is the danger that they will be improperly voted, at which point they will become "active" again and not subject to removal. Indeed, where states or counties are not cleaning their voter rolls, even their *active* registrations become outdated.

One of the main reasons the Carter-Baker Commission identified absentee ballot fraud as "the largest source of potential voter fraud" is simple: it poses fewer risks for a person filling out and mailing a fraudulent ballot. By contrast, a person attempting "impersonation" fraud at a polling site must at least appear to cast the vote and, in consequence, may be found out and detained. Even so, a number of recent stories attest to the practice of mail-in ballot fraud. In July 2020, a West Virginia postal worker pled guilty to manipulating eight voters' absentee ballots. In 2019, an Oakland County clerk outside Detroit was charged with illegally altering 193 absentee ballots. A Minneapolis man was charged with helping thirteen others falsify absentee ballots ahead of the 2018 election. In 2017, a Dallas County, Texas, man was convicted after 700 mail-in ballots were witnessed and signed by a fictitious person. And recently in North Carolina's 9th Congressional District race, a scheme was run to steal 1,200 absentee ballots and fill them out, in a race that was decided by only 900 votes.

As a final point, as of this writing, it is about five months now until Election Day, and the pandemic's infection curve has flattened. Insisting now on all-mail ballot elections seems less like a response to a health crisis and more like a partisan application of the immortal words of Rahm Emanuel: "Never allow a good crisis to go to waste."

Governor Newsom's executive order in California seems particularly cynical. While he has relied on his emergency powers in the face of the pandemic to order all-mail ballot elections, he notably has failed to restrict ballot harvesting under state law, which allows paid employees of public sector unions, among others, to go door-to-door gathering ballots from strangers, even helping those voters to fill them out. Public health, in other words, is cited as a justification when it is convenient, and is ignored when it is inconvenient. This is just the kind of self-interested, partisan game playing that causes American voters to react with disgust at how we conduct our elections.

Also testifying was Stacey Abrams, the failed Democratic gubernatorial candidate from Georgia who has made an issue of falsely alleging the election was stolen from her due to "voter suppression." Her new angle, echoed by leftists throughout the media, is warning that Americans shouldn't have to choose between "dying and voting." This capitalizes on the fear of coronavirus and, as I testified, is actually likely to cause actual voter suppression by needlessly (and, I suspect, purposely) scaring Americans from voting in person!

I fear for our elections this year, as there has been a mad, partisan rush for vote-by-mail despite *not* having systems in place to handle and verify mail ballots.

Judicial Watch is battling against the tide. We must be forthright in describing the problem—the Left wants a free-for-all election system. And such a system will be susceptible to fraud, and as importantly, undermine American's confidence in the administration of our elections. So not only will be elections be less secure, but you can be sure fewer Americans will be willing to participate in elections without basic safeguards. How long can our republic stand this assault on the franchise?

ARE ALIENS GETTING OUT TO VOTE?

The Left is desperate to downplay the reality that aliens vote in our federal elections contrary to law. We have tens of millions aliens, legal and otherwise in the United States. From there, it is a numbers game—

a certain percentage will register to vote and a certain percentage of that number will vote. Honest observers can only argue over the size of the alien voter bloc—not its existence. I explored the issue for our friends at the *Daily Caller*:[2]

> Leftists and their media outlets have been all too eager to dismiss President Donald Trump's charge that as many as 5 million illegal aliens voted in the 2016 presidential election, enough to easily swing the popular vote to Hillary Clinton.
>
> Many of these pundits, backed by an army of so-called "fact-checkers," would have you believe that the number of illegals who are registering to vote and voting is insignificant. Oh, there may be the occasional, misguided "undocumented worker" who inadvertently wanders into the election booth, they seem to suggest. But, surely, not enough to make any difference.
>
> Anyone who thinks that needs to think again.
>
> There are a total of 43 million noncitizens currently living within U.S. borders. Of these, approximately 12 million are illegal aliens. Not only are there well-documented reasons to believe that many of them may be violating election integrity, the fact is many on the left are more than happy to see them do so. A Rasmussen Reports poll last year found that 53 percent of the Democratic Party supports allowing illegal aliens to vote.
>
> Part of the problem is that election laws in the United States are a complicated hodgepodge of federal, state, and local rules, regulations, and red tape. Generally speaking, it is illegal for any noncitizens to cast a vote in any election, and those who do are at least theoretically subject to criminal penalties if they are caught.

But many states do not have a voter ID requirement. Worse yet, many states do not even have a requirement to certify citizenship, other than saying out loud that you are a citizen. All too many of the systems that are in place to prevent unlawful voting are either nonexistent or are so weak that they are useless. We are naïve to think that the millions of people who are present in the United States illegally are all resisting the temptation to cast unlawful votes, especially when so much is at stake—including their being able to continue residing illegally within our borders.

As I point out in my book *Clean House,* in 2014 a disturbing study by political scientists at Old Dominion found that 6.4 percent of foreign nationals residing in the United States voted in the 2008 presidential election. If the key Old Dominion study results on the 2008 election were applied to 2016—1.41 million aliens may have voted illegally, with probably 1.13 million voting for Democrats.

Add to that the 2012 Pew Research Center study noting that "approximately 2.75 million people have active registrations in more than one state." On top of that, the study revealed, more than "1.8 million deceased individuals are listed as active voters." Combine those figures with the number of aliens the Old Dominion study cites, and the Trump allegations may not be so far out of line.

A full-scale, nonpartisan federal voter fraud investigation is long overdue. I'm not aware of any systematic federal investigation of voter fraud—ever. Initially, such an investigation would be a simple matter of analyzing voter registration databases against federal databases of aliens and deceased individuals. Judicial Watch's Election Integrity team, headed up by Robert Popper, former deputy chief of the Voting Section in the Civil Rights Division of the Department of Justice, would be more than happy to help.

The Left wants to downplay the threat of aliens illegally voting. How many aliens illegally voting is too many? 30,000? 10,000? 1,000?

100? Even *one* may be too many if it is *YOUR* vote canceled out by an alien illegally voting!

Voter ID and citizenship verification are needed more than ever to secure our elections.

ASSAULT ON YOUR RIGHT TO CHOOSE—A CANDIDATE

As the cliché goes: "All politics is local."

It's also very partisan and often, very anti-Trump.

In fact, across the country, local politicians, prosecutors, and judges are abusing their powers to target President Trump. Let's call it the politics of sedition—abusing the law to overthrow a duly elected president.

California's version of this get-Trump scheme was to try to lawlessly keep him off the ballot in 2020. Simply put, the state tried to unconstitutionally demand that he disclose to the public his tax returns before allowing him to appear on the presidential primary ballot. Though the law didn't name Trump, no one was fooled as to who it targeted. As with most leftist abuses, there was little concern about the collateral damage to citizens and voters.

We stepped up and filed a federal lawsuit on behalf of four California voters to prevent the California secretary of state from implementing the state law requiring all presidential candidates who wish to appear on California's primary ballot to publicly disclose their personal tax returns from the past five years (*Jerry Griffin et al. v. Alex Padilla* [No. 2:19-cv-01477]).

The suit argued that the law unconstitutionally adds a new qualification for candidates for president. Our clients include a registered Independent, Republican, and Democrat California voter.

Under the law, known as the Presidential Tax Transparency and Accountability Act, candidates who do not publicly disclose their tax returns are barred from having their names printed on California's primary ballots. We argued that SB 27 imposes candidate qualifications beyond those allowed by the U.S. Constitution and impermissibly burdens a voter's expressive constitutional and statutory rights. The lawsuit claimed violations of the U.S. Constitution's Qualifications Clause, the First and Fourteenth Amendments, and 42 U.S.C. § 1983 and 1988.

During the 2017–18 legislative session, then-governor Jerry Brown vetoed a previous version of this law, which California's Legislative Counsel concluded "would be unconstitutional if enacted." In vetoing the 2017–18 tax return law, Brown noted:

> First, it may not be constitutional. Second, it sets a "slippery slope" precedent. Today we require tax returns, but what would be next? Five years of health records? A certified birth certificate? High school report cards? And will these requirements vary depending on which political party is in power? A qualified candidate's ability to appear on the ballot is fundamental to our democratic system. For that reason, I hesitate to start down a road that well might lead to an ever escalating set of differing state requirements for presidential candidates.

Our complaint further alleged the political nature of the law, which is totally divorced from the states' legitimate constitutional role in administering and establishing procedures for conducting federal elections:

> None of the interests proffered by the California legislature for requiring the disclosure of candidates' tax returns is related to election

procedure or administration. Rather, the stated interests incorporate particular, substantive judgments about what is most important for voters to know when considering a candidate, how voters should go about "estimate[ing] the risk" of a candidate "engaging in corruption," and what might assist law enforcement in detecting violations of the Emoluments Clause and crimes "such as insider trading."

―――――――――

Unless SB 27 is enjoined, states will assume the power to create their own qualifications for national candidates seeking to obtain a party's nomination for president. This could lead to as many as fifty distinct and possibly inconsistent sets of qualifications regarding the only national election in the United States. Using rationales similar to California's, states might come to demand medical records, mental health records, sealed juvenile records, driving records, results of intelligence, aptitude, or personality tests, college applications, Amazon purchases, Google search histories, browsing histories, or Facebook friends.

In their zeal to attack President Trump, California politicians passed a law that unconstitutionally victimizes California voters. A state can't amend the U.S. Constitution by adding qualifications to run for president, and, as far as we were concerned, the courts couldn't stop this abusive law fast enough.

President Trump also sued to stop the law—and we won!

A federal judge issued a preliminary injunction at the request of Judicial Watch, President Trump, and other challengers to the law.

California politicians, in their zeal to attack President Trump, passed a law that also unconstitutionally victimizes California voters and the Constitution. A federal court seems to agree and granted our request for a preliminary injunction that stops this scheme from interfering with the 2020 elections.

In his decision, Judge Morrison C. England of the U.S. District Court for the Eastern District of California observed that "there has never been a legal requirement that any candidate for federal office disclose their tax returns." While he noted that SB 27 "was primarily intended to force President Trump to disclose his tax returns," Judge England agreed with Judicial Watch that the law particularly harmed California voters by diminishing their ability "to cast an effective vote" and to select the "presidential candidate of their choice."

Judge England ruled that Judicial Watch was likely to succeed on every one of its claims. He stated that California's scheme "tramples the Framers' vision of having uniform standards" for candidate qualifications. He also found that the public had an "extraordinary" interest in "ensuring that individual voters may associate for the advancement of political beliefs and cast a vote for their preferred candidate for President." And he agreed with President Trump that SB 27 was preempted by the federal Ethics in Government Act.

The law was eventually killed for good by the California Supreme Court. The episode is a dramatic example of a rogue attack on our rights under the Constitution to select our own president. Our republic's law was vindicated, but the blows against it continue, from inside our borders and from outside.

OUR REPUBLIC UNDER ASSAULT . . . AT OUR BORDER

A nation without sovereign and protected borders is no nation at all. It becomes a dangerous no-man's-land where laws are irrelevant and good and decent citizens and lawful residents fear for their safety.

Unfortunately, our borders are now under daily—and if the truth is allowed to be told, hourly—attack.

Judicial Watch's commitment to upholding the rule of law has led it to become the most effective litigator in the country supporting enforcement of our nation's laws against illegal immigration. These laws are under sustained attack by a range of well-funded (many by radical billionaire George Soros) groups . . . and politicians in both parties . . . who are willing to sacrifice our national sovereignty in preference to "open borders," cheap illegal labor, and for raw political advantage. Today, we continue to successfully meet challenges to the enforcement of our laws against illegal immigration across a broad range of fronts, including:

CHALLENGING ILLEGAL
SANCTUARY POLICIES

Judicial Watch is currently scheduled to go to trial against the city and county of San Francisco, challenging their deadly sanctuary policy, which prohibits local law enforcement from cooperating with federal immigration authorities. This taxpayer lawsuit arose out of the shocking death by shooting of Kathryn "Kate" Steinle on a San Francisco pier in 2015. The killer, an illegal alien from Mexico, had been released from custody on a drug charge by San Francisco police; even Immigration and Customs Enforcement (ICE) officials were seeking him to begin deportation proceedings.

San Francisco's sanctuary policy received national attention on July 1, 2015, when Steinle was gunned down at one the city's most popular tourist spots, allegedly by Jose Ines Garcia Zarate (formerly known as Juan Francisco Lopez-Sanchez), an illegal alien who had been released from the San Francisco Sheriff's Department despite a request from ICE that he be detained for possible deportation. Though there was no doubt he shot Steinle, a San Francisco jury acquitted Zarate of murder.

In its court filing opposing then-sheriff Vicki Hennessy's effort to dismiss our lawsuit, Judicial Watch argued:

> Sheriff Hennessy's refusal to share basic information about the release of deportable criminal aliens in her custody—the date, time, and place of their scheduled release—plainly frustrates Congress' clear purpose in enacting section 1226(c). By refusing to share release information, Sheriff Hennessy allows deportable criminal aliens in her custody—aliens Congress plainly intended to be detained upon release from the custody of [law enforcement agencies] such as SFSD—to escape federal immigration officials' grasp. Her restric-

tions enable aliens who have committed aggravated felonies or other crimes deemed sufficiently serious by Congress to warrant detaining them and denying them bond or conditional parole to remain at large pending removal. Not only might such persons pose a further danger to the community—which was one of Congress' main concerns—but federal immigration officials must spend additional time and resources and assume unnecessary risk to themselves, the aliens, and others locating and apprehending them.

In rejecting the attempt to end the lawsuit, presiding Superior Court judge Harold Kahn wrote there is "sufficient support at this stage of the case for Ms. Cerletti's allegation that the Sheriff's policy prohibiting or restricting release information about suspected priority aliens stands as an obstacle to the accomplishment of Congress' asserted purpose of enabling federal immigration officials to gain access to inmates who may have violated federal immigration laws."[1] Though there is a new sheriff, our lawsuit continues and is now in discovery.

And we found a shocking disregard for the rule of law. The San Francisco Sheriff's Department (SFSD) admitted to the following jaw-dropping numbers:

As of October 17, 2019, SFSD was unaware of any instances in which SFSD staff gave ICE information about an individual's citizenship or immigration status despite Title 8, Sec. 1373's requirement that state and local govts not restrict sharing such information with ICE.

Between April 11, 2016, and October 17, 2019, ICE sent SFSD 2,401 requests for notification about a prisoner's release from SFSD's custody.

As of October 17, 2019, only six prisoners in SFSD's custody satisfied the requirements of SFSD's policy for when to respond to an ICE request for notification about a prisoner's release. This doesn't mean ICE will be notified about the prisoner's release because, after it is determined a prisoner meets the requirements of the policy, the Sheriff reviews the prisoner's file to determine, in the exercise of her discretion, whether ICE should be notified of the release.

Then-sheriff Hennessy admitted in her deposition to our Judicial Watch legal team that of the six prisoners who satisfied the requirements of the sanctuary policy, the number of times ICE has been notified of the prisoner's release was zero. However, only three of the six were released. The other three remained in custody and were unlikely to be released.

What a public safety nightmare that breeds contempt all around for nation's borders. We hope to go to trial as scheduled this year, but this being California, we will be lucky to get this issue fully adjudicated even with our dramatic evidence of sanctuary lawlessness.

We've also focused on illegality in Santa Clara County, the heart of California's Silicon Valley.

We filed another taxpayer lawsuit. Santa Clara County Board Policy 3.54(B) requires Immigration and Customs Enforcement (ICE) agents to obtain a "judicial arrest warrant" in order for the county to transfer custody of an alien. Federal law, however, does not require "judicial arrest warrants" for federal authorities to detain aliens, especially for those who had been incarcerated or arrested by local authorities.

Judicial Watch is asking the court to grant an injunction against the sanctuary policy because:

It is an "illegal local regulation of immigration,"

It is "preempted by federal law," and

It is "barred by the doctrine of intergovernmental immunity," which prevents a state from intruding on the federal government's sovereignty.

On February 28, 2019, Bambi Larson, a Santa Clara County resident, was murdered inside her San Jose home. According to court documents, she suffered extensive and deep wounds consistent with a cutting tool. A few weeks later, Carlos Arevalo-Carranza was arrested and charged with Larson's murder. Arevalo-Carranza reportedly had multiple prior convictions in Santa Clara County, including a conviction for burglary in 2015, convictions for battery of an officer, resisting arrest, and entering a property in 2016, and a conviction for false imprisonment in 2017.

He also reportedly had multiple, prior arrests in 2015–18 in both Santa Clara County and Los Angeles County, including arrests for possession of drug paraphernalia and methamphetamine, prowling, and false identification. At the time of Larson's death, Arevalo-Carranza reportedly was on probation for possession of drug paraphernalia and methamphetamine, false imprisonment, and burglary.

ICE officials sent six separate requests to Santa Clara County, when Arevalo-Carranza was about to be released from its custody, asking that he be detained long enough for federal immigration officials to take him into custody for removal proceedings. Each request was ignored because of Santa Clara County's sanctuary policies.

In March 2019, San Jose officials reportedly "criticized so-called sanctuary policies they say prevented federal authorities from detaining a gang member in the country illegally before he allegedly killed a woman." The murderer was a "self-admitted gang member," with a "long criminal history in the San Francisco Bay Area and Los Angeles spanning five years."

Sanctuary policies are illegal and deadly. They encourage more illegal immigration and undermine our borders.

The outcomes of these lawsuits will have national repercussions and may well create models for overturning sanctuary policies across America.

While complete anarchy may be the goal of the Left, it is the enemy of every law-abiding citizen who believes in the values of our nation and the sovereignty of our borders.

President Trump has taken strong action to control the assault on our sovereignty, but he's faced dishonest opposition from anti-Trump activist judges and sanctuary politicians who placed politics over public safety.

But the rule of law is continuously under assault from all quarters. The Supreme Court just ruled this summer that it is illegal for the Obama administration to end Obama's illegal amnesty for so-called Dreamers! The Supreme Court undermined the Constitution by protecting, for now, Obama's decision to provide amnesty for hundreds of thousands of illegal aliens under the Deferred Action for Childhood Arrivals (DACA) program. DACA is unlawful, and the court interfered with the President Trump's duty and absolute right to rescind it.

This is the Alice-in-Wonderland approach to judicial decision-making. Threats to the rule of law come not only from rioters and looters in the streets, but also from activist judges on the bench.

Only Congress can amend the law, not President Obama nor the courts. One cannot help but conclude that this decision is driven more by politics than the rule of law.

Judicial Watch has previously exposed how DACA is not only illegal but a threat to public safety. For example, we uncovered how the Obama administration granted DACA amnesty without the promised background checks.

How about this idea for immigration reform: *Enforce the law!* Almost everyone who is here illegally should go home.

Instead we have sanctuary cities and states where police and other officials are told not to cooperate with federal law enforcement trying to enforce the law. These sanctuary policies are illegal and dangerous.

And I was glad to see the attorney general announce potential criminal investigations of politicians who aid and abet illegal aliens and abuse their offices to protect criminal aliens!

One of the most crucial lessons taught to us by the Wuhan COVID-19 pandemic is that it is essential that first, our borders be more secure than ever, and second, that we know *exactly* who is crossing them into our nation. The main reason of course is that if we have control of our borders, we can ensure that no one who is infected with this virus or any other disease can enter. I'd suggest that a "wall" and secure border are as essential to the public health as any requirement to wear a mask!

There can be no safety and no United States of America without borders. Period.

The Left knows this truth. No borders means no sovereignty—and the end of our republican system of government. And so the organized Left has made it its mission to undermine our borders.

CARAVAN CRISIS—BORDER UNDER ASSAULT

In 2018, America faced an unprecedented assault on its borders from organized caravans of illegal aliens posing as asylum seekers. After initially being overwhelmed and subjected to the propaganda press encouraging the sustained attack on our borders, the Trump administration tightened and more strictly enforced the rules under law and pressured our southern neighbors. The courts tried to intervene to prevent President Trump from defending America but eventually the judicial system vindicated the president's constitutional prerogatives to defend our borders.

Most asylum seekers are now turned back at the border and are required to reside in Mexico (or go home). The border remains largely unsecure, but new wall is being built every day, and President Trump's aggressive response to the caravan crisis saved our southern border from complete collapse, while also saving the lives of the children and other innocents victimized by the drug-cartel-run human smuggling operations that had pervaded the caravans.

Our Judicial Watch team is second to none on expertise on border issues. So when the crisis erupted we began digging and reporting.

My colleagues Chris Farrell and Irene Garcia flew down to Guatemala and partnered with investigative journalist Sara Carter. They began a series of reports that drove the national response to the crisis and angered the Left, which wanted to control the flow of fake information about the caravan assault on our nation. Here is their first report that blew the lid off the caravan crisis:

"Elaborately Planned" Caravan Brings Human Traffickers & Violent Gangbangers to Guatemala

The migrant caravan marching northbound through Central America is an "elaborately planned" movement that's benefiting human smugglers and bringing disturbing numbers of violent gang members and other criminal elements through Guatemala, according to government sources in the capital city. "MS-13 gang members have been detained and coyotes (human smugglers) are joining the march with clients who pay to get smuggled into the United States," a Guatemalan official told Judicial Watch. People from Asian countries waiting to get smuggled into the U.S. through Central America are also integrating with poor Hondurans in the caravan, a high-level Guatemalan government source confirmed. Among them are nationals of Bangladesh, a south Asian Islamic country that's well known as a recruiting ground for terrorist groups such as ISIS and Al-Qaeda Indian Subcontinent (AQIS). "There are lots of dirty businesses associated with this," Guatemalan authorities told Judicial Watch. "There's lots of human trafficking."

Sandwiched between Honduras and Mexico, Guatemala has been overrun with the onslaught of migrants that began their journey last week in the northern Honduran city of San Pedro Sula. At last count around 7,000 have participated in the trek, a great deal of them rowdy, angry men ages 17 to 40. President Jimmy Morales has ordered the military and police to detain all of the migrants and facilitate their safe return back to Honduras, though thousands have already reached the Mexican border. In a morning interview with Judicial Watch at the Guatemalan Ministry of Defense, Secretary of Defense General Luis Miguel Ralda Moreno said more than 2,000 Hondurans have been sent back home on buses. "We're doing everything possible to stop the caravan while still respecting human rights," General Moreno said.

During an afternoon interview at the National Palace, President Morales said that Guatemala has absorbed the huge cost of mobilizing police and military to return thousands of people to Honduras. He would like the United States to help him find the organizers of the caravan so they can face legal consequences. "Mass immigration like this endangers lives," Morales said. "This is unprecedented. We are in the process of investigating who is behind the caravan." Morales assures that Guatemala is doing everything possible to curb illegal immigration and asked for cooperation from the United States.

It has been a delicate and complicated task, Guatemalan officials say, because the caravan is a very organized movement that has been well orchestrated. There are rest points along the route with food, water and shelter for the migrants as well as medical care in some areas. "It's very strategic and extremely organized," a Guatemalan government source told Judicial Watch. "It is very complex, not a simple march. There is nothing spontaneous about it." During a visit to the Guatemalan-Honduran border this week Judicial Watch interviewed multiple migrants who repeated the same rehearsed line when asked who organized the caravan, insisting it was a spontaneous event even though there were clearly organizers shouting instructions in Spanish and putting select persons in front of cameras for interviews. All of them said the caravan was not about politics but rather poverty.

Guatemalan officials disagree, estimating that the caravan is a movement of radicalized forces to destabilize Central American countries. Honduran President Juan Orlando Hernández, a conservative, echoes that assessment. In a local newspaper report published last week Hernández asserted that leftist interests seeking to destabilize the country are manipulating migrants. Women and children are being used without regard to the risks to their lives, Hernández said. "The irregular mobilization was organized for political reasons to negatively affect the governance and image of Honduras and to destabilize the peace of neighboring countries," the president said, adding that many have returned to the country after realizing they've been fooled.

We also angered the Left by daring to do our own reporting, in addition to researching and disseminate Spanish language reporting from the region—all to educate the American people about what we found in terms of the potential terrorist threat from the caravan crisis. For instance, our popular Corruption Chronicles online blog made waves with the following report:

100 ISIS Terrorists Caught in Guatemala as Central American Caravan Heads to U.S.

In a startling revelation, Guatemala's president announced in the country's largest newspaper that nearly 100 ISIS terrorists have been apprehended in the impoverished Central American nation. Why should Americans care about this? A caravan of Central American migrants is making its way north. Let's not forget that Guatemala is one of the countries that bombarded the U.S. with illegal immigrant minors under Barack Obama's open border free-for-all. They came in droves from Honduras, El Salvador and Guatemala through the Mexican border and for years Uncle Sam rolled out the welcome mat offering housing, food, medical treatment and a free education.

A terrorist could have easily slipped in considering the minors, coined Unaccompanied Alien Children (UAC), were not properly vetted and some turned out to be violent gangbangers who went on to commit heinous crimes in their adopted land of opportunity. In fact, the nation's most violent street gang, Mara Salvatrucha (MS-13), was energized by the barrage of UACs. The Texas Department of Public Safety even issued a report documenting how the MS-13 emerged as a top tier gang in the state thanks to the influx of illegal alien gang members that came with the UACs. At the time more than 60,000 UACs—many with criminal histories—had stormed into the United States in a matter of months.

Tens of thousands more eventually made it north.

Guatemala has long been known as a major smuggling corridor for foreigners from African and Asian countries making their way into the United States. Last year Guatemala's largest paper, *Prensa Libra,* published an in-depth piece on the inner workings of an international human smuggling network that moves migrants from Afghanistan, Pakistan, India, Nepal, and Bangladesh to the United States. Individuals are sent to Dubai in the United Arab Emirates then flown to Brazil before heading to Colombia. Once in South America, the migrants are transported to Panama, before moving on to Costa Rica then a central point on Guatemala. One Spanish news report refers to Guatemala as a human smuggling paradise because it's so easy to get fake passports. A few years ago, the head of Guatemala's passport division got arrested for selling fake passports to a group of Colombians, according to a government announcement.

All this makes ISIS terrorists operating in Guatemala incredibly alarming. President Jimmy Morales confirmed it during a recent security conference attended by Vice President Mike Pence and Secretary of State Mike Pompeo as well as the presidents of Honduras and El Salvador and other Latin American dignitaries. Morales said that his administration has captured "close to 100 persons completely involved with terrorists, with ISIS and we have not only detained them within our territory, but they have been deported to their country of origin." Several of the terrorists were Syrians caught with fake documents, according to Guatemala's head of intelligence. At the same event, President Morales also revealed that Guatemalan authorities captured more than one thousand gangbangers, including members of the MS-13.

Many more probably make it into the United States via the Mexican border and a lot of them get released inside the country. In fact, Border Patrol agents in Texas have been ordered to release illegal immigrants caught entering through Mexico because detention facilities have no bed space, according to a news report. Earlier this year Judicial Watch exposed a secret program—started by Obama and continued by Trump—that quietly relocates illegal immigrants to different parts of the country on commercial flights. Years earlier Judicial Watch uncovered a similar DHS initiative that transported illegal immigrants from the Mexican border to Phoenix and released them without proper processing. The government classified them as Other Than Mexican (OTM) and transferred them 116 miles north from Tucson to a Phoenix bus station, where they went their separate ways. The OTMs were from Honduras, Colombia, El Salvador, and Guatemala and a security company contracted by the U.S. government drove the OTMs from the Border Patrol's Tucson Sector, where they were in custody, to Phoenix. Some could have been ISIS operatives.

And after the anti-Trump media moved on from the caravan crisis to the impeachment phase of the coup, Judicial Watch persisted in its vigilance, continuing to expose the ever-present national security threat on our border with Mexico, as reported by our investigative team:

A recent U.S. alert warning Mexico of armed Iranians planning to enter the country through the southern border didn't faze a busy Mexican border city's police chief, who confirms the region is full of Middle Easterners, Africans and Asians heading north. In a Latin American news report published shortly after the U.S. issued the bulletin, Mexicali Police Chief María Elena Andrade Ramírez matter-of-factly said the arrival of people from the Middle East, Africa and Asia as well as the rest of the Americas is "normal" in her California border city of about a million residents. Nevertheless, the chief, who affirmed receiving the U.S. government bulletin, said she planned to cooperate and coordinate with state authorities to "reinforce security."

The alert was issued a few days ago by the Department of Homeland Security (DHS) and largely ignored by the American and Mexican mainstream media. Only a few conservative media outlets in the U.S. reported about the warning after one obtained a DHS document outlining the threat. The document, issued by the Border Patrol's regional intelligence operation center in Arizona, says that a Guatemalan national may try to smuggle five Middle Easterners—including a suicide bomber—into the U.S. through Mexico. The smuggler and four other men and a woman transited through Guatemala and Belize before reaching Veracruz, Mexico, according to the bulletin. The Guatemalan, whose name is redacted in the government document, was deported from California a year ago. The Spanish-language article linked above elaborates that American intelligence officials received the threat after picking up recordings distributed via social media. A Mexicali news story cites Mexican authorities downplaying the situation by assuring citizens that the arrival of people from the Middle East, Africa, Europe, Asia and the rest of the Americas is "something normal."

This new norm creates a serious national security crisis along the famously porous southern border, though Islamic terrorists have long been present in Mexico. Judicial Watch has investigated and reported on it for years, uncovering several operations involving Mexican drug cartels joining forces with Islamic terrorists to enter the U.S. and carry out attacks. Back in the spring of 2015 Judicial Watch broke a story about an ISIS training facility just a few miles from the U.S. border near Ciudad Juárez in the Mexican state of Chihuahua. At the time sources, including a Mexican Army field grade officer and a Mexican Federal Police Inspector, confirmed that "coyotes" engaged in human smuggling—and working for the Juárez Cartel—help move ISIS terrorists through the desert and across the border between Santa Teresa and Sunland Park, New Mexico. A few months later Judicial Watch exposed a separate scheme in which Mexican cartels smuggled foreigners from countries with terrorist ties into a small Texas rural town near El Paso, Texas.

A few years ago Judicial Watch obtained State Department documents showing that the government has long known that "Arab extremists" are entering the country through Mexico. Among them was a top Al Qaeda operative wanted by the Federal Bureau of Investigation (FBI) during his cross-border jaunts. More recently, federal statistics show that unprecedented amounts of migrants from terrorist nations, labeled Special Interest Aliens (SIA) by the government, are entering the U.S. via Mexico. A congressional probe completed in early 2019 found an astounding 300% increase in Bangladeshi nationals attempting to sneak into the country through Texas alone. Bangladesh is a South Asian Islamic country well known as a recruiting ground for terrorist groups such as ISIS and Al-Qaeda Indian Subcontinent (AQIS). Before the year ended, Mexico confirmed that large groups of migrants from terrorist nations are in Tapachula awaiting asylum in the United States. Also, federal authorities in Houston arrested a Mexican-based Bangladeshi smuggler and charged him with bringing in fifteen fellow countrymen through the Texas-Mexico border.

When the Central American caravan got started in the fall of 2018, Guatemalan president Jimmy Morales confirmed that nearly one hundred ISIS terrorists had been apprehended in the impoverished Central American nation. Guatemala has long been known as a major smuggling corridor for foreigners from African, Asian, and Middle Eastern countries making their way into the United States like the Iranians identified recently by the feds. No wonder Mexican authorities are unfazed.

The border crisis on the best of days simmers. On the worst of days (or weeks) it boils over and we're overwhelmed. But there are threads that are uniform throughout:

> The drug cartels run the caravans and human smuggling operations.

> The caravans are aided and abetted by left-wing interest groups.

> The caravans are humanitarian nightmares.

> The largely unsecure border is a national security threat.

In January 2019, the Department of Homeland Security reported:

There are thousands of individuals on the terrorist watch list that traveled through our Hemisphere last year alone, and we work very hard to keep these individuals from traveling on illicit pathways to our country.

We work with foreign partners to block many of these individuals and prevent them from entering the United States. But effective border security is our last line of defense.

The threat is real. The number of terror-watch-listed individuals encountered at our Southern Border has increased over the last two years. The exact number is sensitive and details about these cases are extremely sensitive. But I am sure all Americans would agree that even one terrorist reaching our borders is one too many.

Overall, we stop on average 10 individuals on the terrorist watch list per day from traveling to or entering the United States—and more than 3,700 in Fiscal Year 2017. Most of these individuals are trying to enter the U.S. by air, but we must also be focused on stopping those who try to get in by land.

Additionally, last year at our Southern Border, DHS encountered more than 3,000 "special interest aliens"—individuals with suspicious travel patterns who may pose a national security risk—not to mention the many criminals, smugglers, traffickers, and other threat actors who try to exploit our borders.

Think about that—3,000 special interest aliens who may pose a national security risk. DHS goes on to define this category further:

> Generally, an SIA is a non-U.S. person who, based on an analysis of travel patterns, potentially poses a national security risk to the United States or its interests. Often such individuals or groups are employing travel patterns known or evaluated to possibly have a nexus to terrorism. DHS analysis includes an examination of travel patterns, points of origin, and/or travel segments that are tied to current assessments of national and international threat environments.

Despite the death and lawlessness of sanctuary policies, despite the humanitarian catastrophes associated with open borders, the organized Left has doubled down in attacking our sovereignty. The radical Left now supports voting rights for aliens, welfare and free health care for illegal aliens, the decriminalization of the border (no criminal sanction for crossing the border illegally), and the abolishment of Immigration and Customs Enforcement (ICE).

Never before have we had such extreme support for open borders and the absolute erasure of distinctions under law between citizens and noncitizens. This is a fundamental threat not only to our constitutional republic but to the very nationhood of the United States.

HOW TO PROTECT AND SAVE OUR REPUBLIC

U nfortunately, one critical expression and truism has become much
    more of a cliché than a call to arms over the last few decades. The
Left has seen to that.

That truism: "Freedom isn't free."

Fewer and fewer people ever think about that saying, and only people like us know it to be true.

Obama and Clinton operatives, the Deep State, and their allies were counting on that new and sad reality to help them "take down" President Trump. They failed, but have not given up.

Freedom and liberty does come with a price. Usually, it is a daily cost that each of us can easily cover. Sometimes the price is the steepest of all and is paid for by the heroes in uniform who walk those ramparts to protect us all.

But if we do want to preserve, protect, and maintain our republic as it was so gloriously envisioned and then created by our Founding Fathers, then each of us has to be involved to some extent.

If we don't, then the Left wins and the republic we cherish will fall and fade away.

President Ronald Reagan understood this better than most and spoke to the issue during his farewell address to the nation on January 11, 1989. Said President Reagan in part:

> One of the things I'm proudest of in the past 8 years: the resurgence of national pride that I called "The New Patriotism." This national feeling is good, but it won't count for much, and it won't last unless it's grounded in thoughtfulness and knowledge. An informed patriotism is what we want . . . those of us who are over 35 or so years of age grew up in a different America. We were taught—very directly—what it means to be an American. And we absorbed, almost in the air, a love of country and an appreciation of its institutions. But now . . . for those who create popular culture, well-grounded patriotism is no longer in style. Our spirit is back but we haven't re-institutionalized it. We've got to do a better job of getting across that America is freedom—freedom of speech, freedom of religion, freedom of enterprise. Freedom is special and rare. It's fragile; it needs protection.

Tens of millions of Americans cherish the freedoms articulated by President Reagan. Freedoms they do understand are being taken away from them—seemingly forever—with each passing day. Freedoms that truly do need to be "re-institutionalized" in a hurry . . . or else.

Well . . . as President Reagan was fond of beginning a sentence . . . we *must* be the ones to "re-institutionalize" those freedoms.

If not us, *who*? If not now, *when*?

Every American who believes in our Constitution and the Founders' vision believes the United States must have clearly defined and protected borders, believes in the need for a strong military, believes in the value of hard work and faith, believes in the rule of law, and believes in American exceptionalism must band together to "re-institutionalize" those freedoms and protect them going forward.

Knowing that to be the truth, while massive problems and issues can rarely be solved in the macro sense, they can often be dealt with in the micro sense.

Meaning, while we as individuals or even small groups are not going to necessarily stop the imposing and evolving threats to the welfare of our republic on our own, we can very positively affect those threats at the local level.

Those on the left and the far left and those who have contempt for the rule of law in the Deep State truly do believe that they have an "ace in the hole" when it comes to undoing the United States of America.

The one thing they believe above all others is that those who oppose them will ultimately do nothing to stop them. *Nothing.*

Sadly, and even tragically, many times they have been proven correct.

Way back in 1770, Edmund Burke spelled it out for all of us when he warned: "The only thing necessary for the triumph of Evil is for good men to do nothing."

The good people doing "nothing" scenario has become the largest part of the far-left playbook. They factor that into every single socialist, anarchistic, illegal, and destructive act they take.

The Left and the Far Left have proven time and again that there are few lines they will not cross to achieve their liberty-destroying objectives. Our cities are now facing violent riots from communist insurrectionists, our history is under attack, churches are being defaced, and the very foundations of our country are being questioned by a radical rabble. Even more dangerously, this political violence is being egged on, coddled, and condoned by craven leftist politicians. The assault on our republic is dire—and we are on the precipice of collapse.

There are a number of ways we can protect, defend, and maintain the republic we all love and cherish without descending into the gutter with the Far Left and their army of gangsters.

Thanks to the support of now millions of you, Judicial Watch has been fighting the fight from our nation's capital and across the states. Together with you, we have stood shoulder to shoulder from one end of the United States to the other.

We *are* the force needed to defeat the darkness of the Far Left.

But to win, we must not only never give up the fight, but *expand* it.

Each of you is both a member of a freedom army and a force of one.

Seek out those in your neighborhood, town, and city who think like you. Get involved whenever and wherever you can.

Create your own activist "platoon" of committed patriots to engage in this fight of our lives by supporting, voting, campaigning, and exercising your core First Amendment rights.

Write reports. Share information with each other. Let the authorities know of any wrongdoing. Keep track of the news to make sure the current crisis recedes. If not, increase your activism! Use state and federal FOIA laws and other public information laws to ask questions and demand answers about what your government is up to! It is easy. You can go over to our Judicial Watch website (www.JudicialWatch.org) for our FOIA handbook to help guide you on any public records requests you'd like to make.

Those who cherish your ideals *are* out there. They are out there by the *millions*. But some have been intimidated into silence or compliance by the brutal tactics of the Left.

Let them know they are not alone.

The agents and the operatives of the Far Left believe that most who oppose them will never get involved and instead simply sit at home twiddling their thumbs while saying, "Tsk, tsk, tsk."

Prove them wrong. Every law Judicial Watch seeks to vindicate is also open to everyday citizens. You can demand documents under transparency law, you can demand accountability and clean elections, you can engage in party politics, you can, as the Constitution lays out, petition your government for redress of grievances.

And, of course, support Judicial Watch and get the word out about our work!

The little accountability Hillary Clinton has faced, the thwarting of the coup cabal, the successes for honest elections, and pushback against open borders extremism—all have largely flowed from our rag-tag group.

Our motto and motivation is "Because no one is above the law!"

With that mission in mind—our combined mission—please continue to let your family members, your friends, and your neighbors know about Judicial Watch.

The agents, the operatives, and the goons of the Left and the Far Left truly hate us for a reason. We not only drag them out from their dark and murky shadows, kicking and screaming into the light for all to see their decrepit ugliness, but we also bring them to justice.

We *can't* do it alone. We *are* all in this together.

This *is* the fight of our lives.

We will *not* lose our republic to these agents of anarchy and darkness.

Together, we *will* overcome that evil.

ACKNOWLEDGMENTS

This book is truly the work product of the Judicial Watch team, whose patriotism, work ethic, and vision have built Judicial Watch into one of the most significant civic organizations in the history of our country. Paul Orfanedes, our Director of Litigation and Chris Farrell, our Director of Research and Investigations, have helped me lead our team in achieving success after success for the rule of law. And in further testament to the fact that our country is the best in the world, none of our achievement would have been possible without the generous and voluntary support of millions of Americans who are Judicial Watch supporters and members. Of course, the families of our staff deserve a special note of thanks, as their steadfast support is essential to our success. (I know I am grateful to my patient wife and children for putting up with my trying to run Judicial Watch out of our house because of the insane coronavirus crisis!) And for those of you who helped me directly on *A Republic Under Assault*, thank you for ensuring the success of this essential educational effort.

I am very grateful to the talented and dedicated team at Simon & Schuster, Threshold Editions. This will be our third book together. My editor, Natasha Simons, is a true professional, and her guidance and direction have been invaluable. She, along with assistant editor Maggie Loughran, has helped immeasurably in the process of refining the content for the reader's benefit.

To our publisher, Jennifer Bergstrom, and associate publisher, Jennifer Long: Judicial Watch is honored to entrust our important content to you, and we're grateful for those whom you've assembled to tend to the details of making and marketing this book.

We truly value the efforts of publicity director Sally Marvin and publicist Jennifer Robinson in helping to raise awareness for this title. Thank you for working closely with our team to ensure the best coverage possible for our book.

A special thanks is due to managing editor Caroline Pallotta; production editor Al Madocs; designer Davina Mock; and art director Lisa Litwack and deputy art director John Vairo for investing their talents to fashion and produce a book whose visual and physical attributes are befitting the important content it conveys.

And thanks to Frank Breeden, our literary agent, who has shepherded us patiently through the years in our book endeavors!

APPENDICES

"Electronic Communication" Opening Spy Operation Against Trump Campaign

b6 -1
b7C -1
b7E -1

FD-1057 (Rev. 5-8-10)   (U)

OFFICIAL RECORD

SECRET//ORCON/NOFORN

FEDERAL BUREAU OF INVESTIGATION
Electronic Communication

(U) Title: (S//OC/NF) CROSSFIRE HURRICANE   Date: 07/31/2016   b6 -1
                                                                          b7C -1

CC:

STRZOK PETER P II

From: COUNTERINTELLIGENCE
                                                                          b7E -2
        Contact: STRZOK PETER P II, [_____]

Approved By: STRZOK PETER P II

Drafted By: STRZOK PETER P II

Case ID #: [_____]   (S//OC/NF) CROSSFIRE HURRICANE;   b3 -1
                              FOREIGN AGENTS REGISTRATION ACT -   b7E -1
                              RUSSIA;
                              SENSITIVE INVESTIGATIVE MATTER

DOCUMENT RESTRICTED TO CASE PARTICIPANTS
This document contains information that is restricted to case participants.

(U) Synopsis: (S//OC/NF) Opens and assigns investigation

                    Reason: 1.4(b)
                    Derived From: FBI
                    NSISC-20090615
                    Declassify On: 20411231

                                                                          b7E -3

Details:

(U) (S//NF) An investigation is being opened based on information received   b7E -2
from Legat [____] on 07/29/2016. The text of that email follows:

(U)   SECRET//ORCON/NOFORN

(U) ~~SECRET~~/ ~~ORCON/NOFORN~~

(U)
Title: (X/~~OC/NF~~) CROSSFIRE HURRICANE   b3 -1
Re: [_____] 07/31/2016   b7E -1

BEGIN EMAIL

(U//~~FOUO~~) Legat [____] information from [_____] Deputy   b7E -2
Chief of Mission   b6 per DOS

Synopsis:
(U//~~FOUO~~) Legat [____] received information from the [_____]   b7E -2
[____] Deputy Chief of Mission related to the hacking of the Democratic b6 per DOS
National Committee's website/server.

Details: b6 -1
(U) (X/~~REL TO USA,~~ [____] On Wednesday, July 27, 2016, Legal Attaché (Legat) b7C -1
[_____] was summoned to the Office of the Deputy Chief of b7D -1
Mission (DCM) for the [_____] who   b7E -2
will be leaving [_____] post Saturday, July 30, 2016 and set to soon   b6 per DOS
thereafter retire from government service, advised [____] was called by
[_____] about an urgent matter requiring an in person
meeting with the U.S. Ambassador. [Note: [_____]
[_____] was scheduled to be away from post until mid-August,
therefore [_____] attended the meeting.
(U) (X [_____] [_____] advised that [_____] government
had been seeking prominent members of the Donald Trump campaign in
which to engage to prepare for potential post-election relations should
Trump be elected U.S. President. One of the people identified was
George Papadopolous (although public media sources provide a spelling
of Papadopoulos), who was believed to be one of Donald Trump's foreign
policy advisers. Mr. Papadopoulos was located in [____] so the
[_____] met with him on several occasions,
with [_____] attending at least one of the meetings.
(U) (X [_____] [_____] recalled [_____]
of the meetings between Mr. Papadopolous and [_____]
concerning statements Mr. Papadopolous made about suggestions from the
Russians that they (the Russians) could assist the Trump campaign with
the anonymous release of information during the campaign that would be

(U) ~~SECRET~~/ ~~ORCON/NOFORN~~

(U) ~~SECRET~~/~~ORCON~~/~~NOFORN~~

(U)   Title: ~~S~~/~~OC/NF~~ CROSSFIRE HURRICANE
Re: [   ]   07/31/2016

b3 -1
b7E -1

b6 -1
b7C -1
b7D -1
b6 per DOS

damaging to Hillary Clinton. [   ] provided a copy of the
reporting that was provided to [   ] from [   ] to Legat [   ] The
text is exactly as follows:
[Begin Text]

(U)   ⌧[   ] 5. Mr Papadopolous [

b7D -1
b7E -2

                                      ] also suggested the Trump team had received some
kind of suggestion from Russia that it could assist this process with
the anonymous release of information during the campaign that would be
damaging to Mrs Clinton (and President Obama). It was unclear whether
he or the Russians were referring to material acquired publicly of
through other means. It was also unclear how Mr Trump's team reacted to
the offer. We note the Trump team's reaction could, in the end, have
little bearing of what Russia decides to do, with or without Mr Trump's
cooperation.
[End Text]

⌧[

                                                                           ] (S)

(U)   ⌧[   ] Legat requests that further action on this information
should consider the sensitivity that this information was provided
through informal diplomatic channels from [   ] to the U.S.
Embassy's DCM. It was clear from the conversation Legat [   ] had with
DCM that [   ] knew follow-up by the U.S. government would be
necessary, but extraordinary efforts should be made to protect the
source of this information until such a time that a request from our
organization can be made to [   ] to obtain this
information through formal channels.

b6 -1
b7C -1
b7D -1
b7E -2
b1 per DOS

END EMAIL

(U)   ⌧/~~OC/NF~~ Based on the information provided by Legat [   ] this
investigation is being opened to determine whether individual(s)

b7E -2

(U)   ~~SECRET~~/~~ORCON~~/~~NOFORN~~

3

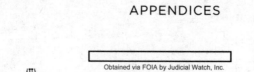

(U) ~~SECRET~~//~~ORCON/NOFORN~~

b3 -1
b7E -1

(U) Title: ~~(S//OC/NF)~~ CROSSFIRE HURRICANE
Re: [   ] 07/31/2016

associated with the Trump campaign are witting of and/or coordinating
activities with the Government of Russia.

◆◆

(U) ~~SECRET~~//~~ORCON/NOFORN~~

4

Andrew McCabe Memo about Rod Rosenstein Offer to Wear a Wire into the Trump Oval Office

b6 -1
b7C -1

SECRET//NOFORN

Tuesday, May 16, 2017

At 12:30 pm on 05/16/2017, I met with Deputy Attorney General (DAG) Rod Rosenstein in his office at the Department of Justice. Also present were Tashina Gauhar and Jim Crowell. The following is a contemporaneous recollection of the main topics we discussed.

I began by telling him that today I approved the opening of an investigation of President Donald Trump. I explained that the purpose of the investigation was to investigate allegations of possible collusion between the president and the Russian Government, possible obstruction of justice related to the firing of FBI Director James Comey, and possible conspiracy to obstruct justice. The DAG questioned what I meant by collusion and I explained that I was referring to the investigation of any potential links between the Trump campaign and the Russian government. I explained that counterintelligence investigations of this sort were meant to uncover any the existence of any threat to national security as well as whether or not criminal conduct had occurred. Regarding the obstruction issues, I made clear that our predication was based not only on the president's comments last week to reporter Lester Holt (that he connected the firing of the director to the FBI's Russia investigation), but also on the several concerning comments the president made to Director Comey over the last few months. These comments included the President's requests for assurances of loyalty, statements about the Russia investigation and the investigation of General Michael Flynn. I also informed the DAG that Director Comey preserved his recollection of these interactions in a series of contemporaneously drafted memos. Finally, I informed the DAG that as a result of his role in the matter, I thought he would be a witness in the case.

The DAG then related his experiences at the White House on Monday, 05/08/2017. He began by stating that he had the feeling that the decision to fire the Director had been made before he arrived. At the White House, he first met with White House Counsel Donald McGahn, who told him that the President had drafted a letter to Director Comey that McGahn did not want the President to send. Shortly thereafter they met with the President and Attorney General Jeff Sessions, and possibly others, in the Oval Office. President Trump told the DAG he had written a letter to Director Comey, asked the DAG if he had seen the letter, and instructed McGahn to provide the DAG with a copy. The DAG described the letter to me as being a long list, possibly several pages, of the President's complaints with Director Comey. Among those complaints was a discussion about the FBI's Russia investigation, as well as a paragraph about the FBI Deputy Director. The DAG indicated to me that he retained a copy of the President's letter. The DAG said he told the President ⬚ ⬚ The President then directed the DAG to write a memo explaining the reasoning for Director Comey's termination and that the DAG should include Russia. The DAG said to the President he did not think this was a good idea and that his memo did not need to include Russia. The President replied that he understood, but that he was asking the DAG to include Russia anyway. As our conversation continued the DAG proposed that he could potentially wear a recording device into the Oval Office to collect additional evidence on the President's true intentions. He said he thought this

b5 per DOJ/OIP

b6 -1
b7C -1

SECRET//NOFORN

SECRET//NOFORN

might be possible because he was not searched when he entered the White House. I told him that I would discuss the opportunity with my investigative team and get back to him.

We discussed the issue of appointing a Special Counsel to oversee the FBI's Russia investigation. The DAG said he has two candidates ready, one of whom could start immediately.

The DAG said that he left a copy of the delegation with Acting Assistant Attorney General for National Security Dana Boente to execute in the DAG's absence if the DAG were suddenly removed from his position.

b5 per DOJ/OIP

He anticipated that he may be terminated when he puts the Special Counsel in place, in light of the president's anger with AG Sessions when the AG recused himself from the Russia investigation. The DAG further stated that he was told that others heard the President tell the AG "you were supposed to protect me."

The DAG related to me that on Sunday, 05/14/2017, the AG asked him to participate in the interview of for the position of FBI Director.

b5 per DOJ/OIP

The DAG told me that he informed the AG that I should remain in my role as Acting Director until the permanent Director was chosen. The DAG opined that my only "problem" was that some people believe that I was involved in my wife's 2015 campaign for State Senate in Virginia. The DAG said it was a "credibility problem" because after having told him during my May 13 interview that I played no role in her campaign and attended no campaign events, the DAG said a staffer had provided him with a photograph found on the internet of me and my wife wearing Dr. Jill McCabe campaign t-shirts. The DAG suggested that this photograph contradicted my statement that I had not campaigned for my wife. I pointed out to the DAG that the photograph he saw was taken not at a campaign event, but rather at I further informed the DAG that I confirmed with my ethics counsel at FBI that the Hatch Act does not prohibit wearing a campaign button or shirt away from the office, and that attending wearing such a shirt does not constitute proscribed political activity.

b6 -2
b7C -2

SECRET//NOFORN

NOTES

SECTION ONE: Our Republic Under Assault . . . from the Deep State

1   Kevin Brock, "New FBI document confirms the Trump campaign was investigated without justification," *The Hill,* May 27, 2020, https://thehill.com/opinion/white-house/499586-new-fbi-document-confirms-the-trump-campaign-was-investigated-without.

2   July 10, 2019: Judicial Watch, "Emails Show Dossier-Connected Top Obama State Department Officials Set 'Face-to-Face' Meeting on 'Russian Matter' in NY in September 2016."

3   September 9, 2019: Judicial Watch, "New State Department Documents Reveal Last-Minute Efforts by Obama State Department to Undermine President Trump."

4   September 19, 2019: Judicial Watch, "Documents Reveal Extensive Relationship between Dossier Author Steele and Top Obama State Department Officials."

5   October 31, 2019: Judicial Watch, "Documents Reveal Extensive Relationship between Dossier Author Steele and Top Obama State Department Officials."

6   January 7, 2020: Judicial Watch:, "State Department Handler for Steele Used Personal Email to Push-Reports."

7   August 14, 2019: "Judicial Watch: New DOJ Docs Show Nellie Ohr Sent DOJ/FBI Anti-Trump Russia Dossier Materials Through Her Husband Bruce Ohr."

8   August 14, 2019: Judicial Watch, "New DOJ Docs Show Nellie Ohr Sent DOJ/FBI Anti-Trump Russia Dossier Materials Through Her Husband Bruce Ohr."

9   August 15, 2019: "Judicial Watch Releases Email Exchanges of Russian-Related Material between Nellie Ohr and DOJ Top Official Lisa Holtyn During the Time Ohr Worked at Fusion GPS."

10 August 19, 2019, *The Washington Examiner*, "FBI used Steele dossier in FISAs despite knowing about flaws and bias."

11 Daniel John Sobieski, July 16, 2019: *The American Thinker*, "Mueller was Weissmann's Sock Puppet."

12 Ibid.

13 March 15, 2018: USAPoliticsToday.org, "Mueller's 'Pit Bull' Andrew Weissmann Busted for Withholding Evidence in Previous Case."

14 May 22, 2018: "Daily Caller—Manafort's Lawyers Suggest Key Mueller Deputy Is Leaking to Media."

15 August 12, 2019: *American Thinker*, "Both Ohrs in Troubled Water."

16 September 11, 2019: "Judicial Watch: Records Show DOJ Effort to Craft Response to Reports on Rosenstein Wearing Wire, Invoking 25th Amendment."

17 September 23, 2019: Judicial Watch, "McCabe memo detailed how DOJ's Rosenstein proposed wearing a wire into Oval Office to record President Trump."

18 April 29, 2020: Judicial Watch, "Emails show extensive communications between senior Defense official and columnist who published leaked info on Flynn calls with Russian Ambassador."

19 October 17, 2017: *The New York Times*, "Andrew Weissmann, Mueller's Legal Pit Bull."

20 FoxNews.com [n.d.]: "Mueller team criticized by fellow attorneys for history of questionable tactics."

21 December 5, 2017: Judicial Watch, "New Justice Department records show strong support by Mueller deputy Andrew Weissmann, other top DOJ officials for Yates' refusal to enforce President Trump travel ban."

22 October 22, 2019: Judicial Watch, "AP Reporters Gave DOJ/FBI Ukraine Info and Code to Private Locker of Paul Manafort in Apparent Effort to Push Criminal Prosecution."

SECTION TWO: Our Republic Under Assault . . . from the Impeachment-Coup Attack Against President Trump

1 April 14, 2017: Judicial Watch, "Judicial Watch Calls upon Office of Congressional Ethics to Investigate Whether Rep. Schiff and Rep. Speier Disclosed Classified Information."

2 January 22, 2020: RealClearInvestigations.com, "Whistleblower Was Overheard in '17 Discussing with Ally How to Remove Trump."

3 February 20, 2020: Judicial Watch:, "CIA, DOJ Refuse to Confirm or Deny Existence of Eric Ciaramella Records."

SECTION THREE: Our Republic (Still) Under Assault . . . from Hillary Clinton

1 November 30, 2017: Judicial Watch, "Judicial Watch Releases 29 Pages of FBI Clinton-Lynch Tarmac Meeting Documents Previously Withheld by Justice Department."

2 March 26, 2020: Judicial Watch, "Strzok's 'Weiner Timeline' shows gap between Clinton email discovery and search warrant."

3   August 23, 2018: Real Clear Investigations.

4   October 17, 2018: Judicial Watch, "FBI Documents detail Weiner laptop/Clinton email find just before the 2016 election."

5   January 4, 2018: Judicial Watch, "At least 18 Classified Emails found on Weiner's laptop."

6   November 22, 2019: Judicial Watch, "Judicial Watch Obtains Strzok-Page Emails Showing FBI's Special Accommodation of Clinton Email Witnesses."

7   November 22, 2019: "Judicial Watch Obtains Strzok-Page Emails Showing FBI's Special Accommodation of Clinton Email Witnesses."

8   July 5, 2016: ABC News, "FBI Probe Contradicts Clinton's Claim She Never Sent Classified Emails."

9   November 12, 2019: Judicial Watch, "Judicial Watch Obtains Strzok-Page Emails Disputing Hillary Clinton's Claim That She 'Never Received nor Sent Any Material That Was Marked Classified."

10 June 3, 2019: "Judicial Watch: New Strzok-Page Emails Reveal FBI Gave Special Treatment to Hillary Clinton's Demands for Email Investigation Information Just Before Election."

11 June 3, 2019: Judicial Watch, "Judicial Watch: New Strzok-Page Emails Reveal FBI Gave Special Treatment to Hillary Clinton's Demands for Email Investigation Information Just before Election."

12 November 17, 2009: "CNN Politics—Bill Clinton Could Pose Cabinet Problem."

13 January 5, 2009: "Senator Hillary Clinton's Letter—Subject: Ethics Undertakings"; https://www.judicialwatch.org/wp-content/uploads/2015/04/Hillary-R -Clinton-Termination-EA.pdf.

14 August 9, 2015: Judicial Watch, Judicial Watch Uncovers New Batch of Hillary Clinton Emails.

15 April 30, 2015: Judicial Watch, "Teneo & the Clinton Machine."

16 January 8, 2010: PBS, "Chasing the Ghosts of a Corrupt Regime."

17 December 18, 2008: *Wall Street Journal*, "Clinton Foundation Donors."

18 February 9, 2010: ABC News, "No-Fly Terror List Includes Big Financial Backer of Clinton; "FBI stops Nigerian with ties to ex-president; allowed to fly after questioning."

19 April 5, 2016: Judicial Watch, "The Clinton Shell Game."

20 January 8, 2010: PBS, "Chasing the Ghosts of a Corrupt Regime; "Gilbert Chagoury, Clinton donor and diplomat with a checkered past."

21 March 25, 2015: *Washington Free Beacon*, "Senator Highlights Clinton Ties to Nigerian Donor."

22 May 10, 2019: Judicial Watch, "Judicial Watch: Records Obtained in Court-Ordered Discovery Reveal Obama White House Tracking FOIA Request for Clinton Emails."

23 May 6, 2015: "Judicial Watch Files Seven New FOIA Lawsuits against State Department to Force Release of Clinton Emails, Other Secret Email Records."

24 October 20, 2016: Judicial Watch, "Clinton Emails with Petraeus Reveal Her

'BlackBerry Blues'; Clinton Tells Then-CENTCOM Commander to Use Her 'Personal Email Address.'"

25   June 26, 2020: Judicial Watch, "Judicial Watch Obtains Secret Service Records Showing Hunter Biden Took 411 Flights, Visited 29 Countries."

26   October 2, 2019: NBC News, "Biden's Trip to China with Son Hunter in 2013 Comes under New Scrutiny."

27   July 8, 2020: "Judicial Watch and Daily Caller News Foundation sue for Joe Biden Senate Records at University of Delaware."

28   May 11, 2020: *The Hill*, "Tara Reade's Attorney Asks Biden to Authorize Search of His Senate Papers."

29   May 1, 2020: *The Independent*, "Biden Senate papers: 3 Things to Know about the University of Delaware Archive."

SECTION FOUR: Our Republic Under Assault . . . at the Ballot Box

1   Executive Order N-64-20 (May 8, 2020) at 2, ¶1.

2   Tom Fitton, January 17, 2017, Daily Caller, "It's Naive to Think Illegal Aliens Aren't Voting—by the Millions."

SECTION FIVE: Our Republic Is Under Assault . . . at Our Border

1   September 4, 2017, "California Court Rejects Attempt to Throw Out Judicial Watch Taxpayer Lawsuit Against San Francisco's Illegal Immigrant Sanctuary Policies."